DISPUTE RESOLUTION

DISPUTE RESOLUTION

Negotiation and Consensus Building

JOHN T. DUNLOP

Harvard University

Auburn House Publishing Company
Dover, Massachusetts

Library of Congress Cataloging in Publication Data

Dunlop, John Thomas, 1914–
  Dispute resolution.

  Includes bibliographical references and index.
  1. Industrial relations—United States. 2. Collective
bargaining—United States. 3. Arbitration, Industrial—
United States. 4. Mediation and conciliation, Industrial
—United States. I. Title.
HD8072.5.D86 1984   331.89'14'0973   83-27531
ISBN 0-86569-123-1

Printed in the United States of America

PUBLISHER'S FOREWORD

John T. Dunlop has an unparalleled experience in the world of industrial relations, beginning intensively in 1943 and continuing without interruption to the present. During this time, in many different roles, he has borne responsibility for consequences and for decisions, and he has had ample opportunity for first-hand observation, discussion, and reflection on dispute resolution processes.

His writings about industrial relations, dispute resolution, and consensus building during these many years have vitally influenced others' thought and have helped to shape and articulate new approaches to action-oriented roles. In the preface to his book, *Industrial Relations Systems*, Professor Dunlop explained, "This writing constitutes, for the author, an attempt to make one world of direct experience in industrial relations and the realm of ideas." Twenty-five years, hundreds of cases, and many new roles later the present volume is designed to help integrate his many direct experiences in dispute resolution, labor-management committees, and agreement-making with the realm of ideas and explanations.

As a practitioner, Professor Dunlop has combined an intensive involvement over an extended period of years, in a number of labor-management relationships (sometimes as a government representative) in both the private and public sectors, with a wide ranging *ad hoc* experience in isolated situations. The continuing relationships made it possible to follow organizations, environments, problems, and personal ties over time and to observe their continuing interactions. These long-term perspectives help one avoid the limitations of the one-time snap-shot.

In the midst of these continuing attachments, he has been invited to resolve disputes and solve problems in a wide-ranging series of independent cases and complex policy issues. A few illustrations will indicate the breadth of this experience, which has afforded him an opportunity to test the range of applicability of ideas generated from the core experiences. He mediated an intense dispute over the terms of a collective agreement between the Massachusetts Teachers Association (an affiliate of the National Educational Association) and its own staff union in 1983. He also arbitrated a grievance case between

v

the Steelworkers and its staff union in 1969 involving Emil Narick. (The latter had been transferred by President I. W. Abel from the general counsel's office to the Research Department, restricting his capacity to travel, after Narick announced he would run for the office of president of the union.) In yet another case, as Secretary of Labor, he had to deal with picketing by a restaurant union—which was supported by most of his employees—inside a new Department of Labor headquarters building when a dispute arose from the letting of a contract (by another agency of Government) to a national firm that operated largely non-union restaurants (1975–1976).

Even within Harvard University he was invited to mediate a policy dispute among deans over the allocation of athletic costs and charges, and he mediated an agreement for the transfer of a major department from one school to another. Problem solving of a special order was required in dealing with many issues raised by faculty and students in the troubled period 1970–1973, while Professor Dunlop was Dean of the Harvard Faculty of Arts and Sciences. This experience concentrated his attention on the requisites and constraints of mediation in unstructured circumstances.

Professor Dunlop had experience in seeking agreement between elements of the black community and the national and local building trades unions in the late 1960s and in accommodating decisions affecting environmentalists and business organizations. The negotiations attendant to the five-year Soviet–U.S. grain agreement in 1975 are still another facet of his experience.* These special cases outside of industrial relations in the ordinary sense are no less instructive as to principles of dispute resolution and consensus building.

Following is a list of major organizations with which John T. Dunlop has been involved in specific dispute resolution and problem solving in industrial relations, with his role in each situation indicated. The enormous breadth of this experience and accomplishment enhances the significance of the writings presented in this volume.

THE PUBLISHER

---

*Roger B. Porter, *Presidential Decision Making, The Economic Policy Board* (Cambridge University Press, 1980), pp. 123–60 and *U.S.–U.S.S.R. Grain Agreement* (Cambridge University Press, 1984).

Stabilization Agencies with Dispute Settlement

1. War Labor Board, 1943–45: Vice-Chairman, Boston Regional Board; Public Member, Wage Adjustment Board (Construction) Office of Economic Stabilization, 1945–47: Staff, Office of Economic Stabilization and Office of War Mobilization and Reconversion
2. Wage Stabilization Board, 1950–53: Public Member
3. Construction Industry Stabilization Commission, 1971–74: Chairman

Stabilization Agencies with Informal Dispute Settlement

1. Cost of Living Council, 1973–74: Director and Chairman of Labor-Management Advisory Committee
2. The National Commission for Industrial Peace, 1973–74: Member
3. Tripartite Pay Advisory Committee, 1979–80: Chairman

Boards of Inquiry: Taft-Hartley Act

1. Bituminous Coal, 1950: Member
2. General Electric Company, Evendale Plant: Member, 1966

Disputes at Critical Installations

1. President's Commission on Labor Relations in the Atomic Energy Installations: Consultant, 1948–49
2. Atomic Energy Labor Relations Commission: Member, 1949–53
3. Secretary of Labor's Advisory Committee on Labor-Management Relations in Atomic Energy: Member, 1954–57
4. Missile Sites Labor Commission: Public Member and Chairman of Construction Panel, 1961–67
5. Nevada Test Site Committee: Member, 1965–67

Railroads and Airlines

1. Emergency Board 109, Conductor's Case: Member, 1954–55
2. Emergency Board 130, Non-operating case: Chairman, 1960
3. Presidential Railroad Commission: Member, 1960–62
4. Emergency Board 167, American Airlines and Transport Workers Union of America, AFL–CIO: Chairman, 1966
5. Special Mediation Panel Appointed by the President, Shop craft case: Member, 1967.

Construction

1. Wage Adjustment Board, 1943–47 (World War II dispute settlement and wage stabilization machinery): Public member representing the War Labor Board
2. National Joint Board for Settlement of Jurisdictional Dispute: Impartial Chairman, 1948–57
3. Special Mediator, United Brotherhood of Carpenters and Joiners of America and the International Association of Machinists, 1953–57
4. Atomic Energy Labor Relations Panel, 1948–53: Member of 5-member governmental panel for atomic agency disputes, with special responsibility for construction disputes
5. Construction Industry Stabilization Commission (1951–53): As a public member of the Tripartite Wage Stabilization Board in the Korean period, was responsible for subsidiary tripartite agency in construction
6. Construction Industry Joint Conference, 1959–68: Impartial chairman of private joint labor-management group to deal with a variety of construction industry problems
7. Missile Sites Labor Commission, 1961–67: Public member, chairman of the construction tripartite panel to resolve disputes affecting missile sites
8. Appeals Board, Jurisdictional Disputes, 1965–68: Chairman of private appeals body to resolve jurisdictional disputes
9. Construction Industry Collective Bargaining Commission, 1969–71: Public member of governmental tripartite commission to deal with wide range of construction problems (Executive Order 11482)
10. Construction Industry Stabilization Committee, 1971–74: Chairman, 1971–73; Member, 1973–74 of Tripartite Committee to Control Wages and Resolve Disputes (Executive Order 11588)
11. Umpire and Mediator, Nuclear Power Construction Stabilization Agreement, 1977–   (Collective agreement developed by major construction firms, electric utilities, and building trades unions to apply to nuclear electric generating plants)
12. Umpire, Bricklayers and Mason Contractors Association, 1982–   (National agreement to resolve collective bargaining disputes over the terms of local agreements)
13. Arbitrator on Jurisdictional Issues, 1981–   (Alaska oilfields construction agreements)

Private Umpire-Arbitrator (various years)

1. St. Louis Dress Industry and International Ladies' Garment Workers Union

2. Pittsburgh Plate Glass Company and United Glass and Ceramic Workers of North America
3. Glass Bottle Manufacturers Association and Glass Bottle Blowers Association of the United States and Canada
4. Scoville Brass Company and United Automobile Workers of America
5. Eastern Air Lines and Air Line Pilots Association, System Board
6. Ad hoc arbitrator

Private Labor-Management Committees: Neutral Member or Umpire

1. Kaiser Steel Company and United Steelworkers of America (Long-Range Sharing Plan): Public Member, 1959–67
2. Trucking Association and International Brotherhood of Teamsters, Chauffeurs, Warehousemen and Helpers of America (Master Freight Agreement): Neutral chairman, 1977–79
3. Joint Labor Management Committee of the Retail Food Industry—Retail Food Chain Stores and United Food, and Commercial Workers International Union and Teamsters): Coordinator, 1974, and chairman of joint staff committee, 1981–
4. Tailored Clothing companies and Amalgamated Clothing and Textile Workers of America: Chairman, 1977–
5. Bricklayers and Mason Contractors Industrial Relations Committee: Impartial umpire, 1981–
6. Six National Organizations concerned with medical care costs, access, and quality of care (American Medical Association, American Hospital Association, Blue Cross–Blue Shield, Health Insurance Association of America, The Business Round Table and AFL–CIO): Coordinator, 1980–
7. Ad hoc maritime committee: Neutral, 1977–80
8. The Labor-Management Group, Coordinator, 1973–   in various forms (Comprised of eight chief executive officers of the Business Round Table companies and the President and Secretary-Treasurer of the AFL–CIO and six members of the Executive Council)

Public Sector Committees

1. Governor's Committee on Public Employee Relations, New York State, 1965–69: Member
2. Joint Labor-Management Committee for Municipal Police and Fire, Commonwealth of Massachusetts: Chairman, 1977–
3. Task Force on Public Pensions and Disability, Commonwealth of Massachusetts: Chairman, 1982–

AUTHOR'S PREFACE

The interplay of reflection and action, or analytical constructs and public or private policy, has been an abiding interest from the outset of my professional education. On the title page of *Wage Determination Under Trade Unions* (1944) is a quotation from Alfred North Whitehead, "All the world over and at all times there have been practical men, absorbed in irreducible and stubborn facts. All the world over and at all times there have been men of philosophic temperament who have been absorbed in the weaving of general principles. It is the union of passionate interest in detailed facts with equal devotion to abstract generalization which forms the novelty in our present society."

It was the War Labor Board, however, that provided both the initial opportunity to learn the trade of mediation and the vision of the potentials for dispute resolution and consensus building in a democratic society. The syndicalist concerns of Henry Simons were likewise to constitute an early reminder against peace at any price and to emphasize the importance of the quality of settlements.

The Publisher's Foreword provides a summary of some of the activities that the War Labor Board experience initiated for me in the dispute resolution field and gives a perspective for both the writings over the years and the new chapters included in this volume. But the extended experience inevitably also involves a number of limitations. Notably I have never worked for a private business enterprise, save as a director of GTE for seven years; neither have I worked for a labor organization. Indeed, it is important to recognize that one can have only a small speck of the total universe of industrial relations experiences; there is always a further list of cases or situations it would have been insightful and instructive to have experienced. It follows that theory, generalization, and analysis are the more essential, as ideas are compelled steadily to confront changing experience.

The role of a neutral is further constrained by inhibitions on taking public positions on many issues on which it would be natural to express policy judgments or appraisals of one party or another and to engage in public debate. There are few fields in which press and media are so addicted to passing fads and in which the quality of thoughtful reporting has so declined. But an active public discourse on wide-ranging issues is no doubt incompatible with the confidence and acceptability requisite to being an effective neutral. General views and evaluations, however, can be judiciously expressed in informal forums and more formal papers, as well as in the course of private access to the parties. Overall, the restraint on public discourse or controversy has not been a major concern since—as experience teaches—most decisive discussions between labor and management, between business and government in the executive or legislative branches, or between labor and government in both branches is non-public. Public statements and true positions on serious disputes are often far apart, and it serves little purpose to comment on formal positions that are not the real positions. Press and media coverage is likely to be a certain sign of formality and posturing, whereas exclusion of the press and media is likely to be associated with the stage of serious negotiations.

The experiences of a neutral do not constitute a single undifferentiated role, in formal status or in actual performance. In some circumstances, with some parties and at some times, the assignment may be to help generate ideas for resolution of a problem; or to pronounce and legitimate an agreement (decision); or to help formulate the issue for an agreement or decision; or to assist in gathering the facts about a problem area; or to assist with factional groups or dissenting views or even the lawyers in the agreement-making process; or to formulate and to express subtly the basis and rationale for an agreement; or to assist in explaining and selling a potential agreement to various constituencies and groups outside the negotiating parties.

The neutral is not one role; it varies in each situation, and no two neutrals will behave the same way in a given setting. The neutral may use sweet talk or tough language. The role may be highly active or passive; it may be factually oriented, be a reminder of history and precedent, or treat issues conceptually. The role may be genuine leadership or simply hand-holding. It is likely to be influenced according to the circumstances by which the neutral entered the situation, the formal assignment, the mutual acceptability of the neutral, and the history of the relationship of the parties.

The art of dispute resolution and the analysis of the process in particular cases for me was influenced by working closely with George W. Taylor and David L. Cole. We were involved together in a number of common and related situations for almost thirty years. Our discussions afforded the all-too-rare opportunity to compare notes frankly, to test techniques as practitioners, and to share reactions to generalizations and analytical schemes.* The process of mediating 36 national agreements on work jurisdiction between national construction unions and the related national contractor associations was no less instructive in mediation at an early stage. The writings and ideas in this volume have also been shaped by the opportunity of editing the Wertheim Series in Industrial Relations over the past forty years.

Part One presents in a single chapter an analytical perspective, closely rooted in experience, of the negotiation process among representatives of continuing organizations, such as unions or public and private managements, and of the mediation process. Part Two, Chapters 2–6, describes the industrial relations system of the United States in which labor and management organizations negotiate and the ways that system and its environment have evolved and shaped the negotiations process and its outcomes. Part Three, Chapters 7–13, concerns the mechanisms designed by labor, management, and governments to resolve various classes of disputes. In order to appreciate any dispute resolution process, it is essential to understand the larger context in which the parties interact, the history of their relationships, and the features of their relations that generate conflict. Part Four, Chapters 14–17, treats with joint consultation, labor-management-government committees, and a social contract designed to generate consensus and problem-solving and to achieve the potentials of opportunities developed through cooperation.

I am indebted to Claire Brown, Librarian of the Sumner H. Slichter Industrial Relations Collection, for readily producing materials that I have often only vaguely identified; I have thus been able to utilize or cite them herein for references. Carol Fields typed the manuscript and helped see it through to publication, above and beyond her usual role of overseeing effectively a variety of diffused office responsibilities. Such dedicated performance is deeply appreciated.

Acknowledgment is made of the permission granted to reprint copyrighted materials, with some modifications to provide up-to-date information, as follows: The Macmillan Company (Chapter 3);

---

*See, John T. Dunlop, "Themes on George Taylor" in *Scope of Public Sector Bargaining*, Walter Gershenfeld, J. Joseph Lowenberg, and Bernard Ingster, Eds. (Lexington, Mass.: Lexington Books, 1977), pp. ix–xiii; Edward B. Shils, *et al.*, *Industrial Peacemaker, George W. Taylor's Contribution to Collective Bargaining* (University of Pennsylvania Press, 1979); and David L. Cole, *The Quest for Industrial Peace* (New York: McGraw-Hill Book Company, 1963); David L. Cole, *Oral History Interview*, November 18, 1974 (Federal Mediation and Conciliation Service, Washington, D.C., Tape Numbers 57, 58, 76, 77 and 78).

Daedalus, Journal of the American Academy of Arts and Sciences (Chapter 5); Industrial Relations Research Association (Chapters 6 and 8); Harper and Row, Publishers (Chapter 7); The American Foundation on Automation and Employment, Inc. (Chapter 9); and The Free Press (Chapter 10).

I am also pleased to acknowledge the financial assistance of the Rockefeller Brothers Fund in connection with the support of younger persons interested in the interactions of business, labor, and government involved in negotiations and labor-management committees referred to in Parts One and Four of this volume.

Part One presents in a single chapter an analytical perspective, closely rooted in experience, of the negotiation process among representatives of continuing organizations, such as unions or public and private managements, and of the mediation process.

Part Two, Chapters 2–6, describes the industrial relations system of the United States in which labor and management organizations negotiate and the ways that system and its environment have evolved and shaped the negotiations process and its outcomes.

Part Three, Chapters 7–13, concerns the mechanisms designed by labor, management, and governments to resolve various classes of disputes. In order to appreciate any dispute resolution process, it is essential to understand the larger context in which the parties interact, the history of their relationships, and the features of their relations that generate conflict.

Part Four, Chapters 14–17, treats with joint consultation, labor-management-government committees, and a social contract designed to generate consensus and problem solving and to achieve the potentials of opportunities developed through cooperation.

JOHN T. DUNLOP

CONTENTS

Part One

INTRODUCTION

Chapter 1

THE NEGOTIATIONS ALTERNATIVE IN DISPUTE RESOLUTION

In Western societies there have been two approved arrangements over the past two hundred years for resolving conflicting interests among groups and organizations, and among their constituent members: the give-and-take of the market place and government regulatory mechanisms established by the political process. Markets in various institutional forms[1] bring together buyers and sellers, without visible hand, to set prices of goods, services, and various factors of production, including land and capital assets. Markets provide the terms of exchange and thus resolve—largely impersonally—disputes between potential buyers and sellers over the countless features of transactions. Adam Smith described the situation in the *Wealth of Nations* more than two hundred years ago:

> *Give me that which I want, and you shall have this which you want, is the meaning of every such offer; and it is in this manner that we obtain from one another the far greater part of those good offices which we stand in need of. It is not from the benevolence of the butcher, the brewer, or the baker that we expect our dinner, but from their regard to their own interest. [Book I, Ch. 2]*

Beyond providing markets with legal status, the political process has established government institutions, from courts to administrative tribunals, to resolve many other conflicts and differences of interests and to restrain methods of conflict. Further, the political process has set up and nurtured the "public household,"[2] or public sector, that in part compliments and in part competes with and displaces or transforms the private market economy.

It is not the present purpose to recount or to explain the development of markets or the growth of the "public household," including regulatory institutions, in Western societies generally or in the United States.[3] Rather the present starting point is to note that the received ideas and institutions designed to resolve conflicting interests consist of both markets and the public household including governmental regulation.

A Trend Away from the Market Place and Regulation

There is abundant evidence that the American community since the Great Depression places less reliance on markets to achieve social purposes, including the resolution of conflicting interests, despite the deregulation movement of the past decade.[4] In international trade, for instance, the doctrinaire support for free trade and free markets for international commerce has been supplemented or replaced by a complex network of reciprocal and bilateral agreements negotiated in various forums as reflected in the arrangements for sugar, coffee, tin, wheat, textiles and apparel, steel and other manufactured goods, maritime cargos, and airplane fares, not to mention movement of people across national boundary lines. In the labor market, the presence of collective bargaining, minimum wage regulation, and health and safety, pension, and non-discrimination requirements testify to the extent reliance on the market has been qualified. The regulations of the S.E.C., Federal Reserve System, Comptroller of the Currency, and the housing finance agencies, as well as fair housing rules and the Internal Revenue Code, constrain capital flows and money markets. The complex of regulations affecting specific product markets, from public utilities through consumer and producer goods and agricultural products, has greatly expanded, thereby constricting buyers and sellers and changing the nature of these markets. Moreover, wage and price controls—or other forms of income policy—were in effect for 22 of the 43 years that followed 1940.

The costs of these regulatory mechanisms, as measured by the extent to which they result in distorted decisions, financial outlays, litigation, delays, and uncertainty, have come to be increasingly recognized as a heavy burden and as a complication in the resolution of conflicting interests.[5] The uneconomic consequences of some regulations have helped policy makers to rediscover the market in the past decade and to advance deregulation, as in developments affecting airlines, trucking, and communications. The deregulation movement may still expand. Although it is difficult to see it growing faster than the political propensity to regulate, the main thrust of the past generation must clearly be characterized as away from reliance upon the market place.

Negotiations and negotiation processes appear to be in the ascendancy as compared with resolution in the market place and, in recent years, even with public regulation. It is not uncommon, for instance, for private corporate suits, as in the instance of a telecommunication antitrust case after more than 12 years, to be settled by direct negotiations between the companies or with the government. The major disputes involving the price and supply of uranium between Westinghouse and certain utilities have been settled by direct negotiations and the withdrawal of court suits. The device of plea bargaining on economic questions likewise is illustrative of the general distrust of pure regulation and public agency decision and of the tendency to resort to negotiations to limit uncertainty, to speed resolution, and to assure greater attention to features of a settlement that are of special concern to each party. Contestants often achieve a more satisfactory and less risky settlement by direct negotiations, or with the staff of a public agency, than would be likely were the proceedings to run their full litigious course.

A variety of specialized mediation and arbitration devices also have been developing in recent years to facilitate agreement-making and to reduce litigation and formal court processes in fields outside the industrial relations arena, where such methods have been used for many years and where the institutional arrangements are well established. New areas in which disputes have been submitted to mediation or arbitration under voluntary arrangements developed and administered by the American Arbitration Association include malpractice suits; controversies over home or product warranties; differences over price or product among owners, contractors, and architects in construction; differences between manufacturers and converters in textiles and apparel; or some controversies over equal employment opportunities. A number of courts have experimented with special mediators, including the Bronx Housing Court in disputes between landlords and tenants, as well as courts handling divorce cases. A number of organizations have sprung up to encourage the settlement of complex controversies between environmentalists and businesses by direct negotiations and mediation.[6] In all these cases, procedures that are faster, less expensive, and more subject to the interests of the contending parties are replacing more formal and legalistic determinations. It can be expected that these methods of dispute resolution will spread and be more extensively utilized.

But negotiations have not only extended into the resolution of individual cases and disputes; they are also utilized to resolve controversies over public regulation and rule making[7] and indeed, to reach accommodation of differences over legislation itself. The procedures used to enact the Arab Boycott legislation, the 1979 trade liberalization act, and the 1983 Amendments to Social Security are illustrative of the successful resort to negotiations procedures prior to and outside of the established process. The Massachusetts legislation that reformed the administration of public employee pensions (including those for disability) and created the Public Employee Retirement Administration was negotiated and mediated among various private and governmental interests, including legislators, and then enacted (Chapter 630 of the Acts of 1982 and Chapter 661 of the Acts of 1983).

One needs to be careful, nevertheless, in considering what is meant by the statement that negotiations are an alternative or have replaced markets and governmental determinations. It is easy to see that there has been a change in form or appearance, but the reality is more complex. As with wage and price controls or collective bargaining, market forces are not entirely displaced or entirely replaced, and they operate, limit, and shape sooner or later, to some degree, the decisions made through the new institutions. It is erroneous to assert either that the new institutions make no difference or that the decisions are entirely different since the market or the regulations have been altered to a negotiations form. The reality is rather that the old market forces and the new ones generated by the new institutions now operate through the new institutions, yielding more or less different results which must be assessed in each situation.

Collective bargaining, for instance, does change the performance of labor markets in many ways not well captured by econometric studies. The tendency of collective agreements in many industries to be set for three-year terms, the differences between parties in pure bargaining skills and power, or the institutional interests in fringe benefits or union security may be expected to result in somewhat different terms and conditions of employment over time than would arise through markets or under governmental dictation. The quality of management and its policies, as well as the characteristics of the labor force, are altered. But it would be simplistic to hold that market considerations have been entirely displaced or eliminated. The substitution in form, from market to a negotiations form, yields complex results that differ significantly from purely market results.

The penetration of negotiations into the arena of governmental determinations similarly is not simply a change in institutional form. The costs and time of settlement are likely to be less than those of protracted litigation. The opportunity to influence more directly the outcome and to secure attention to issues of most vital concern is often greater. These factors are likely to yield different results through negotiations than through litigation or other formal processes. But it must be remembered that the possibility of reverting in the course of negotiations to court, to an administrative agency, or to a legislative body is likely to be a continuing influence in such negotiations; accordingly the emerging precedents of litigation are likely to influence relative positions and bargaining tactics. With regard to negotiations on some issues subject to regulatory decisions, as in employment discrimination or protected activity cases, it is to be recognized that agreements or settlements are subject to attack and to displacement in the very tribunals the negotiations are intended to circumvent. But it cannot be denied that negotiating a settlement with one or more adversaries, or with a governmental administrative agency or in a court, is a different process with somewhat different results than a commitment to litigation and formal processes.

The field of industrial policy has come to be an area of intense ideological debate over various issues, including the role of negotiations and tripartite committees to establish and administer policies relating to economic growth and industrial configuration. A *Business Week* editorial on strategy for rebuilding the economy urges that "the leaders of the various economic and social groups that compose U.S. society should agree on a program for reindustrialization and present that program to Washington."[8] The AFL-CIO has repeatedly proposed a tripartite National Reindustrialization Board "to carry forward a national industrial policy."[9] Against such views stands the editorial position of the *Wall Street Journal*: "The only industrial policy we need is one that offers the maximum possibility for individual decision makers to apply their initiative and imagination, take their risks, and reap their rewards when their judgments are correct. As a group they will be right far more often than government bureaucrats not subject to the disciplines and incentives of the market."[10] Secretary of the Treasury Donald T. Regan has disparaged the idea of a tripartite commission: "Do we really believe that either waste or greed can be abolished by good men and women sitting around a conference table in Washington? It is the kind of scene that makes 'Utopia' seem like a rough-and-tumble operation." (*New York Times*, October 15, 1983, p. 35).

These introductory observations have been intended to call attention to the growing importance of negotiations in resolving real or potential conflicting interest among groups in our society. Negotiations have been making inroads on both markets and governmental mechanisms. These changes are more complex than the apparent changes in form. The expansion of negotiations brings with it growing controversy over the independent consequences of negotiations. The study of markets and, more recently, regulation are both well established and embedded in the disciplines of economics and law. The negotiations process deserves to be much better and more widely understood.

Approaches to Negotiations

There are a variety of approaches to explicate the negotiations process. First, a considerable literature utilizes formal models seeking to explain bargaining generally and collective bargaining negotiations in particular.[11] At one time, for example, I developed a model of bargaining power (with Benjamin Higgins) based upon different degrees of competition in related product and labor markets and the "pure" bargaining power of negotiators to determine a wage rate.[12]

There are, however, at least two major difficulties with the applicability of abstract models of negotiations. The first is that they are typically simplified to a single issue, such as money, or they assume that other issues are translatable into money on some stable trade-off, effectively recreating a single issue. The second difficulty arises from the usual presumption that the negotiators constitute monolithic entities, with no significant internal differences among the constituent members of the negotiating organizations or between these members and their negotiator and that any internal differences are entirely constant throughout the negotiations. These simplifications, essential to analytical rigor, are too abstract to be very helpful in providing much insight into the class of negotiations that are of central concern in this volume.

A second approach to explicate negotiations is through the use of experimental or simulated bargaining games.[13] In some instances a class is divided into groups to represent the negotiating parties, initial positions are defined for each, and rules of play are specified. The process can generate substantial interest and apparent involvement of the participants.

Third, there has been some effort to use econometric methods to measure aspects of arbitration or collective bargaining. Public sector bargaining has been used most often in view of the availability of data.[14] The results appear to me to be unimpressive; situations are always changing in some respects, and these studies do not appear to center on fundamentals.

Finally, there is an approach to negotiations that constitutes an almost verbatim account of the exchanges from the earliest stages of negotiations to the achievement of a settlement.[15] In recent years more condensed case studies of negotiations have been developed for courses in schools of business, law, and public policy.[16]

A somewhat different approach is developed in this chapter: to limit the types of negotiations considered and then to outline a number of key principles central to an understanding of the negotiations process. These principles grow out of reflecting on experience; they seek to blend analysis and art forms.

The types of negotiations considered in this chapter have at least three characteristics that eliminate some negotiations from our concern in the universe of all negotiations. *First,* parties or organizations expect to continue to be engaged and to interact over a future period. Thus, the direct sale/purchase of a house between individuals who are unlikely to have any interaction in the future ever again, or a transaction by a visitor to a garage sale, are a species of negotiations excluded from these principles. In the negotiation under consideration in this volume, events during negotiations, in the agreement-making process, or in the breakdown of negotiations are likely to be significant to the performance of the parties in following negotiations. *Second,* the negotiators represent organizations or groups within which there are important differences in preferences among members, and these relative preferences for bargaining objectives may even shift during the course of negotiations, particularly when they are protracted. The parties to our negotiations are *not* monolithic. *Third,* the negotiators are concerned with more than a single issue, or with one that can be decomposed into more than one issue. Thus, whenever money is an issue, there is the issue of effective dates of any change in money.

Compensation typically has a variety of dimensions. While one issue may be more significant to one party as compared with others, I have yet to meet a single-issue real dispute, recognizing that issues typically are broken down into a variety of dimensions or components. The framework for analysis of negotiations outlined in the next section may provide some insight into these excluded classes of negotiations, although that is not the present primary purpose.

Labor-management negotiations in the United States are characterized by the three inclusions defined above, although few private negotiations are so precisely specified by public policy. The labor organization is certified by law as the exclusive representative of the employees in a precisely defined job territory. The management is clearly identified by law. The subjects the parties are required (or *not* required) to bargain over are also defined by law. The obligation to bargain in good faith has been defined by statute and case law in great detail. The labor organization has the obligation to represent all employees in the bargaining unit fairly and without "hostile discrimination," including any minority group of employees confronting a majority of employees. Negotiations are to begin a specified number of days before the expiration of the old agreement. Some methods of conflict in negotiations (for example, relating to picketing, a boycott, or violence) are permissible by law, while others are prohibited.

A Framework for Analyzing Negotiations

It is difficult for those who merely observe negotiations through the press or second-hand accounts or who only see reports of isolated events in negotiations to have a good understanding of direct negotiations and the role of associated mediation. Despite a spate of recent volumes that advertise how one can learn to "negotiate agreement without giving in" or "get the best out of bargaining," I am inclined to believe that the art of negotiation can only be learned by experience—often, hard experience. Indeed, no outsider can ever fully participate in ongoing negotiations or a mediation process.

A framework for analysis and a statement of principles may, however, provide a perspective on what happens in negotiation and reduce the learning time—or, perhaps, the pain of experience.[17] The framework presented below is not highly abstract or elegant. But it does reflect a first approximation of experience and analysis of the roles of various negotiating parties in diverse settings.

Diverse Internal Interests

Each group or organization that is party to negotiations to seek an agreement has diverse internal interests, and an internal consensus or formal approval by each party is required to permit the consummation of a negotiated agreement. Thus, in the instance of two parties, it takes three agreements to achieve one agreement—that is, an agreement within each party as well as one across the table. In the instance of three parties, it takes four agreements to achieve one agreement. This simple proposition is fundamental to agreement-making.

The parties to negotiations among continuing groups or organizations are never a monolith. Attention to the conflicting interests and internal governance for negotiations is essential to observe agreement-making perceptively or to participate effectively in the process. A great deal of the negotiations process is devoted subtly to communications about internal priorities and reactions to various proposals and counter-proposals.

In the negotiations in 1975 over the five-year grain agreement between the Soviet Union and the United States, for instance, there were diverse interests within the United States over the volume of grain to be sold in 1975 and beyond, the urgency of reaching an accommodation, the consequences for domestic living costs, the problem of how to resolve a longshore work stoppage and achieve the use of American tonnage in grain shipments, and the need to include in an agreement with the Soviets oil purchases below the OPEC price. These divergent interests were in part reflected in the different agencies of government—including the Departments of State, Agriculture, Labor, and Commerce, the OMB, and the White House, among others—involved in making recommendations to the President on the positions in negotiations. Although the United States negotiators may have had less hard information, it could be presumed there were some internal differences at some levels to be accommodated within even the Soviet government on questions of immediate needs, agricultural policies, storage capacity, shipping rate structure, and oil prices.[18] In the end the United States had to abandon any linkage to oil if it was to achieve an agreement and the Soviets were under some pressure to reach a negotiated settlement if it was to secure the grain volume it sought. The grain agreement and the related shipping agreement required considerable internal accommodation and congruent internal positions within each side: three agreements to achieve one formal agreement.

The private collective bargaining process well illustrates the same principle. Ordinarily the negotiating proposals of a labor organization are put together initially from the aspirations of a wide range of members and subsidiary groups, as are management's counterproposals. The union comprises diverse interests: Younger workers may be more interested in health care, older workers in pension benefits, and retired workers in adjusting pensions for increased living costs. Workers in various departments or plants may place high priorities on local working conditions. Women or minorities may give top priority to new elements in an affirmative action program. And unemployed workers may be most concerned with supplemental unemployment benefits and the extension of health care benefits. In multi-company bargaining the marginal company employees may be concerned with job security and employment, in contrast to the high priority for wage increases among the employees of the higher-profit companies. The collective bargaining and negotiations process requires the labor organization (and management) to assess these competing opportunities and to seek a settlement, before or after a work stoppage, with a "package" congruent with management's (and the labor organization's) internal necessities. The negotiation process eliminates many of the initial aspirations of both sides and seeks mutually consistent items and magnitudes—three agreements to achieve the agreement ratified by the internal procedures of each party and made public.

The diversity in management is evident most clearly in public sector negotiations, where mayors and city councils or boards of selectmen, finance committees, and personnel boards may be at odds. These differences, which are exacerbated by partisan and personality rivalries, materially complicate agreement-making and ratification.[19]

The emphasis on the internal diversity and complexity of each organization party to the negotiations suggests that each negotiator appreciate the informal governance of each side in order to understand the proposals and counter-proposals made in the negotiations. It is vital to sense the priorities sought by each side and the severity of their opposition to proposals, in truth rather than merely in formal positions or in public pronouncements. Each negotiator, and indeed each mediator,[20] needs to be sensitive to the possibilities of putting together "packages" of items to constitute an acceptable settlement in view of the respective priorities and negative evaluations of particular proposals. Indeed, negotiations or mediation is often the art of putting together packages that recognize the true priorities on each side that will "sell" to both parties informally as well as in any formal ratification process. Again, it takes three agreements to resolve the dispute.

Initial Proposals for Agreement

In negotiations, the initial proposals for an agreement by any party tend to be large or extreme relative to eventual settlement terms, save in the case of a very few negotiators. It is important for observers or negotiators to understand the reasons for such inflated proposals and the functions that large initial proposals play in the negotiations process. They should not be simply dismissed with moral indignation as unreasonable; they often reveal a great deal about the internal complex of the side making them.

Many initial proposals are large because they reflect the way they were put together—that is, simply assembling the aspirations of the divergent groups which comprise each party to the negotiations. In order to cut back or scale down proposals, it is essential to establish priorities among groups within the negotiating organizations, as suggested in the first principle. While some culling of raw proposals may be made initially, the process of priority setting and scaling back proposals for one party or another is often an integral part of the bargaining process itself.

Initial proposals may be extensive or large as a deliberate act on the part of negotiators to secure the reactions of the other side. At the outset it is not always clear which items or proposals may be of interest or be most acceptable to the other side or to elements of the other side. A wide and diverse menu may permit explorations that otherwise will not take place. Some proposals are also planted for future years. John L. Lewis initially proposed the novel idea of royalty per ton of coal mined for health care of miners as a means to compel the diversified owners to study the approach seriously for the next negotiations.

When negotiations may be protracted or when the environment of the negotiations may be expected to change significantly, the initial proposals are sometimes large to accommodate such circumstances. Parties are likely not to want to make proposals that may appear grossly inadequate to their constituencies after six months or a year of negotiations; hence larger or more extreme initial proposals protect the negotiations from drastic changes in circumstances.

Initial proposals may be substantial also in order to facilitate a negotiations strategy calling for the abandonment or reduction in some items in response to movement by the other party. If a negotiator has advanced only a minimum or final position, it will not be possible to make concessions to see what effects such a change may have on the other party. The need to maneuver in negotiations also encourages large initial proposals.

As observed above, there are a few situations in which initial proposals for an agreement by a negotiator may be close to the final settlement. Such a strategy may be followed, in my experience, by a negotiator with very considerable authority and prestige so that there is creditability and likely strong support for the approach within the organization represented. The tactic has the advantage that, once successfully established in a previous negotiation, it may contribute to its own success in future negotiations. But it has very limited applicability. The position of take-it-or-leave-it from the beginning of negotiations is a dangerous ploy for all but the strongest and most prescient. Movement from large initial proposals is the ordinary course of negotiations.

Changing Positions

Negotiations constitute the process by which authorized representatives, starting from positions that are initially often far apart, change those positions to achieve a procedural or substantive agreement. A procedural agreement would settle a dispute, for instance, by referral to arbitration or to some other tribunal for resolution.

The change in the formal position of a party in negotiations is always accomplished with a certain amount of difficulty because a concession may be interpreted as a weakness and invite expectations for further yielding. Yet changes in positions by negotiators—

ordinarily substantial—are required if the differences between the parties are to be narrowed and an agreement is to be achieved. But each apparent concession tends to create on the other side the impression of a willingness to yield further in continuing negotiations. If a negotiator has reduced (or raised) his offer ten cents an hour, the other side will argue that a further movement is appropriate to close the remaining gap between the parties on that issue. Moreover, an explicit concession once made is almost impossible to withdraw as a practical rather than as a formal or legal matter. It should be no surprise that concessions from initial or previous proposals are often accompanied by the refrain, "This is our last offer!" or "This is our last proposal!" before some deadline or projected breakoff in negotiations.

At the outset of negotiations, after the lists of formal proposals have been submitted, each negotiator is likely to enjoy the full support of his organization, and there are sharp conflicts across the table. The positions are far apart and each side has a united constituency on rather extreme proposals. In the course of negotiations, as spokesmen change their positions and make concessions, more and more tension tends to arise within each group while it may ease across the bargaining table. As each initial proposal is dropped or modified, internal support may be lost from additional constituencies. Indeed, it is a practical rule-of-thumb that one is nearing agreement across the table when there is more difficulty within each side than between the leading spokesmen across the table. Each principal negotiator is often as much preoccupied with handling the internal conflicts and shaping proposals to satisfy the internal necessities as with controversy with the opposing negotiator. Changing positions creates internal tensions, making internal agreement more difficult.

The way in which negotiators for organizations change their positions in order to move toward a settlement is an art form incorporating considerable style in handling tensions both internally and across the table. In my experience the characteristics that most distinctively separate experienced from inexperienced negotiators are the way in which they are able to effectuate changes in positions without creating the expectation of further concessions and the way they can "read" suggestions of the other side for possible changes in previous positions. These differences in talents and skills do make a difference in the substantive outcomes of negotiations. An absolutely essential ingredient to the art of changing positions is the capacity to listen perceptively and to read between the lines. A good sense of timing and understanding the moods on the two sides are likewise critical factors in effective negotiating.

In the early stages of negotiations, it would not be unusual for a change in position to be reflected in the withdrawal or scratching of some items from the agenda of one or both sides. But as the negotiations proceed, the discussions are often centered around various "packages" of proposals. While a change in position may be reflected in a modification in the magnitudes of the items in the "package," a change may also be signaled by discussing a "package" modified to exclude some items or to add some items more desirable to the other side. These combinations may not be presented as formal offers or modifications in positions but only as different "packages" for exploration. Only later may a formal change in position or a withdrawal of an item be conceded.

There is often considerable ambiguity over the status of various package proposals and their composition. At a given stage of the negotiations it may be quite uncertain as to what is in dispute and what, if anything, has been agreed upon, particularly since an axiom of negotiations ordinarily is that there is no agreement until all items in dispute have been resolved one way or the other, unless otherwise explicitly specified. The negotiations process ordinarily consists of steps involving changes in position or an indication of willingness to change, while preserving positions should the negotiations fail to reach a settlement in the current round or forum of negotiations. But regardless of how artful or clumsy in execution, negotiations is the process of changing positions in movement toward a resolution of the dispute.

Role of a Deadline

A deadline serves a vital function in negotiations, compelling each side to reach decisions and establish priorities that would not otherwise occur—at least, not so rapidly. The temptation to procrastinate and to hope the issues will go away or can be postponed is recurrent. In the absence of a deadline, as during a strike or a lockout in collective bargaining or during a court proceeding or other mandated decision-making in government regulatory agencies, the negotiators or mediators often create artificial deadlines to try to bring issues "to a head" and to resolution.

The passage of time is not ordinarily neutral with respect to the interests and fortunes of each party. Time may run more towards one party than the other, and one or the other may hope for a more favorable setting in which to settle or reach agreement. A deadline is an institutional design in negotiations with the purpose of reducing dilatory postponement; it can be a natural deadline, as in the expiration of an old collective bargaining agreement, or a synthetic one created by no less a necessity than the desire to catch an airplane or report to another scheduled meeting.

The question is repeatedly asked as to why negotiations are not settled until a deadline—often at midnight or in the wee hours of the morning—even after a symbolic stopping of the clock. An appreciation of this distinctive feature of negotiations involves the series of points made above concerning the essential nature of negotiations between continuing organizations. The "end game" of negotiations involves concessions, from one side or the other or both, that are more vital than those changes in position previously made, and they are likely to prove more difficult to make. The less valuable "chips" have already been played. Moreover, settlement involves complex trade-offs, often in "principle," between one group of the constituency and others as they involve different aspirations of the same constituency that is now required to face more realistically the opportunity costs of any priority—that is, what they have to give up to achieve their objective.

These internal decisions involve complex communications and often sharp differences of internal views which are likely to have become acute as negotiations have continued and more concessions have been made. A deadline requires reconsideration of the easy view that the other side is likely to "blink" first, and it forces a hard review of the consequences of non-agreement. These consequences are more realistic when they are imminent than when viewed in anticipation months or even hours ahead. A deadline is an essential ingredient to such hard choices and decisions. Students well understand that it often takes a deadline to produce a term paper.

End-Play

The end-play of negotiations poses distinctive problems and opportunities that may facilitate agreement or freeze positions into obdurate obstacles to settlement. In the end-stage of negotiations the number of issues is reasonably limited and defined and the distances between the parties are moderate. The critical problem is that each side would prefer the other to move to avoid a further concession itself, and that any move may create the impression of being willing to move all the way to the position of the other side. The negotiating situation is delicate. As explained in the next section, a mediator can play a vital role. In the absence of a neutral, it is common for the one or two key persons from each side to meet privately at lunch or elsewhere, even without the advanced knowledge of their colleagues, to span the remaining gap. The final steps are seldom taken at the table, although they must be confirmed there and by ratification.

Ronald Reagan, in his autobiography, reports on his experience in negotiations as President of the Screen Actors Guild:[21]

> *I was surprised to discover the important part a urinal played in this high-altitude bargaining. When some point has been kicked around, until it swells up bigger than the whole contract, someone from one side or the other goes to the men's room. There is a kind of sensory perception that gives you the urge to follow. . . . Then, standing side by side in that room that levels king and commoner, comes an honest question, "What do you guys really want?" . . . Back in the meeting, one or the other makes an offer based on this newly acquired knowledge. . . . Then the other returnee from the men's room says, "Can our group have a caucus?" That is the magic word, like the huddle in football—it's where the signal is passed.*

A Judgment: Serious or Sham?

An essential feature of all negotiations is the determination by each negotiator whether the parties are serious about reaching an accommodation at the current "table" or whether they are going through the motions as prelude to some subsequent further negotiations in some other forum with some other representatives, or are engaging in a sham to conceal a prospective conflict designed to end in the extinction of one party. This judgment is often not easy to make, but it has decisive effects upon the negotiations. There are many negotiations that are perceived by both sides to be preliminary to further negotiations; as long as both sides have the same perceptions, serious difficulties may be avoided. Different expectations, however, can be the source of major conflict and charges of bad faith.

It is axiomatic that negotiations recognized to be preliminary to a further stage are unlikely to elicit best offers, although very important functions relating to factual information, exploration of priorities among issues, alternative approaches, and sensing of internal considerations may be achieved. In some labor-management negotiations it is possible to envisage a succession of "tables" at which the dispute may be negotiated. Local parties may be followed by national and headquarters representatives of the two organizations; top officials may participate; a succession of mediators and government officials may seek to mediate the dispute; formal fact-finding with recommendations may be voluntarily agreed to or required by legislation; a succession of further negotiations and mediation may follow fact-finding; the physical locale of the negotiations may shift a number of times. The White House or the Governor may intervene in certain disputes. The negotiators will want to anticipate such shifting "tables" because the timing of concessions is vital to the negotiators, and mediators may expect additional flexibility in positions.

Some negotiations, at least on the part of one side, may be regarded as a way to secure delay, to postpone legal proceedings, or to secure a lapse of time thought to be favorable to one's position. In such instances the procrastinating side is likely to pay scrupulous attention to the form and protocol of negotiations but to avoid problem solving. It is vital for an observer or a participant to know whether a case has these characteristics, although the determination is often not easy to make.

Among continuing organizations that deal with each other on an ongoing basis, negotiations may at the outset take on the character of mutual problem solving. The process involves careful development of the factual basis of a problem, delineating areas of agreement or disagreement over the facts, including the need for further investigation. Both the more objective character of the problem and the organizational concerns of both parties are to be explored. There follows consideration of alternative resolutions of the problem, as redefined, and of the costs and acceptability of each approach to each party. An accommodation, formally or informally, may then be accepted for a temporary or a longer period. In this mode negotiations are problem solving; the negotiators are not characterized simply as traders seeking a sharp advantage. The difference is vital to long-term constructive relationships between the organizations or groups. Labor-management committees are discussed in detail in Chapters 14 and 15.

Overt Conflict

Negotiations do not preclude overt conflict, and both may take place simultaneously. Thus, negotiations may begin or continue concurrently with a strike or lockout, with litigation, or with political activity, or while public campaigns are also under way. It may be difficult for an organization to conduct warfare and diplomacy simultaneously, but separate representatives of an organization are often involved. In these circumstances conflict is another form of pressure directed to the bargaining table, and bargaining strategy may take on the form of another element of conflict. It must, of course, be recognized that overt conflict, in the circumstances of ongoing negotiations, may in the course of the conflict or as a consequence of the results of conflict, alter the position of one side or the other in negotiations. Indeed, that is typically the purpose of the conflict: to facilitate agreement on more favorable terms or more rapidly.

Going Public

Negotiations cannot be fruitfully conducted in the press or in the media. Indeed, it is an indication that negotiators are serious about reaching a settlement or willing to explore their problems in earnest when they exclude the press and refrain from public comment save in the most general terms, such as, "We met for so many hours," and "We explored our mutual proposals constructively." In public sector bargaining, negotiations are ordinarily excluded from the requirements of conducting public business under the open meeting laws. It is important to be analytically clear as to why negotiations need to be conducted in private.

Negotiators desire to explain the concessions they make and the terms they have achieved directly to their constituents rather than have the press or media initially make that explanation and state the merits or deficiencies of the settlement. The negotiators know their own constituents and the political alignments within the group. Moreover, performance of negotiators, as indicated by an appraisal of the results of negotiations, is a major feature of the political life of an organization's leaders. Since negotiations may affect different members of a group somewhat differently, the leadership will want to deal with these differences directly rather than have the media or press present their views.

The injection of the press into negotiations would make it even more difficult for the principal negotiator or the committee to change positions, because those opposed would be encouraged by the press reports to generate hostility as the negotiations proceeded before the settlement could be considered as a whole. Moreover, as has been noted, much of negotiations is contingent upon over-all agreement; thus, initial proposals and counter-proposals may not even appear in the final settlement.

The proclivity of the press and media to highlight particular items or give a special cast to events does not appear to well serve the success of negotiations in process, particularly when an agreement is subject to ratification. The public report of the settlement after the fact, with any desired editorial comment, does not of course affect the outcome.

Implementing the Settlement

The negotiation process that has ended in an agreement typically needs a procedure to administer or to interpret the terms of the settlement. It is literally impossible to provide for all details, circumstances, or contingencies. Sometimes minor gaps are deliberately left in an agreement because a full understanding cannot be achieved; resolution is left to a future process of administration or adjudication. Some questions can be resolved only in the light of future developments. Specialists or those subordinately involved in particular operations may be more qualified to resolve the application questions than the principals involved in the negotiations. And, of course, the long hours of tiring negotiations may result in a problem being overlooked.

In many instances the procedures for interpretation or administration may simply constitute a reconvening of the negotiating committees or a sub-group thereof. In other situations there may be resort to arbitration on a question of meaning or application of the original agreement, or the parties may agree on voluntary arbitration after a period of future negotiations over the issues raised subsequent to the agreement.

In a continuing relationship the process of interpretation and administration of any agreement develops a substantial body of cases, questions and answers, issues, interpretations, and applications that come to constitute, with the original negotiated agreement, a complex and expanding body of common understandings. The terms of those understandings may involve different levels of the organizations' parties to the original agreement, from the top level to the lowest operating level in each. These processes provide the "flesh and blood" of the interaction of the organizations over the "bare bones" of the formal agreement. In a sense, the negotiations process and the administrative process create a complex interrelation of the organizations on a day-to-day basis and not merely the written words of the formal agreement or protocol.

The Personal Ingredient

There is at least one facet of the negotiations process about which it is most difficult to generalize in principle: the importance of personal relationships among the principal negotiators. Agreements are made not merely among organizations but also among individuals acting in behalf of these organizations. Some individuals in these settings get along well and some do not, and this factor of personality, experience, skill, chemistry, attitude, and demeanor, as well as status in the organization, does not tend to make much difference in the agreement-making process in some situations while in others it matters very much. It is not unusual in negotiations for the chief negotiator of each side—sometimes with an aide—to talk "off-the-record" about procedures, timing, or substance, or to "try on for size" next moves or proposed settlements, or even to compare notes on constituencies. Accordingly these personal relationships may be pivotal. Even with respect to entirely professional negotiators, the factor of personality influence is often not inconsequential.

While it may not be possible to adjudge the quantitative impact of the personality and the interaction of the principal negotiators, a careful observer or mediator will carefully appraise it and take it into account. The reference to this factor may not be analytically neat, but it does reflect a principle of practical import in many instances.

In summary, the framework developed to elucidate negotiations among continuing organizations that expect to continue to relate to each other involves the following propositions:

1. In two-party negotiations, it takes an agreement within each side to reach an agreement across the table; that is, it takes three agreements to make one.
2. Initial proposals in negotiations are typically large compared with eventual settlements, for a variety of reasons. Priorities within each side are often actually established in the course of negotiations.
3. Negotiations is the process of changing positions and making concessions from initial positions in the course of moving toward an agreement.
4. A natural deadline or a designed one is an essential feature of most negotiations. Time is not neutral in its effects on the relative position of the negotiators.
5. The end-stages of negotiations are delicate when issues are limited and the distances apart are not large. Private discussion between one or two key persons on each side is often used to close the gap in the absence of a mediator.
6. Negotiations will be significantly influenced by the fact of whether the negotiating table is the final one or merely a step toward further negotiations, in new locales, with other higher-ranked negotiators or with neutrals.
7. Negotiations and serious conflict may be carried on simultaneously; the purpose of the overt conflict is typically to serve as a tool of agreement-making, although the conflict and its results may affect the bargaining objectives and priorities of the negotiators.
8. Agreement-making in negotiations does not flourish in public, with press and media, because serious negotiations require that the leaders at the table first communicate directly with their constituents concerning settlement and explain their recommendations in terms of the internal political life of the organization.
9. An agreement typically reflects the need for a recognized procedure to resolve questions on the meaning and application of the agreement or to fill in lacunae.
10. The personalities of negotiators and the way they relate to one another does affect the outcomes in some instances.

The Course of Negotiations

There is one further set of ideas that may be insightful in interpreting negotiations from the perspective of the observer or the negotiator. Ordinary negotiations tend to follow a pattern or course, and it may be helpful to locate a given session or point in time in this succession of stages or life cycle. A number of stages have been reflected in the above discussion.

In the initial stage, each side presents its credentials, identifies for whom it speaks, and states its authority to settle or to recommend settlement. Each organization then formally presents its proposals for an agreement, with supporting facts and argument.

The next stage involves each side in asking questions about the proposals, seeking to understand how they would operate, and probing the reasons for the proposals and searching for the true priority items for the current negotiations. Factual material may be developed and side-tables or sub-committees may be asked to generate data on particular issues in dispute.

Some effort may next be made to narrow the number of issues or reduce the magnitudes involved, following which will be an attempt to develop a package or alternative packages of proposals for a settlement. This process involves a search for relative priorities and trade-offs. The internal tensions within each side complicate this process.

The end-play stage of negotiations, closing the gap, often involves side-bar and private discussions among principal negotiators or with a mediator. Seldom is agreement reached directly at the negotiating table. There is typically considerable emotional release on reaching agreement—the joy of settlement.

An agreement usually must be reduced to "legal" language checked by both counsels. The appropriate ratification and approval processes need to be accomplished.

Not every day or night at the negotiating table is the same. There is typically a beginning and an end, as well as a sense of flow or a process through stages toward an agreement. While there is often a good deal of backing and filling, and even starting over again, the negotiators and close observers need a sense of location or stage in the course of the negotiations process.[22]

The Role of Mediation

The framework of the negotiation process among continuing organizations, summarized above, provides a setting to consider the questions: What do mediators do to facilitate agreement-making? What are the potentials and the limitations of the mediator?

There are various types of mediation and mediators, and the extent of penetration into the substantive bargaining discourse, as well as into the bargaining process, varies a great deal. Moreover, just as among negotiators, personality factors and status may be significant factors with some mediators. Some mediators may do little more than preside over meetings and maintain a modicum of order, while others may be deeply involved in proposing packages for settlement and in seeking acceptance of these proposals. But whatever the role of mediator in an individual situation, the mediation process in negotiations may be analyzed as follows.

1. The strategic position of the mediator relates fundamentally to the communication flow between the parties and on occasion (depending on location and time) between the principal negotiators and their larger committees and constituencies. Particularly in mediation in which the parties are separated and meet separately with the mediator—a situation existing at the most critical stages of most negotiations with mediation—the control over information flow between the parties is in the hands of the mediator.

This control is a substantial and significant tool. What the parties know of each other's changing positions, the explanations and rationales for changes, any view as to how far apart the parties may truly be, the status of internal conflicts of view, and critical attitudes and feelings all are within the control of the mediator. An encouraging or dismal picture may be portrayed to one or both sides. The way in which this control over information is utilized is the first principle in understanding the function of mediation in negotiations. Some information that is available to the mediator might have been transmitted by the parties to each other across the table, but some is known to one side and the mediator alone as a consequence of private discussions with that side. In other words, the mediator occupies a position of confidence and trust with each side. If, on the other hand, the parties communicate directly with each other, around the mediator, they are signaling the mediator's limited usefulness, probably restricting his role to housekeeping functions.

2. The mediator function often involves the development of mutually acceptable factual data to provide a setting for more informed and dispassionate discussion of particular issues. In some cases, the costing of various proposals and the validation of data regarding other settlements or levels of wages and benefits may be significant to settlement. The costing of complex pension plans or health care arrangements may be done with the mediator or with agreed-upon outside experts or sub-committees. It is difficult to exaggerate the importance and effectiveness of working through background factual material in a dispassionate mode with the parties.

3. The mediator serves as a private, informal advisor to each side

in the delicate art of putting together packages for consideration by the other. This role involves a sensitivity to the internal priorities and constituencies of each party. It also requires a sympathetic interpretation of each side's problems and aspirations to the other.

4. The mediator has the opportunity to formulate a distinctive and imaginative package proposal on his own from an independent and creative perspective. He is free to suggest ideas without having to reveal their origin to either party. These avenues are important because the parties may have pursued particular solutions or courses to the neglect of new or original ideas that may be more acceptable to both sides. Mediators differ greatly in their willingness to take such initiatives, although the most distinguished in the past generation, such as George Taylor or David L. Cole, were never bashful in this respect if the option appeared to offer an alternative for settlement.

5. The mediator has a special opportunity in the "end-game" of negotiations. When the parties are relatively close to settlement and are aware of it, the final steps may be very difficult. Each side may well believe that the other should make the final concessions. The dispute may appear particularly intractable at this juncture. Each side has made many moves that have hurt, and the internal hostility to a further accommodation is likely to be very high. In these circumstances a third party may greatly facilitate agreement. The separate conditional acceptance to the mediator by one side of a proposal does not prejudice the position of that side if there is no agreement. It is not unusual for a mediator to secure the separate acceptance of each side to a "package" of the mediator's design and then to bring the parties together to announce that, even if they do not know it, they have an agreement.

6. A critical factor affecting the role of the mediator is the circumstances by which he or she entered the dispute. In general, the strongest possible position derives from a joint invitation of the parties to the mediator to assist in the resolution of the controversy. The past relationship of the parties with the mediator, if any, is also likely to be a factor. A mediator may have so sought to induce agreement in a previous case as to be unacceptable to both parties, or to one side, in another situation.

7. A mediator may be asked to serve as an arbitrator with authority to determine a settlement on one or more specified issues. While arbitration is a different proceeding and bears a different relationship to negotiations than mediation, there is a class of arbitrations that involve the mediator in formally decreeing an agreed-upon settlement which the parties for one reason or another desire to be formally specified as an arbitration award. The arbitration format of a settlement may be more acceptable to certain internal constituencies or external groups.

8. Finally, mediators may play a role in settlement of some disputes by asserting a moral authority or assuming a role in the public interest. Such a role may be supported by public officials, by the press, or by interests among affected businesses or communities. In some limited circumstances this role may help to induce settlement, although rarely has this factor alone been very effective.

In summary, in the negotiations process among established organizations as analyzed earlier, mediation may play an independent role in achieving settlement. The analytical process of mediation achieves its outcomes through the following processes:

1. Control of the communication patterns among the parties, and the use of these flows to encourage settlement.
2. The dispassionate development of factual material thought to be relevant to the issues in negotiation.
3. Assistance to the parties in developing settlement package proposals.
4. Development of distinctive settlement packages different from those initiated by the parties.
5. Facilitating settlement in the "end-game" of negotiations without prejudicing the positions of the parties when further movement is required.
6. Molding of the role of the mediator by the circumstances and sponsorship under which he or she entered the dispute.
7. Facilitating acceptance of a settlement by issuing an arbitration award.
8. Exertion of moral authority or reflection of a public interest in the resolution of a dispute.

The Case for Negotiations in Dispute Resolution

As a means for the resolution of conflict between organizations, negotiations and agreement-making have a variety of advantages compared with litigation, governmental fiat, or warfare to extinction, although there are some agreements that may be unacceptable to the society expressed in its political and legal processes. The significant feature of an agreement is that both parties are committed to live by it rather than to continue conflict and warfare after a decision unacceptable to one side. There is simply no decision so precise or detailed that parties cannot continue to fight about its meaning, application, and scope if they choose to do so. There is an important sense in which no decision among groups can genuinely resolve a controversy unless the parties agree to accept it. The likelihood of parties enforcing their own agreement is far greater than their accepting a decision adverse to one party.

Beyond the basic superiority of genuinely settled controversy, an agreement achieved by negotiations has the virtue of eliminating or reducing the high costs of litigation, reducing the time required for a resolution, and avoiding uncertainty in the resolution. Further, the two sides are ordinarily capable of more imaginative solutions to problems than any outsiders, since they presumably know more about their problems and controversies than do others. It is also increasingly the case that many conflicts among groups are so complex or the groups are so powerful relative to each other that issues cannot be decided with a winner and a loser. The negotiations process often discovers a viable form of accommodation not previously evident. Negotiations can be creative and problem-solving, while most litigation tends to be formalistic and sterile.

These observations suggest that an understanding of the general principles of negotiations and some attendant rudimentary skills are essential features of the education of managers of public, non-profit, and business organizations alike. The traditional educational emphasis placed on an appreciation of markets and governmental processes including litigation, for practitioners and officers alike, needs to be shifted to some degree toward negotiations and agreement-making. The latter play a growing role in conflict resolution today, and they are likely to be even more significant in the future for private organizations and public policy. As Georg Simmel wrote in 1908: "On the whole, compromise, especially that brought about through exchange, no matter how much we think it is an everyday technique we take for granted, is one of mankind's greatest inventions."[23]

Endnotes

1. For a discussion of the institutional forms of markets, see John T. Dunlop, "Economic Vitalization and Market Competition," a paper presented at the International Productivity Symposium in Tokyo, Japan (Japan Productivity Center, May 11, 1983).
2. The term is that of Daniel Bell, *The Cultural Contradictions of Capitalism* (New York: Basic Books, Inc., 1976), pp. 220–27.
3. See Alfred D. Chandler, Jr., *The Visible Hand, The Managerial Revolution in American Business* (Cambridge, Mass.: Harvard University Press, 1977); Charles E. Lindblom, *Politics and Markets, The World's Political-Economic Systems* (New York: Basic Books, Inc., 1977); Charles L. Schultze, *The Public Use of Private Interest* (Washington, D.C.: The Brookings Institution, 1977).
4. See John T. Dunlop, "The Limits of Legal Compulsion" (November 11, 1975), reprinted in *Issues in Health Care Regulation*, Richard S. Gordon, Ed. (New York: McGraw-Hill, Inc., 1980), pp. 184–91; Murray L. Weidenbaum, *The Future of Business Regulation* (New York: Amacon, A Division of American Management Association, 1979).

5. *Cost of Government Regulation Study for Business Roundtable*, a study of the direct incremental costs incurred by 48 companies in complying with the regulations of six federal agencies in 1977 (Arthur Andersen and Company, March, 1979); Edward F. Denison, "Effects of Selected Changes in the Institutional and Human Environment upon Output per Unit of Input," *Survey of Current Business* (January 1978), pp. 21–44.

6. See also Gerald W. Cormick and Leota K. Patton, "Environmental Mediation: Defining the Process Through Experience," paper prepared for American Association for the Advancement of Science, Symposium on Environmental Mediation Cases (Denver, Colorado; February, 1977). The authors are associated with the Institute of Environmental Mediation, University of Washington; *Where We Agree: Report of the National Coal Policy Project*, Center for Strategic and International Studies, Georgetown University, 1981; The Conservation Foundation's newsletter, *Resolve*, is devoted to "environmental dispute resolution."

7. Lawrence S. Bacow, *Bargaining for Job Safety and Health* (Cambridge, Mass.: MIT Press, 1980); Philip J. Harter, "Negotiating Regulations: A Cure for Malaise," *Georgetown Law Journal*, October, 1982, pp. 1–118.

8. *Business Week* (June 30, 1980), p. 146.

9. *The AFL–CIO American Federationist* (January 8, 1983), p. 8; "Rebuilding America, A National Industrial Policy," *The AFL–CIO American Federationist* (October 22, 1983).

10. *The Wall Street Journal* (October 19, 1982), p. 34.

11. See for instance J. Pen, *The Wage Rate Under Collective Bargaining* (Cambridge, Mass.: Harvard University Press, 1959) (English edition, translated by T. S. Preston); Carl M. Stevens, *Strategy and Collective Bargaining Negotiation* (New York: McGraw-Hill Book Company, Inc., 1963); Ingolf Stahl, *Bargaining Theory* (Stockholm: The Economic Research Institute, 1972); Wallace N. Atherton, *Theory of Union Bargaining Goals* (Princeton, New Jersey: Princeton University Press, 1973), pp. 3–30. See Gerd Korman and Michael Klapper, "Game Theory's Wartime Connection and the Study of Industrial Conflict," *Industrial and Labor Relations Review* (October 1978), pp. 24–39.

12. John T. Dunlop and Benjamin Higgins, "'Bargaining Power' and Market Structures," *Journal of Political Economy* (February 1942), pp. 1–26.

13. Howard Raiffa, *The Art and Science of Negotiations* (Cambridge, Mass.: Harvard University Press, 1982). Angelo S. DeNisi and James B. Dworkin, "Final-Offer Arbitration and the Naive Negotiator," *Industrial and Labor Relations Review* (October 1981), pp. 78–87.

14. See Richard J. Butler and Ronald G. Ehrenberg, "Estimating the Narcotic Effect of Public Sector Impasse Procedures," *Industrial and Labor Relations Review* (October 1981), pp. 3–20.

15. See for instance, Edward Peters, *Strategy and Tactics in Labor Negotiations*, National Foreman's Institute (1955); Ann Douglas, *Industrial Peacemaking* (New York: Columbia University Press, 1962). Also see Harvard Business School case materials.

16. James J. Healy, ed., *Creative Collective Bargaining* (Englewood Cliffs, N.J.: Prentice-Hall, Inc., 1965); Benjamin M. Selekman, Sylvia K. Selekman, and Stephen H. Fuller, *Problems in Labor Relations*, 3d ed edition (New York: McGraw-Hill, 1964).

17. For earlier formulations see John T. Dunlop and James J. Healy, *Collective Bargaining: Principles and Codes,* Revised Edition (Homewood, Illinois: Richard D. Irwin, Inc., 1953), pp. 53–68 and unpublished manuscript (August 29, 1979).

18. For a detailed account and analysis of the negotiations see Roger B. Porter, *Presidential Decision Making, The Economic Policy Board* (Cambridge University Press, 1980), pp. 123–56 (The U.S.–U.S.S.R. Grain Agreement).

19. See Jonathan Brock, *Bargaining Beyond Impasse* (Boston: Auburn House Publishing Company, 1982).

20. See William E. Simkin, *Mediation and the Dynamics of Collective Bargaining* (Washington, D.C.: The Bureau of National Affairs, Inc., 1971); Deborah M. Kolb, *The Mediators* (Cambridge, Mass.: MIT Press, 1983).

21. Ronald Reagan and Richard G. Hubler, *Where's the Rest of Me?* (New York: Dell Publishing Company, 1965), p. 225.

22. The discussion of negotiations and mediation in this chapter has significant implications for public policy. The NLRB and the courts as well as public sector agencies in various states, have created the concept of "impasse" in negotiations to authorize a variety of unilateral actions. An employer may be free, for example, to make unilateral changes in working conditions or to withdraw from an association engaged in collective bargaining if an "impasse" exists. This is an utterly unsatisfactory and ambiguous standard. The parties may not be able to settle the dispute directly; they may be able to settle with one mediator but not with another; the dispute may remain one night but be settled in a further week. An "impasse" may be largely in the eye of the beholder, or it may be merely an excuse to destroy the other side. As a mediator I am unwilling to recognize a permanent "impasse" or even to announce one. For a summary of the law see Charles J. Morris, Editor-in-Chief, *The Developing Labor Law, the Board, the Courts, and the National Labor Relations Act* (Washington, D.C.: The Bureau of National Affairs, Inc., 1971), pp. 330–32.

23. Georg Simmel, *Conflict* and *The Web of Group-Affiliations,* Translated by Kurt H. Wolff (Glencoe, Ill.: The Free Press, 1955), p. 115.

Part Two

THE U.S. INDUSTRIAL RELATIONS SYSTEM AND ITS TENDENCIES

The discussion of negotiations and mediation in Chapter 1 implicitly presumed the industrial relations setting of the United States. The roles of labor organizations, business, and government reflect our domestic setting. The procedures of negotiations, the roles of labor and management organizations, and the status of government officials would be somewhat different in Australia, for instance, with its Commonwealth Conciliation and Arbitration Commission, or in Canada where separate provincial statutes govern the largest proportion of industrial relations, or in Great Britain with its union-management structure and voluntary conciliation bodies and courts of inquiry constrained by a tradition of private settlement. One also needs to appreciate the way in which the U.S. industrial relations system and its component actors have changed and evolved over the years in their internal policies, in their interactions, and in the consequences of their behavior.

The five chapters in Part Two are concerned explicitly with the larger industrial relations setting in which collective bargaining, negotiations, and joint consultation among labor organizations, managements, and governments arise in the United States. These chapters sketch the analytical concept of an industrial relations system and describe the characteristics of the U.S. arrangements, their past developments, and their future tendencies. Any full understanding of negotiations, dispute resolution, or cooperative activities as in labor-management committees requires an appreciation of the larger industrial relations systems in which these activities play roles.

29

Chapter 2

AN INDUSTRIAL RELATIONS SYSTEM

There are marked differences in industrial relations among enterprises, industries, and countries. While each work place is to a degree unique, there are groups of situations with common industrial-relations features. A participant—be he manager, worker, representative of workers, neutral, or government agent—moving from one place to another will recognize familiar arrangements; other moves will reveal strange surroundings. Practical experience in the United States would identify a distinctive pattern of industrial relations within the railroad industry, the maritime field, basic steel, a construction site, the plants of General Motors, the newspaper offices in metropolitan New York City, the Bank of America in California, or the offices of federal government departments. Each of these cases constitutes a system of industrial relations. For some purposes these illustrations may be broken down into smaller and more distinctive systems, and for other purposes they may be integrated into still larger systems. Those with industrial relations experience identify and distinguish among systems on the basis of rules of thumb developed out of experience.

Practitioners recognize that within a single industrial relations system there are common problems, distinctive from those posed in other systems; there tend to be distinctive solutions. A system has a certain unity; changes in one part of a system affect other parts of that system more directly than they affect other systems. The participants are more attuned to developments within the system than without;

From *Industrial Relations Systems* (New York, Henry Holt and Company, 1958), pp. 1–28.

they share distinctive common beliefs and prejudices. The perceptions of the sensitive practitioner are no substitute for systematic analysis, but they are a suggestive starting point.

The literature on industrial relations has begun to make explicit use of the term "system," particularly to describe features characteristic of one country and distinguished from others.[1] Two studies are illustrative: *The System of Industrial Relations in Great Britain*[2] and "The American System of Industrial Relations."[3] "System" in these writings does not mean a planned order. ". . . We have chosen to deal with so vital a matter as the relations between employers and employed in an extremely involved and haphazard fashion. This is, after all, an age of planning. Yet in no part of our economic life is planning so strongly opposed by all classes in the community."[4] "The ardent advocates of economic planning may be shocked by the haphazard consequences of our voluntary system; they see power overriding equity, tradition barring the way to rational change, and muddled compromise being preferred to ordered consistency."[5] "Perhaps it is wrong to designate as a 'system' a group of arrangements that has grown up without being planned as a whole. . . . Our arrangements in the field of industrial relations may be regarded as a system in the sense that each of them more or less intimately affects each of the others so that they constitute a group of arrangements for dealing with certain matters and are collectively responsible for certain results."[6]

The present interest in industrial relations systems is to be sharply distinguished from classifications of union-management relationships in the spectrum of labor peace and warfare.[7] These typologies use such terms as open conflict, armed truce, arms-length bargaining, and full cooperation; in one sense each may be regarded as a different system of relationships between parties. The concern with labor peace or warfare probably has stimulated interest in the larger subject of industrial relations systems, but such classifications have almost no relevance to the present inquiry.

What meaning, then, is to be given to an "industrial relations system"? In what sense is a "system" involved? Can the term be given rigorous and analytical definition, or shall it remain a perceptive phrase corresponding to the insights of practical experience? Are there characteristics common to all industrial relations systems? What factors distinguish one industrial relations situation from another? Can the same concept be used to facilitate analysis among sectors within a country and also among countries? These questions are suggestive of the major problem of this chapter: to provide *analytical* meaning to the idea of an industrial relations system.

Industrial Relations and Industrial Society

In primitive and agrarian societies the analogue of industrial relations problems arise—such as, who shall perform what work, what standards of discipline shall be applied at the work place, or how shall the fruits of labor be divided. These issues are typically handled within the extended family which is closely integrated into the society. In the plantation slave society the corresponding problems are met by the political institutions that maintain slavery.[8] Thus, industrial relations problems of a general type are not unique to modern industrial society. But industrial society, whatever its political form, creates a distinctive group of workers and managers. The relations among these workers and managers and their organizations are formally arranged in the industrial society outside the family and distinct from political institutions, although the family and political institutions may in fact be used to shape or control relations between managers and workers at the industrial work place.[9]

The full range of the complex interactions among groups and persons in a modern industrial society does not admit of ready description or explanation. The social system as a whole is ordinarily regarded as the province of sociology. Economics has carved out from the fullness of social action certain limited facets of behavior. Within the confines of these abstractions, it has developed rigorous theoretical models and analytical propositions relevant to these limited aspects of total social behavior. There is no purely economic behavior, but economists have developed significant and useful propositions about the economic aspects of behavior. They have also organized specialized collections of facts, often built around special-purpose concepts and definitions such as the national income accounts or input-output tables. Thus has economics become highly developed as a discipline.

The economic system can be regarded as a subsystem of the more general total social system. Few scholars have explored the interrelations and boundary lines between a general system of social action and economics more comprehensively or persistently than has Professor Talcott Parsons.[10] While it would be interesting to apply directly the general analytical scheme developed by Professor Parsons and various associates to the industrial relations features of industrial society,[11] such an exercise is not the central interest here. Nonetheless, the analogy of economics, an economic system, and the relations between the economic aspects of behavior and the totality of social action is suggestive for organizing insights and observations about the industrial relations aspects of behavior in industrial society.

1. An industrial relations system is to be viewed as an analytical subsystem of an industrial society on the same logical plane as an economic system, regarded as another analytical subsystem. The industrial relations system is not coterminous with the economic system; in some respects the two overlap and in other respects both have different scopes. The procurement of a work force and the setting of compensation for labor services are common centers of interest. A systematic explanation of production, however, is within economics but outside the scope of industrial relations. The full range of rule-making governing the work place is outside the scope of an economic system but central to an industrial relations system.

2. An industrial relations system is not a subsidiary part of an economic system but is rather a separate and distinctive subsystem of the society, on the same plane as an economic system. Thus, the theoretical tools designed to explain the economic system are not likely to be entirely suitable to another different analytical subsystem of society.

3. Just as there are relationships and boundary lines between a society and an economy, so also are there between a society and an industrial relations system. All analysis of the economy makes some assumptions, explicitly or implicitly, about the remainder of the social system; so also must an analysis of an industrial relations system make some assumptions about the rest of the social system.

4. An industrial relations system is logically an abstraction just as an economic system is an abstraction. Neither is concerned with behavior as a whole. There are no actors whose whole activity is confined *solely* to the industrial relations or economic spheres, although some may approach this limit. Neither an economic system nor an industrial relations system is designed simply to describe in factual terms the real world of time and space. Both are abstractions designed to highlight relationships and to focus attention upon critical variables and to formulate propositions for historical inquiry and statistical testing.

5. This view of an industrial relations system permits a distinctive analytical and theoretical subject matter. To date the study of industrial relations has had little theoretical content. At its origins and frequently at its best, it has been largely historical and descriptive. A number of studies have used the analysis of economics particularly in treating wages and related questions, and other studies, particularly of factory departments, have borrowed the apparatus of anthropology and sociology.[12] Although industrial relations aspires to be a discipline, and even though there exist separate professional societies, industrial relations has lacked any central analytical content. It has been a crossroads where a number of disciplines have met—history,

economics, government, sociology, psychology, and law. Industrial relations requires a theoretical core in order to relate isolated facts, to point to new types of inquiries, and to make research more additive. The study of industrial relations systems provides a genuine discipline.

6. Three separate analytical problems are to be distinguished in this framework: (a) the relation of the industrial relations system to the society as a whole, (b) the relation of the industrial relations system to the subsystem known as the economic system, and (c) the inner structure and characteristics of the industrial relations subsystem itself. These questions have not ordinarily been separated in industrial relations discussion, and what is given and what is variable accordingly has not been clearly stated. These issues are quite distinct. The next section considers the structure and characteristics of the industrial relations subsystem of industrial society.

Structure of an Industrial Relations System

An industrial relations system at any one time in its development is regarded as comprised of certain actors, certain contexts, an ideology which binds the system together and a body of rules created to govern the actors at the work place and work community.

The Actors in a System

The actors are (1) a hierarchy of managers and their representatives in supervision, (2) a hierarchy of workers (nonmanagerial) and any spokesmen, and (3) specialized governmental agencies (and specialized private agencies created by the first two actors) concerned with workers, enterprises, and their relationships. The first two hierarchies are directly related to each other in that the managers have responsibilities at varying levels to issue instructions (manage), and the workers at each corresponding level have the duty to follow such instructions (work).

The hierarchy of workers does not necessarily imply formal organizations; they may be said to be "unorganized" in popular usage, but the fact is that wherever they work together for any considerable period, at least an informal organization comes to be formulated among the workers with norms of conduct and attitudes toward the hierarchy of managers. In this sense workers in a continuing enterprise are never unorganized. The formal hierarchy of workers may be organized into several competing or complementary organizations, such as works councils, unions, and parties.

The hierarchy of managers need have no relationship to the ownership of the capital assets of the work place; the managers may be
public or private or a mixture in varying proportions. In the United
States, for instance, consider the diverse character of management
organizations in the executive departments of the federal government, local fire departments, the navy yards, the Tennessee Valley
Authority, municipal transit operations and local utilities, govern-
ment-owned and privately operated atomic-energy plants, railroads
and public utilities, and other private enterprises. The range of combinations is greater where governments own varying amounts of
shares of an enterprise and where special developmental programs
have been adopted. The management hierarchy in some cases may
be contained within an extended or a narrow family, and its activities
largely explained in terms of the family system of the society.

The specialized government agencies as actors may have functions
in some industrial relations systems so broad and decisive as to over-
ride the hierarchies of managers and workers on almost all matters. In
other industrial relations systems the role of the specialized governmental agencies, at least for many purposes, may be so minor or
constricted as to permit consideration of the direct relationships between the two hierarchies without reference to governmental agencies, while in still other systems the worker hierarchy or even the
managerial hierarchy may be assigned a relatively narrow role. But in
every industrial relations system these are the three actors.[13]

The Contexts of a System

The actors in an industrial relations system interact in a setting that
involves three sets of givens. These features of the environment of an
industrial relations system are determined by the larger society and
its other subsystems and are not explained within an industrial relations system. These contexts, however, are decisive in shaping the
rules established by the actors in an industrial relations system. The
significant aspects of the environment[14] in which the actors interact
are (1) the technological characteristics of the work place and work
community, (2) the market or budgetary constraints which impinge
on the actors, and (3) the locus and distribution of power in the larger
society.

The technological features of the work place have very far-reaching
consequences for an industrial relations system, influencing the form
of management and employee organization, the problems posed for
supervision, many of the features of the required labor force, and the
potentialities of public regulation. The mere listing of a few different
work places reveals something of the range of industrial relations

systems within an industrial society and the influence of the techno-logical characteristics: airlines, coal mines, steel mills, press and wire services, beauty parlors, merchant shipping, textile plants, banks, and food chain stores, to mention only a few. The technological char-acteristics of the work place, including the type of product or service created, go far to determine the size of the work force, its concentra-tion in a narrow area or its diffusion, the duration of employment at one locale, the stability of the same working group, the isolation of the work place from urban areas, the proximity of work and living quarters, the contact with customers, the essentiality of the product to the health and safety or to the economic development of the community, the handling of money, the accident potential, the skill levels and education required, the proportions of various skills in the work force, and the possibilities of the employment of women and children. These and many other features of the technology of the work place are significant to the type of managerial and worker hierar-chies and government agencies that arise. They also pose very differ-ent types of problems for the actors and constrain the types of solu-tions to these problems that may be invented and applied. Significant differences among industrial relations systems are to be attributed to this facet of the environment, and, in turn, identical technological environments in quite different national societies may be regarded as exerting a strong tendency upon the actors (modified by other factors) to create quite similar sets of rules.

The market or budgetary constraints are a second feature of the environmental context that is fundamental to an industrial relations system. These constraints often operate in the first instance directly upon the managerial hierarchy, but they necessarily condition all the actors in a particular system. The context may be a market for the output of the enterprise or a budgetary limitation or some com-bination of the two. The product market may vary in the degree and character of competition through the full spectrum from pure competition, monopolistic competition and product differentiation to oligopoly and monopoly. A charitable institution or a nationalized plant is no less confronted by a financial restraint than a private business enterprise, and the harshness of the budgetary strictures which confront managements vary among nonmarket units in the same way that degrees of competition vary among market-oriented enterprises. These constraints are no less operative in socialist than in capitalist countries. The relevant market or budgetary constraints may be local, national, or international, depending on the industrial relations system; the balance of payments constitutes the form of the market restraint for nationwide systems.

The product market or budget is a decisive factor in shaping the rules established by an industrial relations system.[15] The history in the past generation of the textile and coal industries around the world is testimony to the formative influence of the market or budgetary influence on the operation of industrial relations systems. The contrasts between industries sheltered or exposed to international competition is another illustration. The interdependence of wage and price fixing in public utilities gives a distinctive characteristic to these systems of industrial relations. The degrees of cost and price freedom in monopolistic industries permeate these industrial relations systems. The market or budgetary context also indirectly influences the technology and other characteristics of the work place: the scale and size of operations and the seasonal and cyclical fluctuations in demand and employment. An industrial relations system created and administered by its actors is adaptive to its market and budgetary constraints.

The locus and distribution of power[16] in the larger society, of which the particular industrial relations complex is a subsystem, is a third analytical feature of the environmental context. The relative distribution of power among the actors in the larger society tends to a degree to be reflected within the industrial relations system; their prestige, position, and access to the ultimates of authority within the larger society shapes and constrains an industrial relations system. At this juncture the concern is not with the distribution of power *within* the industrial relations system, the relative bargaining powers among the actors, or their controls over the processes of interaction or rule setting. Rather the reference is to the distribution of power outside the industrial relations system which is given to that system. It is, of course, possible that the distribution of power within the industrial relations system corresponds exactly to that within the contextual society. But that this need not be so is illustrated by numerous instances of conflict between economic power within an industrial relations system and political power within a society, or by the tendency for an actor to seek to transfer a conflict to the political or economic arena in which his control over the situation is thought to be relatively greater. The general strike and French and Italian experience for a period after World War II particularly illustrate the point. The dominance of an army group, a traditional and dynastic family elite, a dictator, the church, a colonial administrator, a political party, or public opinion are types of power orientation in the larger society that tend to shape an industrial relations system.

The distribution of power in the larger society does not directly determine the interaction of the actors in the industrial relations system. Rather, it is a context that helps to structure the industrial relations system itself. The function of one of the actors in the industrial relations system, the specialized governmental agencies, is likely to be particularly influenced by the distribution of power in the larger society. Industrial relations systems national in scope as different as those in contemporary Spain, Egypt, USSR, Yugoslavia, and Sweden call attention to the distribution of power within the larger society. Industrial relations systems of a lesser scope, such as those at the plant level, are also shaped by the distribution of power within the system that is exterior to the plant level. Thus, the industrial relations system at a plant level which is part of a highly centralized industry-wide arrangement is quite different from one which is decentralized to the plant level. The distribution of power in the society exterior to the industrial relations system is regarded as given to that system and helps to shape its operations.

The full context of an industrial relations system given for the three actors consists at a given time in the development of that system of (1) the technological and work-community environment, (2) the market or budgetary constraints, and (3) the distribution of power in the contextual society.

The Establishment of Rules

The actors in given contexts establish rules for the work place and the work community, including those governing the contacts among the actors in an industrial relations system. This network or web of rules[17] consists of procedures for establishing rules, the substantive rules, and the procedures for deciding their application to particular situations. The establishment of these procedures and rules (the procedures are themselves rules) is the center of attention in an industrial relations system. Just as the "satisfaction of wants" through the production and exchange of goods and services is the locus of analysis in the economic subsystem of society, so the establishment and administration of these rules is the major concern or output of the industrial relations subsystem of industrial society. In the course of time the rules may be expected to be altered as a consequence of changes in the contexts and in the relative statuses of the actors. In a dynamic society the rules, including their administration, are under frequent review and change.

There is a wide range of procedures possible for the establishment and the administration of the rules. In general terms the following ideal types can be distinguished: The managerial hierarchy may have a relatively free hand uninhibited in any overt way by the other two actors; the specialized governmental agencies may have the dominant role without substantial participation of the managerial or worker hierarchies; the worker hierarchy may even carry the major role in rule fixing; the management and worker hierarchies in some relationships may set the rules together without substantial participation of any specialized governmental agency; and, finally, the three actors may all play a consequential role in rule setting and administration. The procedures and the authority for the making and the administration of the rules governing the work place and the work community is a critical and central feature of an industrial relations system, distinguishing one system from another.

The actors who set the web of rules interact in the context of an industrial relations system taken as a whole, but some of the rules will be more closely related to the technical and market or budgetary constraints, while others will be more directly related to the distribution of power in the larger society. Thus maritime safety rules are related primarily to the technology of ships, while rules defining the relative rights of officers and crew aboard ship are related primarily to the distribution of power in a larger society. But safety rules are also influenced to a degree by the distribution of power in the full community, and the obligations and rights of officers and crew aboard ship are clearly conditioned to a degree by the technical problems of running a ship. While the context is an interdependent whole, some rules are more dependent upon one feature of this context than others.

A vast universe of substantive rules is established by industrial relations systems apart from procedures governing the establishment and the administration of these rules. In general, this expanse can be charted to include (1) rules governing compensation in all its forms, (2) the duties and performance expected from workers including rules of discipline for failure to achieve these standards, and (3) rules defining the rights and duties of workers, including new or laid-off workers, to particular positions or jobs. The actual content of these rules varies enormously among systems, particularly, as will be shown, as a consequence of the technological and market contexts of the systems.

One of the major purposes of this inquiry is to determine the extent to which similar rules are developed in different industrial relations systems with common technological contexts and similar market or budgetary constraints. The inquiry also seeks to isolate in systems otherwise similar the separate influence of the locus of power in the larger society, the form of organization of the actors, and their relationships upon the substantive rules. In general terms the rules, including the procedures for establishing and administering them, may be treated as the dependent variable to be "explained" theoretically in terms of other characteristics of the industrial relations system.

Whatever the specific content of rules and regardless of the distribution of authority among the actors in the setting of the rules, the detailed and technical nature of the rules required in the operation of an industrial society tends to create a special group of experts or professionals[18] within the hierarchies of the actors. This group within each hierarchy has the immediate responsibility for the establishment and the administration of the vast network of rules. The existence of job-evaluation plans, incentive or piece-rate systems, engineering time studies, pension plans, or many seniority arrangements is ample evidence of the role of experts or professionals in rule-making. Indeed, one of the major problems within the hierarchies of actors is the difficulty of communication and genuine understanding between such experts and the rest of the hierarchy. There may be on occasion a greater community of interests and understanding among such experts in different hierarchies than between them and the lay members of their own hierarchy.[19]

The experts tend to place the interaction among organizations of workers and managers and special governmental agencies on a more factual basis with careful technical studies made within each of the various hierarchies, or on a cooperative basis. These expert or professional ties on specialized issues tend to add to the stability of the system and to bind the actors closer together. The resort to a study by experts is an established method of reducing, at least for a period, tensions that arise among the actors.

The rules of the system may be expressed in a variety of forms: the regulations and policies of the management hierarchy; the laws of any worker hierarchy; the regulations, decrees, decisions, awards, or orders of governmental agencies; the rules and decisions of specialized agencies created by the management and worker hierarchies; collective-bargaining agreements, and the customs and traditions of the work place and work community. In any particular system the rules may be incorporated in a number of these forms; they may be written, an oral tradition, or customary practice. But whatever form the rules may take, the industrial relations system prescribes the rules of the work place and work community, including the procedures for their establishment and administration.

The Ideology of an Industrial Relations System

An industrial relations system has been described so far in terms of actors who interact in a specified context and who in the process formulate a complex of rules at the work place and work community. A further element is required to complete the analytical system: an ideology[20] or a set of ideas and beliefs commonly held by the actors that helps to bind or to integrate the system together as an entity. The ideology of the industrial relations system is a body of common ideas that defines the role and place of each actor and that defines the ideas which each actor holds toward the place and function of the others in the system. The ideology or philosophy of a stable system involves a congruence or compatibility among these views and the rest of the system. Thus, in a community in which the managers hold a highly paternalistic view toward workers and the workers hold there is no function for managers, there would be no common ideology in which each actor provided a legitimate role for the other; the relationships within such a work community would be regarded as volatile, and no stability would likely be achieved in the industrial relations system. It is fruitful to distinguish disputes over the organization of an industrial relations system or disputes that arise from basic inconsistencies in the system from disputes within an agreed or accepted framework.

Each of the actors in an industrial relations system—managerial hierarchy, worker hierarchy, and specialized public agencies—may be said to have its own ideology.[21] An industrial relations system requires that these ideologies be sufficiently compatible and consistent so as to permit a common set of ideas which recognize an acceptable role for each actor. Thus, in the industrial relations system of Great Britain[22] the philosophy of "voluntarism" may be said in a general way to be common to all three actors; this accepted body of ideas defines the role for manager and worker hierarchies and defines their ideas toward each other within the system; it also prescribes the limited role for specialized public agencies. The ideologies which characterize the industrial relations arrangements, for instance, of India[23] and the Soviet Union[24] are each different from the British.

The ideology of an industrial relations system must be distinguished from the ideology of the larger society; but they can be expected to be similar or at least compatible in the developed industrial society. In the process of industrialization, however, there may be marked differences between the ideology (relevant to the role of managers, workers, and public agencies) of the actors within the industrial relations system and other segments of the larger society which may even be dominant, such as the ideology of the traditional agricultural landholders. Nonetheless, the ideology of an industrial relations system comes to bear a close relationship to the ideology of the particular industrial society of which it is a subsystem. Indeed, in the absence of a general consistency of the two ideologies, changes may be expected in the ideologies or in other facets of the industrial relations system.

The term ideology may convey a more rationalized and formalized body of ideas than is intended. The actors in the system are often inclined to be pragmatic and may hold ideas that are to a degree inconsistent or lack precision. But hierarchies of managers and workers (when formally organized) and public agencies also tend to develop or adopt intellectuals, publicists, or other specialists concerned with articulating systematically and making some form of order out of the discrete ideas of the principal actors. These statements, preachments, and creeds tend to be reworked and reiterated, and in the process even a fairly explicit ideology may emerge. Each industrial relations system contains its ideology or shared understandings.

An Illustration

The preceding section has been concerned with developing in general outline the analytical concept of an industrial relations system—a formal and definitional exercise. No one looks for precise correspondence between the world of construct and the world of experience, but the concept may be clarified, and the unity and interdependence of a system may be more simply portrayed, if an illustration is very briefly presented at this stage of the exposition.

The railroads in the United States have a distinctive system of industrial relations. It gradually evolved over the past century to its present form and has been relatively stable for almost three decades; there have been some changes in rules, of course, but the main structure of the system is well established. The actors are the Class I carriers, the national railway labor organizations, and the specialized governmental agencies including the National Mediation Board, the divisions of the National Railroad Adjustment Board, emergency boards, and the Railway Retirement Board.

The carriers above the management hierarchies of individual railroad companies are organized into the National Carriers' Conference Committee representing the major railroads in collective bargaining on an industry-wide basis. Within a single railroad the management structure is organized into divisions according to operating requirements, length of track, and other technological factors. At each level in the hierarchy from a division to all carriers as a group there are specialized personnel concerned with the formulation or administration of rules.

The labor organizations are comprised of some twenty-three national craft organizations which are federated together in several ways: the six shop crafts operate together on many problems of common concern in the repair shops; the fifteen nonoperating unions, including the shop crafts, negotiate together on general wage changes and fringe compensation; the operating unions have negotiated singly or in various combinations, but in no fixed grouping; almost all the organizations are affiliated with the Railway Labor Executives' Association. The union and management hierarchies from the division to the top levels have corresponding and opposite numbers at each level, and rule formulation and administration takes place at each level appropriate to the generality of the issue.

The specialized governmental agencies were established by national legislation in which both parties were actively involved in discussions and proposals, and on occasion the legislation reflected the agreed-upon views of the management and employee hierarchies. These agencies determine the bargaining representative for the craft or class, decide disputes over the administration of rules that cannot be directly resolved, and mediate and make recommendations on issues of new rules that cannot be otherwise settled. A separate retirement system and agency exists for railroad employees. The parties are both very much involved in the processes by which policy-making appointments to these agencies are made.

The technological context of railroads has many distinctive features affecting the relations of managers and workers: The train operating divisions use small crews working together and in movement far from close and immediate supervision; complex and expensive equipment is utilized with a high ratio of capital to worker; the technology has produced steadily increasing speeds and longer trains; a very high degree of responsibility (and considerable skill) is required of the major operating positions; the costs of accidents can be consequential; the hours of operations for equipment may be around the clock, and they do not conform to normal factory schedules, although repair shops and many clerical operations conform to conventional work-weeks; the transportation services are regarded as vital to many other industries and to the community generally; there is a high degree of continuity of operations in many departments, and the public utility status of the railroads requires the maintenance of published service; there is intimate contact with the public in the train service and in the selling of tickets and at corresponding points with freight customers.

The market context may be characterized by the governmental determination of commodity and class freight rates and passenger fares (product prices), by the keen competition of other forms of transport, and by a high sensitivity to fluctuations in general levels of business activity.

The locus and distribution of power in the American community has had significant impacts on the structuring of the railroad industrial relations system. The relatively larger role of governmental processes (legislative and administrative) in railroads for a very long period has led to the development of managerial and employee hierarchies particularly sensitive to and knowledgeable of the legislative and administrative bodies concerned with railroad matters as compared with most other management and labor organizations. The wide distribution of railroad workers across the country, even in agricultural states, combined with the significance of governmental agencies for railroads, has resulted in a legislative and administrative influence and expertise unrivaled among American labor organizations.

The ideological aspect of an industrial relations system is likely to be most distinctive in considering a system of a whole country, and it has been suggested that the ideological character of a particular system within a country shares both many of the ideological features of the full industrial relations system of the country and the ideological character of the whole society. The American railroad industrial relations system does share much of the ideology of the American collective-bargaining system and society. All three actors have consistent ideas of their roles and the functions of the other actors. There are some distinctive ideas and interests that further help to bind this system together: The common concern with the growing competition of other forms of transportation has led on occasion to mutual discussions of common interests and to proposals for common action on such matters as state laws regulating the length of trains. There is some development of a sense of a common stake in a livelihood threatened by competition. Then, large sections of railway management have come from the ranks, perhaps more than in most industries, and this provides some sense of a common experience and a mutuality in looking at problems.

The rules developed by the railroad industrial relations system are related to the contexts already noted: the historic rules on rates of compensation for operating personnel involve the "dual method of pay," under which elapsed time and mileage traveled affect earnings. The weight of engines and the length of train also affect earnings of some operating crafts. Nonoperating personnel have more conventional methods of compensation. These various methods of pay are tailor-made to the technological and market contexts. The rules regarding the rights and duties of employees are significantly affected by the continuity of railroad operations, by the difficulties of comparing individual workers over a whole railroad property, and by the large element of responsibility in many jobs. As a consequence "seniority" in specified "districts" has a distinctive role to play, and it permeates the whole system of rules. The rules on promotion, layoffs, and transfer were evolved from the technological and market contexts and are consonant with them and the rules on compensation. The procedures used for the administration of the complex of rules ending in the divisions of the boards of adjustment are likewise congenial to the other rules and to the geographical diversity of operations; the procedures work very slowly, for there is less imperative for speed than in most other industrial relations systems, and "retroactivity" to the date a claim is filed is a significant feature to the operation of the system. The procedures established by statute providing for the unique role of the government in the making of agreements, in the event the parties fail to agree (emergency boards), is derived from a common recognition within the system of the essential nature of railroad transportation to the national community. The absence of a fixed duration to collective-bargaining agreements and rules, except as occasionally otherwise specifically bargained, is a distinctive feature of the system attributable to the lengthy procedures used in making contracts and to the system of setting railroad rates and fares.

The railroad industrial relations system has its own social customs. As distinct from formal channels, there are important informal and personal lines of communications among persons in all three groups of actors. The professionals in each group particularly develop distinctive habits in their interactions in conferences and formal hearings, in their places of meeting, and even in their social gatherings. "There is a great deal of affinity between those who were engaged in the same occupation . . .", ". . . the employers and workers . . . were bound together by a common experience and a common love for their occupation. . . ."[25] The railway industrial relations system is a very human institution; flesh and blood soften analytical bones.

Such a brief description of the American railroad industrial relations system cannot adequately convey its distinctive features and internal unity, since no systematic comparisons or contrasts have been drawn with other industrial relations systems.[26] It is in the perspective of other systems that the reality and the distinctive characteristics of a system can be more fully appreciated and understood.

Some Implications of an Industrial Relations System

In the preceding discussion, an industrial relations system has been used on occasion to refer to a subsystem of a national society, at times to a system of industrywide scope, and in other settings to a system in a single enterprise. The term is designed to be applied to each, depending on the scope of the discussion. The smaller the unit to which the term is applied, the larger the context and, in general, the larger the influence of givens outside the system. This multiple usage of the term requires only that the reference to scope be made clear in each instance. The formulation has the merit of facilitating comparisons (and contrasts) within a country, between comparable sectors of different countries, and between industrial relations systems of countries taken as a whole.

The usage that has been developed recognizes that a group of allied systems may be integrated into a larger sector or into a national system. In turn many systems may be subdivided into specialized smaller systems, depending upon the purpose at hand. The American railroad industrial relations system is an integral part of the larger national system; it is also meaningful to explore the industrial relations system on the Baltimore and Ohio Railroad or some other separable road and even in particular shops or a division. It must be recognized, however, that not all industrial relations systems are equally compatible or divisible and that combinations and separations cannot be made arbitrarily which destroy the sense of unity in the resultant grouping.

The preceding formulation calls attention to the fact that a national industrial relations system has a variety of more limited systems within it. They are not all the same, and the features that are ordinarily regarded as distinctive to a national system do not all enter equally into each industrial relations system within its borders. It becomes evident that the industrial relations system characteristic of a country or a region may arise because of the dominance of a particular industry. For instance, the relative influence of the automobile industry in Detroit and basic steel in Pittsburgh give industrial relations in these metropolitan areas a distinctive coloration. A company town is another illustration. In general terms, the industrial relations system of any aggregate will be shaped by the relative prevalence of different types of the component systems.

The import of the discussion is that international comparisons of industrial relations systems may be less fruitful, or even misleading, if confined solely to countrywide systems. It is essential to examine for comparable sectors and industries the component industrial relations systems in the various countries. In such comparisons, with the technology and the market contexts relatively constant, it should be possible to highlight more sharply the separate effects and characteristics of the national industrial relations systems. A comparison of systems across countries in such industries as maritime, coal mining, aviation, automobiles, textiles, basic steel, and construction, to mention a few which appear to have rather distinctive and decisive technological and market contexts, should permit some testing of the impact of national systems in these cases. Are the rules developed in these industries similar among countries or do they vary substantially? Which rules show considerable similarity and which reflect the diverse influences of the national industrial relations systems? It may be suggested for exploration that in some industries, such as those just noted, the similar technological and market contexts result in a number of comparable rules, overriding the influence of national peculiarities, while in other sectors the influence of the national system is more paramount overriding any similarities in the technological and market context or reflecting significant differences in these elements of the context. A comparison of national industrial relations systems and systems for particular sectors across national lines should accordingly prove of considerable theoretical interest.

It is suggested for further exploration that for industrial relations systems of a lesser scope than a country (thus for an industry) the technological and market (or budgetary) contexts are likely to be most significant in influencing the comparative rules which emerge, and that in the comparison of national systems the locus and distribution of power in the larger communities, as given to the industrial relations systems, is likely to be most significant in influencing the characteristics of the distinctive national rules. It may also be inferred that there is a higher degree of uniformity in the substantive content of rules among countries in comparable industries that concern the duties of employees, discipline, safety, and many aspects of compensation in the work place than the degree of similarity among rules concerning the establishment and administration of substantive rules.

The simple description of industrial relations in several countries (or in several industries in one country) tends to be concerned with institutional shapes and forms rather than with substantive operations of the systems. A description of practices in Great Britain, for instance, would point out that rule making is determined in some industries by voluntary private collective bargaining, in other industries by publicly established wages councils, and in still others by joint industrial councils (JIC). The description would go on to elaborate the differences in form, origins, and legislative background and the procedures that are used by these bodies. While these institutional variants are of interest for some administrative and historical purposes, they tend to obscure the unity of the British industrial relations system. Allan Flanders has well said, "It is difficult to know where statutory regulation ends and voluntary regulation begins; it is still more difficult to discover any practical significance in the distinction between industries with JIC's and those with some other arrangements for collective bargaining."[27] The attention to rule making in industrial relations systems provides a common denominator for the comparative analysis of systems of different forms.

The idea of an industrial relations system implies a unity, an interdependence, and an internal balance that is likely to be restored if the system is displaced, provided there is no fundamental change in the actors, contexts, or ideology. Industrial relations systems show considerable tenacity and persistence. The essential unity of an industrial relations system raises doubts about the transfer of rules, practices, or arrangements from one system to another. There is, for example, a prima-facie case against the export of the terms of American collective-bargaining agreements or American-style trade unions to industrial relations systems with essentially different actors, contexts, and ideologies. The same may be said, of course, for the export of features of any other industrial relations system, except that in the spectrum of world experience the American arrangements are likely to be relatively more specialized.

In the preceding discussion, an industrial relations system was developed at one moment in time. But an industrial relations system may also be thought of as moving through time, or, more rigorously, as responding to changes that affect the constitution of the system. The web of rules can be expected to change with variations in the three features of the context of the system. Changes may be expected in the complex of procedural and substantive rules with alterations in the technological context, in the market or budgetary constraints, and in the locus and distribution of power in the larger society. Changes may originate within the organizations of the actors, and the task of analysis is to indicate the consequences for the complex of rules. The formal analysis also suggests that changes in ideology, as a response to the larger society, may also come to have an impact upon the rules established by an industrial relations system. An industrial relations system provides a means of organizing inquiry into changes over time in the rules and other features of industrial relations.

This chapter has set forth a formal theoretical framework with which to approach industrial relations aspects of experience. The test of this concept of an industrial relations system is to be found not primarily in its elegance (or lack of it) or even in its internal consistency but rather in the process of making detailed studies of industrial relations systems among countries, on a countrywide and industry basis, and within a single country among different sectors. Only its application to particular situations will effectively show whether it usefully calls attention to significant relationships and enlightens new and neglected features of experience. The test of a model ultimately is in its use.

Endnotes

1. The term is used in the following works: Walter Galenson, *The Danish System of Labor Relations: A Study in Industrial Peace* (Cambridge, Mass.: Harvard University Press, 1952); Paul H. Norgren, *The Swedish Collective Bargaining System* (Cambridge, Mass.: Harvard University Press, 1941).

2. Edited by Allan Flanders and H. A. Clegg (Oxford: Basil Blackwell and Mott, 1954), pp. v, 260, 285.

3. Sumner H. Slichter in *Arbitration Today, Proceedings of the Eighth Annual Meeting, National Academy of Arbitrators* in Boston, Massachusetts on January 27–28, 1955 (Washington, D.C.: BNA Inc., 1955), pp. 167–186.

4. Flanders and Clegg, *loc. cit.*, p. 260.

5. *Ibid.*, p. 315.

6. Slichter, *loc. cit.*, p. 168.

7. Benjamin M. Selekman, "Varieties of Labor Relations," *Harvard Business Review* (March 1949), pp. 175–199; F. H. Harbison and J. R. Coleman, *Goals and Strategy in Collective Bargaining* (New York: Harper and Brothers, 1951); National Planning Association, *Causes of Industrial Peace* (New York: Harpers and Brothers, 1955).

8. W. Arthur Lewis, *The Theory of Economic Growth* (London: George Allen and Unwin, 1955), pp. 107–113.

9. Clark Kerr, Frederick H. Harbison, John T. Dunlop, and Charles A. Myers, "The Labour Problem in Economic Development," *International Labour Review* (March 1955), pp. 223–235. Also see Clark Kerr, John T. Dunlop, Frederick Harbison, and Charles A. Myers, *Industrialism and Industrial Man, The Problems of Labor and Management in Economic Growth* (Cambridge, Mass.: Harvard University Press, 1960).

10. Talcott Parsons and Neil J. Smelser, *Economy and Society, A Study in the Integration of Economy and Social Theory* (London, Routledge and Kegan Paul, 1956). A social system is defined as ". . . the system generated by any process of *interaction,* on the socio-cultural level, between two or more actors." The actor is either a concrete human individual [a person] or a collectivity of which a plurality of persons are members." (p. 8)

11. For a suggestion in this direction see the brief note in John T. Dunlop, *Industrial Relations Systems* (New York: Henry Holt and Company, 1958), pp. 28–32.

12. W. H. Scott, J. A. Banks, A. H. Halsey, and T. Lupton, *Technical Change and Industrial Relations, A Study of the Relations between Technical Change and the Social Structure of a Large Steelworks* (Liverpool: Liverpool University Press, 1956), pp. 263–281.

13. The term "actor" may have the limitation that it conveys the unreality or pretense of the stage. But "participant" is too passive and other terms are no more satisfactory. "Actor" is used in the sense of doer or reagent.

14. ". . . There does always exist some organization of living matter whose function is to maintain itself in direct interaction with its environment. In the terminology of modern genetics, we may speak of this as the phenotypic system." Julian Huxley, "Evolution, Cultural and Biological," in *New Bottles for New Wine* (London, Chatto and Windus, 1957), p. 63.

15. John T. Dunlop, *Wage Determination under Trade Unions* (New York: The Macmillan Company, 1944), pp. 95–121.

16. S. K. and B. M. Selekman, *Power and Morality in a Business Society* (New York: McGraw-Hill Book Company, 1956).

17. Clark Kerr and Abraham Siegel, "The Structuring of the Labor Force in Industrial Society: New Dimensions and New Questions," *Industrial and Labor Relations Review* (January 1955), pp. 163–164.

18. The term "professional" does not mean a member of one of the generally recognized established professions with access by formal education.
19. George W. Brooks, "Reflections on the Changing Character of American Labor Unions," *Proceedings of the Ninth Annual Meeting, Industrial Relations Research Association* (December 28 and 29, 1956), pp. 33–43.
20. The term "shared understandings" has been suggested by Clark Kerr to characterize the English and American social scene. See Reinhard Bendix, *Work and Authority in Industry, Ideologies of Management in the Course of Industrialization* (New York: John Wiley & Sons, 1956), p. xii.
21. For a discussion of managerial ideologies see *ibid.*
22. Flanders and Clegg, *loc. cit.*, p. 260.
23. Charles A. Myers, *Labor Problems in the Industrialization of India* (Cambridge, Mass.: Harvard University Press, 1958).
24. Isaac Deutscher, *Soviet Trade Unions*, London, Royal Institute of International Affairs, 1950; Joseph S. Berliner, *Factory and Manager in the USSR* (Cambridge, Mass.: Harvard University Press, 1957), pp. 25–44, 271–278.
25. International Labor Office, *Minutes of the Ninety-first Session of the Governing Body, London, 16–20 December 1943*, p. 54; *Minutes of the 94th Session of the Governing Body, London, 25–31 January 1945*, p. 61. (Sir Frederick Leggett, discussing the proposal of Mr. Ernest Bevin for industry committees.)
26. For a more detailed treatment see Jacob J. Kaufman, *Collective Bargaining in the Railroad Industry* (New York: King's Crown Press, 1954).
27. Flanders and Clegg, *loc. cit.*, pp. 288–289.

Chapter 3

THE DEVELOPMENT OF
LABOR ORGANIZATION:
A THEORETICAL FRAMEWORK[1]

"The facts" do not tell their own story; they must be cross-examined. They must be carefully analyzed, systematized, compared and interpreted."[2] This conclusion is an indictment of the all-too-frequent approach to the development of the labor movement,[3] in which "history" and "theory" are separate and non-permeable compartments.

Under the caption of "history of labor" are chronicled what purport to be collections of fact and sequences of fact. Under the heading of "theory of labor organization" are found "explanations" conjured out of inner consciousness with only occasional and convenient reference to the past. The "history" and "theory" of the labor movement can have little meaning in isolation.[4] But it is particularly the failure of theoretical apparatus that accounts for the lack of greater understanding of the development of the labor movement and the paucity of significant research. Indeed, despite all the epoch-making growth in labor organization in the 1930's and 1940's there was virtually no contribution to the "theory."[5]

Let us here re-examine the fashions of thinking in theories of the labor movement, proceeding from the initial conviction that any theory of the labor movement must first establish its criteria. Just what questions is a theory of labor organization supposed to answer? Only after this task has been explicitly recognized can there be critical discussion of the development of the labor movement.

The body of economic theory attempts to explain the allocation of

From *Insights into Labor Issues*, Richard A. Lester and Joseph Shister, Eds. (New York: The Macmillan Company, 1948), pp. 163–93.

resources.[6] Business cycle theories present systems of propositions to make intelligible the fluctuations of the economic system. In similar terms, what is the *pièce de résistance* of a theory of the labor movement? By what standards or tests is it possible to prefer one theory to another? What behavior must such a theory explain to be judged a "closer fit" than another model?

Explanations of the Labor Movement

The literature on theories of the labor movement, if carefully analyzed, reveals at least four questions that have been the concern of investigators. As far as can be determined, however, nowhere are these questions posed explicitly.

1. How is one to account for the origin or emergence of labor organizations? What conditions are necessary and what circumstances stimulate the precipitation of labor organization? Why have some workers organized and others not?
2. What explains the pattern of growth and development of labor organizations? What factors are responsible for the sequence and form in which organizations have emerged in various countries, industries, crafts, and companies? Since there is great diversity in the patterns of development, any theory of the labor movement must account for these differences.
3. What are the ultimate goals of the labor movement? What is its relationship to the future of capitalism? What is its role in the socialist or communist state?
4. Why do individual workers join labor organizations? What system of social psychology accounts for this behavior of the employee?

Most writings on theories of the labor movement have in effect been concerned with one or several of these questions. They show a tendency to seek a single and usually oversimplified statement of the development of labor organization. But the labor movement is highly complex and many-sided. The "history" does not readily lend itself to any single formula.

The pages immediately following constitute a brief summary of the principal contributions to theories of the labor movement. No attempt will be made to present a detailed appraisal of these views; the summary cannot be an exegesis. The discussion is necessarily sketchy. It may be helpful, however, to have in brief compass a summary of views since none exists. Brevity at times has the virtue of concentrating on and compelling attention to essentials.

Frank Tannenbaum[7]

To Tannenbaum "the labor movement is the result and the machine is the major cause."[8] The machine threatens the security of the individual worker and the wage earner reacts in self-defense through a union to attempt to control the machine. The individual worker seeks to harness the machine and to stem the tide of insecurity by which his life is menaced.

He intends little more than this security when joining a union, but ". . . in the process of carrying out the implications of defense against the competitive character of the capitalist system he contributes to the well-being of present-day society—a contribution which represents a by-product of the more immediate and conscious attempt to find security in an insecure world."[9] Tannenbaum sees the labor movement ultimately displacing the capitalistic system by "industrial democracy," "an achievement which is implicit in the growth and development of the organized labor movement."[10]

Tannenbaum provides an answer of sorts to at least three of the four questions posed above; he does not examine the pattern of growth of the labor movement. While not concerned with historical detail, Tannenbaum finds the origin of labor organizations in a reaction to the machine (question 1). The labor movement creates a new society (question 3). The individual worker joins the union in self-defense in quest of security (question 4).

Sidney and Beatrice Webb[11]

A trade union is a "continuous association of wage earners for the purpose of maintaining or improving the conditions of their working lives."[12] Its fundamental objective, according to the Webbs, is "the deliberate regulation of the conditions of employment in such a way as to ward off from the manual-working producers the evil effects of industrial competition."[13] The labor organization utilizes, in the well-known schema of the Webbs, the "methods" of mutual insurance, collective bargaining, and legal enactment. The labor organization chooses among these "methods" depending on the stage of development of the society. An era of the master system requires the enforcement of common rules against "industrial parasitism"; the existence of trusts makes legal enactment the only effective method in many cases. The assumption by government of responsibility for social risks, such as old age and unemployment, greatly curtails the use of the method of mutual insurance on the part of labor organizations.

In the view of the Webbs, trade unionism is ". . . not merely an incident of the present phase of capitalist industry, but has a permanent function to fulfill in the democratic state."[14] The special function of the trade union is in the democratic administration of industry. While consumers acting through cooperatives or entrepreneurs may determine *what* is produced, the democratic society requires a labor organization to provide for the participation of workers in the conditions of sale of their services. In the type of democratic society the Webbs eventually expected (the little profit-taker and the trust superseded by the salaried officer of the cooperative and by government agencies), the unions would more and more assume the character of professional associations.

The Webbs use the term "theory of trade unionism"[15] not to refer to answers to any of the four questions posed in the preceding section but as a statement of the economic consequences of a labor organization, virtually a theory of wages or collective bargaining. The trade union is pictured as having only two "expedients" for the improvement of conditions of employment:[16] the restriction of numbers in the trade and the establishment of uniform minimum standards required of each firm. The Webbs condemned the former monopolist policy. They endorsed the latter application of the Common Rule, for it transfers competition from wages to quality. The device of the Common Rule envisages the gradual improvement in these minimum standards of wages and conditions. It is the duty of the labor organization to strive perpetually to raise the level of its common rules. This process may be carried on by collective bargaining or by the use of legislation.[17] Such is the Webbs' "theory of trade unionism," an economic rationalization for the establishment of minimum standards.

What the Webbs called their "theory of trade unionism" would not ordinarily be called a theory of the development of the labor movement. While the Webbs made fundamental and pioneer contributions to the study of trade union government and the narrative of labor organization history, they formulated no systematic, conceptual answers to the first two questions posed in the previous section (the emergence of labor organization and the patterns of development). As for ultimate goals (question 3), the Webbs see the labor union as an instrument of the democratization of both the work community and the wider society as a whole.

Robert F. Hoxie[18]

Hoxie starts from the proposition that wage earners in similar social and economic environments tend to develop a "common interpretation of the social situation."[19] The union emerges when group sentiments have been crystallized. It appears as a "group interpretation of

the social situation in which the workers find themselves, and a reme-
dial program in the form of aims, policies, and methods. . . ."[20] To
Hoxie, the union constitutes a common interpretation and set of
beliefs concerned with the problems confronting the worker and a
generalized program of amelioration. Such a persistent group "viewpoint or interpretation"[21] Hoxie calls a *functional* type of unionism. His name has come to be associated almost exclusively with classification of the functional types he suggests (business unionism, uplift
unionism, revolutionary unionism, predatory unionism, and dependent unionism) to the detraction of an understanding of his significant
contribution.

The account of the origin of labor organizations which Hoxie
gives—a crystallization of group viewpoint and programme of action—leads him to question whether the labor movement has any
unity: "Seen from the standpoint of aims, ideals, methods, and theories, there is no normal type to which all union variants approximate,
no single labor movement which has progressively adapted itself to
progressive change of circumstances, no one set of postulates which
can be spoken of as *the* philosophy of unionism. Rather there are
competing, relatively stable union types . . ."[22]

Since the labor movement is nonunitary, Hoxie rejects interpretations that look upon trade unionism as fundamentally an economic
manifestation of changing methods of production or market developments.[23] The fact of different functional types compels Hoxie to re-
nounce any explanation in environmental terms alone. The subjective
factor emphasized in the concept of functional types is equally important.

Hoxie provides an answer to the problem of the emergence of labor
organization (question 1) in terms of "group psychology." He accounts
for the divergent forms of unionism but is comparatively unconcerned
with an explanation of historical development. One of the factors
affecting the classification of functional types is the program for social
action developed by the group. In this sense, Hoxie indicates the
different answers that have been posed to the problem of the relation
of the labor movement to the future of capitalism (question 3). But
again there is no sense of historical development, for Hoxie is reticent
to generalize to a "labor movement as a whole" from his "functional
types."[24]

Selig Perlman[25]

Perlman finds that in any "modern labor situation" three factors may
be said to be operative: "first, the resistance of capitalism, determined by its own historical development; second, the degree of
dominance over the labor movement by the intellectual's 'mentality,'

which regularly underestimates capitalism's resistance power and overestimates labor's will to radical change; and, third, the degree of maturity of a trade union 'mentality'."[26] By this last factor Perlman means the extent to which the trade union is conscious of job scarcity. "It is the author's contention that manual groups . . . have had their economic attitudes basically determined by a consciousness of scarcity of opportunity . . . . Starting with this consciousness of scarcity, the 'manualist' groups have been led to practicing solidarity, to an insistence upon an 'ownership' by the group as a whole of the totality of economic opportunity extant, to a 'rationing' by the group of such opportunity among the individuals constituting it, to a control by the group over its members in relation to the conditions upon which they as individuals are permitted to occupy a portion of that opportunity . . . ."[27]

Perlman suggests that there are three basic economic philosophies: those of the manual laborer just indicated, the businessman, and the intellectual. In the United States a "stabilized" unionism was delayed until the labor movement developed job consciousness, until it came to assert a "collective mastery over job opportunities and employment bargains," until wage earners dissociated themselves from "producers" generally who were inbued with the doctrine of abundance and who organized under the slogan of antimonopoly. The American Federation of Labor constitutes a shift in the psychology of the labor movement, a recognition of the scarcity of opportunity.[28]

Perlman apparently gives a certain primacy to the role of job consciousness in the labor movement. In fact a labor organization can be regarded as fundamentally a manifestation of "economic attitudes" (see quotation cited above in note 27, page 74). Nonetheless, labor history cannot deny a "truly pivotal part" to the intellectual. The character of the labor movement in any particular country must depend on the particular combination of the role of the intellectual, the resistance of capitalism, and the development of job consciousness.

Perlman is seen to treat in one way or another all four criteria posed in the previous section. Labor organizations develop from a concern with the scarcity of job opportunities (questions 1 and 4). The pattern of development of organization in a particular country depends upon the particular combination of the three factors operative in any "modern labor situation" (question 2). The relation of the labor movement to the future of capitalism is peculiarly influenced by the role of the intellectual (question 3).

John R. Commons[29]

Commons believed that labor history should be understood in terms of the interaction of "economic, industrial, and political conditions

with many varieties of individualistic, socialistic, and protectionist
philosophies."[30] He treats labor history as a part of its industrial and
political history.

Commons' thinking on the origin and emergence of labor organization involved an appraisal of the writings of Marx, Schmoller, and
Bucher. He posed the problem of explaining the emergence of the
labor movement in terms of the growth of new bargaining classes—
the wage earner and the employer. He traced the gradual evolution
of the employee-employer relationship from the merchant-capitalist
dealings with a journeyman. The growth of the market separates from
the merchant-capitalist the functions of the custom merchant, the retail merchant, and the wholesale merchant. The employer remains.[31]

While Commons recognized that the changing modes of production influenced to some extent the emergence of labor organization,
he attached primary importance to the market expansion. "The extension of the market took precedence over the mode of production as an
explanation of the origin of new class alignments."[32]

The pattern of uneven growth in the American labor movement
was attributed by Commons to the fluctuations in economic conditions. Periods of prosperity produced organization, while depressions
saw the labor movement subside or change its form to political or
social agitation.[33]

The theoretical system of Commons seems to have been concerned
only with the emergence and the pattern of development of the labor
movement (questions 1 and 2 above).

The Marxist View

To Karl Marx, the trade union was first and foremost an "organizing
center."[34] It provided the locus for collecting the forces of the working class. Without organization, workers competed with each other
for available employment. "The trade union developed originally out
of the spontaneous attempts of the workers to do away with this
competition, or at least to restrict it for the purpose of obtaining at
least such contractual conditions as would raise them above the status
of bare slaves."[35]

The labor organization provided for Marx the focal point for the
functional organization of the working class toward a change in the
structure of society. Just as the medieval municipalities and communities were the center of organization of the bourgeoisie, so the
trade union for the proletariat. Thus, in addition to its original tasks,
the trade union was to learn to take on additional duties, to become
the center for organizing the working class for its political eman-
cipation.[36]

It is imperative to distinguish the role of the trade union under capitalism from that after the successful revolution of the proletariat. Left to themselves, labor organizations would remain within the capitalistic framework. Lenin has put this point succinctly, "The spontaneous labour movement, able by itself to create (and inevitably will create) only trade unionism, and working-class trade-union politics are precisely working-class bourgeois politics."[37]

In terms of the fundamental questions posed above, it is apparent that Marx and Lenin, insofar as they formulated a theory of the labor movement, were concerned with the origin or emergence of labor organizations (question 1) and their ultimate relationship to capitalistic society (question 3).

A critical comparison of these views is beyond the scope of this chapter. There are important similarities of analysis and emphasis that appear at once and more that would be evident save for differences in language. A rather sharp cleavage emerges, however, between writers such as the Webbs and Commons, who look upon the labor movement primarily as the manifestation of economic developments, and those such as Perlman and Hoxie who choose to emphasize the habits of mind of wage earners. Compare the *key concepts* of "common rule" (Webbs) and "expansion of the market" (Commons), on the one hand, with "job consciousness" (Perlman) and "functional type" (Hoxie, a persistent exponent of the group viewpoint or interpretation), on the other. The Webbs and Commons built their models of the trade union out of changes in observable economic institutions. Hoxie and Perlman were imbued with the necessity of a "psychology" of the labor movement and hold the notion that the outlook of the worker upon his world and his destiny is the cornerstone of a model of trade union development.

This cleavage represents a fundamental failure in the formulation of "theories of the labor movement." For certainly, there are significant interrelations between the outlook of members of a community and the economic institutions. Consider, for instance, the shedding of the "producer class" complex of the American labor movement. Commons explains the development in terms of the final development of the national market while Perlman emphasizes that job consciousness and the belief in scarcity of work opportunities had asserted itself. These developments are clearly not independent.

The following sections are intended to present a more generalized and more integrated understanding of the development of the labor movement. The next section provides a scaffolding or generalized theoretical framework for an approach to the labor movement.

The Determinants of Labor Organization

The labor movement, or any similarly complex social organization, may be fruitfully explored by an examination of four interrelated factors: (1) technology, (2) market structures and the character of competition, (3) community institutions of control, and (4) ideas and beliefs.

Technology. This term includes not only changes in machinery and in methods of production but concomitant developments in the size and organization of production and distribution units.

Market Structures and Character of Competition. The term comprehends the growth of markets, the changes in the locus of financial control as distinguished from the size of production units, the development of buying and selling institutions in both product and factor markets, and the emergence of specialized functions and personnel within these organizations.

Wider Community Institutions. This phrase is intended to include among others the role of the press, radio, and other means of communication in the society, the formal educational system for both general and vocational training, the courts, governmental administrative agencies, and political parties and organizations.

Ideas and Beliefs. This caption is a short-cut for the value judgments and mores that permeate and identify a social system.

Such a comprehensive scaffolding or method of approach does not in itself constitute a theory of the labor movement. It claims only to facilitate the development of such a theoretical system. It compels reflection on the range of mutual influences operative in any society. Such a comprehensive framework of reference assists in asking significant questions; the complex interrelations between the labor movement and any society are sharpened. The labor movement is seen in the context of its "total" environment. This fourfold scheme is a set of preliminary tools through which the labor movement may be reconnoitered and analyzed. The facts of labor history may more readily be cross-examined.

It must be emphasized that these four factors are intended not merely to facilitate the cross-sectional study of the labor movement at any one given time but even more to assist in the analysis of the growth and change of the labor movement over time. The interaction among technological and market factors, community institutions, and ideas and beliefs must be used to account for the development of the labor movement.

Social systems or institutions go through periods of relative stability and through other periods of spectacular and tortuous change. Periods of stability may be regarded as involving a certain equilibrium among these four factors. That is, a given system of technology and markets requires or is compatible with only a limited number of community institutions and value judgments and ideas. The converse is equally true; a given system of ideas and community organization is compatible only with particular types of market and technological arrangements. In these terms, equilibrium in the social system may be said to exist when these four groups of factors are compatible one with another. Equilibrium may involve an unchanging condition or rates of change among the factors which are congruous. Change the technology of a system and alterations are required in the other three factors or in the value judgments and ideas of a community; and there must be changes in market systems and technology.

The actual course of history does not disclose the isolated reaction to the change in a single factor any more than a series of prices reveals directly the unique effects of shifts in demand or movements along demand schedules. A comprehensive theory of a society should indicate the result of varying one of these factors (the others unchanged) when the system as a whole is in initial equilibrium. The actual course of events consists in continuous and inseparable interaction between the secondary effects of the initial change and new impacts on the social system.

The procedure suggested in this section would analyze the labor movement by indicating the change in each of these four factors over the past and the consequent impact on the emergence and the manner of growth of the labor movement. The labor movement is seen as the product of its total environment. As labor organizations grow they become an independent factor affecting the course of their own destiny.

Long-Run Trends in Union Growth

In thinking of the development of the labor movement, it will be helpful to distinguish between long-term trends and variations around these tendencies. The evolution of social institutions does not take place at a uniform rate. The process is more like waves eating away at the base of a cliff, which eventually crashes into the sea.[38] The present section will be concerned with the trend aspects of the development of the labor movement, while that which follows will adapt this analysis to the pulsation of growth of labor organization.

No working community is ever completely unorganized. Any group of human beings associated together for any length of time develops a community in which there are recognized standards of conduct and admitted leaders. ". . . in industry and in other human situations the administrator is dealing with well-knit human groups and not with a horde of individuals."[39] A group of workers who continue together will establish standards of a "fair" day's work and acceptable norms of behavior in the views of the working group as a whole. Not everyone, of course, will conform to these standards, but there will be recognized norms. In the same way one worker will soon be recognized as a person whose judgment is sought on personal problems; another will be regarded as having superior skill, whose advice on the technical aspects of the job is highly regarded; still another will be accepted as spokesman in expressing the feelings of the group to management. At times these functions may be combined in the same person. Whenever human beings live or work together the informal group develops. This fact is true today; it no doubt preceded the first formal labor organization.

Formal trade union organization has on many occasions been precipitated out of this type of informal organization. Some danger to the stability and security of the informal group frequently serves as the immediate occasion for formalizing an organization. The threat may come from the management in the form of a wage reduction or a substitution of women on men's jobs, or the arbitrary discipline of a member of the work community. The threat may have its origin outside the firm, as in the introduction of machinery made necessary by competitive conditions.

The formal group may be assisted and encouraged by outside organizers. The initiative may be taken by the professional organizer, or he may be called in after an initial step. The congealing of these informal organizations into formal structures follows no uniform pattern. The "intellectual" does not here receive the prominence in the development of the labor movement subscribed to by some writers. There can be little doubt that, in any going institution, "rationalizations" are developed—a task necessarily intellectual in content. Such formal statements often help in extending organization. The processes of rationalization are here treated as an essential step in the growth of the union movement, but the "intellectual" does not have a dominant role.

Wage earners join unions for a great many different reasons. They generally involve various aspects of the relation of the individual workman to his immediate work community and, at times, his relation to the larger locality and national life.[40] The fundamental point, however, is that any analysis of the development of labor organizations must proceed from the recognition that work communities, prior to formal organization, are not simply random aggregates of individual workmen. Typically, informal coagulations exist. While every labor organization probably has not grown out of nor adopted the leadership of the informal group, it is difficult to conceive of a labor organization that has not been substantially influenced by these basic facts of any work community.

There have been, no doubt, many cases in which the informal organization has been precipitated into dramatic formal action, only to lapse quickly and pass away. There have been many such outbursts against arbitrary behavior and substantial grievances. But in some circumstances continuing organization has developed and in others it has lapsed. The discussion which follows suggests, with reference to the American scene, two factors that were necessary to the emergence of organization historically and two that have been decisive in determining the trend of development.

Strategic Position

How is the student of labor organization to account for the location in the productive process of the emergence of continuing unions? Successful organization has required that workmen occupy a *strategic* position in the technological or market structures. In any *technological* process for producing and distributing goods and services there are some workers who have greater strategic position than others; that is, these workers are able to shut down, to interrupt, or to divert operations more easily than others. They furnish labor services at decisive points in the productive stream where the withdrawal of services quickly breaks the whole stream. The productive process has its bottlenecks. Frequently these workers are skilled. The term strategic, however, is not identical with skill. It means sheer bargaining power by virtue of location and position in the productive process. Locomotive engineers, loom fixers in the textile industry, molders in the casting industry, and cutters in the garment industry well illustrate the concept. The withdrawal of the services of these relatively few men almost immediately compels, for technological reasons, the complete shutting down or diversion of operations of the plant.

Analogously, in the *structure of markets* there are firms, and consequently there are employees, who are in strategic positions to affect the whole stream of production and distribution. Employees are technologically strategic by virtue of their position *within* an individual firm. Workers are in a strategic position, marketwise, by virtue of their position in the structure of markets. In the market framework they can most readily exact a price. Not only are the teamsters in a position to tie up operations (technological position) but also their employers are in a position to pass on cost increases to their customers (market position). Another illustration would be a craft, such as the bricklayers, where cost increases may be passed on to the small house-builder whose bargaining position is such as to force absorption. Musicians constitute probably an even better example. The technological and market strategic positions are never completely disassociated, although it is helpful to make the conceptual distinction.

Labor organization emerges among employees who have strategic market or technological positions. They have bargaining power. They can make it hurt. These strategic employees may be regarded as "points of infection" or "growth cones," to borrow the latter term from embryology, for the spread of labor organization.

How far will organization spread around the original "point of infection"? In some instances organization is confined to these most strategic workers and a pure craft union may result. In other instances, these workers become the nucleus of the organization that encompasses other workers in the same plant. The cell wall of the organization may be pushed coextensively with the plant, resulting in an industrial union. The boundary line may be drawn any place in between and may in fact fluctuate a good deal over time. The analogous point applies to the growth of unions in different types of firms. The boundary line of the union may be stopped from crossing into firms with different product market conditions. The phenomenon of a union organized in commercial building but unable or uninterested in pushing into housing is familiar in construction.

There are barriers to extending the cell wall of organization that arise within the strategic group of workers themselves as well as from the opposition of those outside this nucleus. On occasions, the most strategic group will prefer to remain so purist that developments resulting in differentiation of work among these strategic workers will produce a split in the cell and two organizations result. Expanding the group would dilute the gains of organization for the existing nucleus. Labor organizations in the printing industry in this country have taken this pattern of development. From the original group of strategically positioned printers have split off the pressmen, the photoengravers, the stereotypers, the bookbinders, and others, as specialized operations have developed.

Resistance to the expansion of the strategic group may arise from the fact that those outside the nucleus may have such high rates of turnover as to make organization impossible. Thus the butchers in retail outlets did not originally include part-time employees around these stores. The boundary line of the union may be confined because those outside may feel that they can enjoy any benefits won by the strategic group without the costs of organization. It is a mistake to interpret historically the structure (in the sense of boundary lines) of American trade unionism, primarily in terms of a slavish following of the "principle of craft unionism." This analysis suggests a more general view.

Necessary to the emergence and growth of permanent labor organizations have been workers who are located in strategic positions in the market or technological framework. Organization may be treated as expanding from these centers in different patterns and to varying extents. It may be helpful to illustrate this formal analysis with examples from the early growth of labor organizations. In both the men's and women's clothing industry the first group organized was the cutters.[41] Their key position in the technological operation of the making of garments gave them a dominant position in early organizations in these industries. For a while, organization was concentrated in this group. Later the cutters became the nucleus in the women's garment industry for the International Ladies' Garment Workers' Union.

Consider the development of the coal mining industry. Organization was first significant among the contract miners. As a "petty contractor," the miner owned his own tools, purchased his own powder, and worked without supervision. Starting from these strategic employees in the early coal mining industry as a nucleus, organization among the miners gradually expanded to include in a single organization all employees, including those who worked above ground as well as underground.[42]

In the cotton textile industry, the loom fixer has had a position of technological prominence. The failure to keep the looms in running order would soon force the shutdown of the weaving shed. There are other strategic groups of employees, such as the spinners and the slasher tenders. In a sense, one finds multiple points of organization in this industry. In some cases the craft-like union resulted and in others the nucleus expanded to include sufficient other groups to be designated as a semi-industrial arrangement.

In the steel industry, the Amalgamated Iron, Tin, and Steel Workers Union was formed out of strategically located groups in various branches of the industry. The boilers and puddlers in the making of iron, and the heaters, rollers, and roughers from the finishing operations, formed the bulk of organization.[43] This nucleus failed to expand and in fact could not maintain its own position until the emergence of the CIO. These illustrations could be multiplied many times: the linemen in the growth of the Brotherhood of Electrical Workers,[44] the jiggermen and kilnmen in the pottery industry,[45] and the blowers, gatherers, flatteners, and cutters in the flat glass industry.[46] A union leader described an organizing drive as follows: ". . . we had all of the polishing department, and those men were the core of our whole organization."[47] Such instances provide flesh and blood to the formal scheme outlined above. The simple notion again is a strategic nucleus, which may expand in different patterns, depending on conditions and ideas within the union and the environment without.

The analysis that has just been outlined must be thought of as applicable to the task of understanding the development of the American labor movement in the context of community institutions which prevailed prior to the Wagner Act. Organization by ballot rather than by the picket line places much less emphasis upon strategic employees in the technological and market scene. Organization may proceed instead from those most susceptible to union appeals for votes. Furthermore, the unit or boundary which a union would select for an election is apt to be quite different from that which it would select to defend on the picket line. It has not been generally recognized that the Wagner Act has had as much effect on the organizing strategy and structure of labor organizations as upon relations with the employer.[48]

The concept of strategic workers cannot be as useful to an understanding of the development of the labor movement today as it is for the explanation of the past. Still it may help to explain stresses and strains within unions and particular wage policies.

The Employee Perspective

A second necessary condition in the emergence of organization is the view of the employees that they shall look forward to spending a substantial proportion of their lifetime as workmen. This factor has been gradually developing over the past hundred years and has been influenced by the rate of increase in gainful employment. It is also necessary that a substantial proportion in any given work community look forward to remaining in the same or similar work community. Negatively, organization is difficult if not impossible, where individuals expect to work themselves out of the status of wage earners, or where they expect to remain wage earners but a short time because of anticipated withdrawals from the labor market, or where the rate of turnover and migration is so rapid and so erratic and random as to preclude stability in organization. In a period or in situations in which individual employees expect to become foremen and then owners of their own business, permanent and stable organization is virtually impossible. One of the problems of organizing women arises when they expect only a short working life and plan to retire to the more arduous duties of the household. Migratory labor has been notoriously difficult to form into permanent organizations.[49]

Community Institutions

Certain types of community institutions stimulate, and others retard, the emergence and growth of labor organizations. ". . . there had developed, in effect a double standard of social morality for labor and capital. . . . The story of the gradual modification of this double standard can be read in the history of labor organization and in the record of social legislation on state and federal governments over the past fifty years."[50] The legal system may actually preclude organization, as would have been the case had the doctrine of the early conspiracy cases been generally applied. This is not to suggest that the passage of a law could have wiped out all organization. Such a legal doctrine, however, acted as an obstruction to the growth of organization. Analogously, a policy of government to encourage organization, such as adopted in the Wagner Act, tends to accelerate the growth of labor unions.

The role of the wider community influence on the emergence and pattern of growth of the labor movement must be more broadly conceived than the legal system.[51] Both the struggle for free public schools and the impact of widespread general and technical education have left their mark on the American labor movement. The labor press has drawn heavily on the conventions of the daily newspaper. The hostility of the ordinary press to labor organizations over much of the past in this country in turn helped to set the tone of the labor press.

The *emergence* of labor organizations has been related in preceding pages to the strategic position of wage earners in a market and technological setting. But the subsequent form of the labor organization will be decisively molded by the environment of these wider community and national institutions. In some contexts the labor organization has developed into an almost exclusively political body; in others political activity is minor. Special local or industry conditions, such as prevail in the field of municipal employment, may lead to substantial political activity even though the dominant pattern in the country may involve little such action.

The relation of the labor movement to the future of capitalism (question 3) must not be viewed narrowly as an issue of the extent or character of political activity. The growth in modern technology in the setting of the business corporation has gradually yielded a society predominately made up of wage and salary earners. Wage earners have constituted a minor element in previous communities made up largely of self-employed farmers, serfs, slaves, or peasants. Unique in human history has been the creation of a society where the vast majority of persons earn a livelihood as wage and salary earners. (Two-thirds of the national income is wage and salary payment). Under these circumstances when wage earners organize into labor organizations, as traced in previous sections, these bodies may be expected to exercise considerable political power in the community. The center of political power ultimately shifts as the character of the groups within the community changes.

If the locus of political power shifts to the degree that the labor organization becomes the dominant political power, there is growing evidence that the function and role of the union changes. The attitude toward the right to strike, compulsory arbitration, and production drives shifts away from the customary patterns under capitalism. This transition cannot but involve serious controversy within the labor movement.

Community Values

Over and above these technological, market, and community influences on the labor movement has been the system of values, the ethos, and the beliefs of the community. Professor Arthur M. Schlesinger has summarized the traditional attributes of the American most noted by foreign observers: "a belief in the universal obligation to work; the urge to move about; a high standard of comfort for the average man; an absence of permanent class barriers; the neglect of abstract thinking and of the aesthetic side of life . . ."[52] Many of these characteristics are to be traced to the "long apprenticeship to the soil."

It should not be hard to understand why labor organization would be difficult in a day in which men believed that individual advancement was to be achieved solely by work,[53] where leisure was a vice, where economic destiny depended solely upon one's ability to work and save, where poverty could only be the reward for sloth, where the poor deserved their fate, and where the public care of the impoverished was regarded as encouragement of idleness. As Poor Richard says:

Employ thy Time well, if thou meanst to gain Leisure;
And, since thou art not sure of a Minute, throw not away an Hour.

Trouble springs from Idleness, and grievous Toil from needless Ease

For Age and Want, save while you may,
No Morning Sun lasts a whole day.

I think the best way of doing good to the poor, is, not making them easy
in *poverty but leading or driving them* out *of it.*

These admonitions of Benjamin Franklin[54] are hardly the ideal text for the organization of a labor union. This set of ethical standards which has pervaded the ethos of the American community until recently places the economic destiny of a workman in his own hands rather than in a labor union.

The political and economic philosophy of the founding fathers, beyond standards of individual behavior, came to be adapted to the advancing order of corporate business. "This ideology was derived in part from deep-rooted folk ideas, in part from the sanctions of religion, in part from concepts of natural science. But whatever the source, its arguments rested upon the concepts of individualism, equality of opportunity, and the promise of well-being under a profit economy. The conservative defense, crystallized by business leaders and by allied members of the legal, educational, and literary professions, was popularized in sermons, speeches, novels, slogans, and essays. It became part and parcel of American popular thought."[55]

Moreover, the dominant economic thinking on the determination of wage rates (the wage-fund doctrine), by the community, could hardly have been favorable a hundred years ago to the growth of labor organizations. ". . . there is no use in arguing against any one of the four fundamental rules of arithmetic. The question of wages is a question of division. It is complained that the quotient is too small. Well, then, how many ways are there to make a quotient larger? Two ways. Enlarge your dividend, the divisor remaining the same, and the quotient will be larger; lessen your divisor, the dividend remaining the same, and the quotient will be larger."[56] There was no place for a union; it could serve no legitimate function. The intellectual climate of political economy changed and became more conducive to labor organization over the years.

The *trend* of standards of personal morality and social and economic philosophy has moved in directions more congenial to the flowering of unionism. Contrast the entreaties of Poor Richard and Horatio Alger with the admonitions of Sir William Beveridge! Leisure is now a virtue rather than a vice; saving may be a community vice rather than the epitome of individual morality; the economically less fortunate are to be sustained by comprehensive social security rather than to be left to sink or swim. The trade union has a more nourishing ethos.

The dominant ethical judgments pervading the community have been a vital factor influencing the growth of labor organization not only as they affect the individual workman but also as they shape and mold the character of the labor organization itself. The primacy of property rights in the American tradition is partly responsible for the dominance of the concept of exclusive jurisdiction in the American Federation of Labor constitution. Each union "owns" its jurisdiction in the same way that a businessman owns a piece of property. These community values have also decisively determined the attitude of the community toward social insurance. It is no accident that the American Federation of Labor was opposed to a program of compulsory insurance until 1932.[57]

The environment of ideas and beliefs in which the labor organization developed has included the special role of the labor intelligentsia or the intellectual. "Capitalist evolution produces a labor movement which obviously is not the creation of the intellectual group. But it is not surprising that such an opportunity and the intellectual demiurge should find each other. Labor never craved intellectual leadership but intellectuals invaded labor politics. They had an important contribution to make: they verbalized, supplied theories and slogans for it, . . . made it conscious of itself and in so doing changed its meaning."[58] The formulation of a creed or folklore or rationalization is an important function in the development of the labor movement, just as in any organization. The function needs to be kept in proportion. In the American scene this process seems not to have been the province of a special class nor fashioned through different means in labor organizations than in other groups in the community. The English and Continental experience is different in this respect.

This section has sketched some suggestions toward an analytical view of the emergence and development of the labor movement out of its total environment, regarding that environment as the technological processes, the market structure, the community institutions, and the value judgments of the society. The emphasis has been upon the long-term *trend* of development.

Short-Run Variations in Trade Union Membership

The growth of the labor movement has not been uniform and the four factors which have been used to approach the long-term trends in the labor movement were not all operative at the same rate. This section is concerned with the deviations from trend, in particular the periods of advance and stagnation in labor organization.

Even a cursory view of the American labor movement identifies seven major periods of rapid expansion in organization. The following tabulation identifies these periods; it also notes the estimated membership[59] of the organizations at the end of a given period.

Periods[60]	Dates	Membership
Awakening	1827–1836	300,000
Nationalism	1863–1872	300,000
Great Upheaval	1881–1886	1,000,000
Mass Advancement	1896–1904	2,000,000
First World War	1917–1920	5,000,000
New Deal	1933–1937	8,000,000
Second World War	1941–1945	14,000,000

These seven periods can be divided into two distinct types. The dominant characteristics of a period do not preclude some elements of the opposite type. The first group of periods were years of wartime, with rapid increases in the cost of living and stringency in the labor market. This group includes the periods of Nationalism (1863–1872), Mass Advancement (1896–1904), the First World War (1917–1920), and the Second World War (1941–1945). The rapid expansion in membership is to be explained almost entirely by developments in the labor market: the rapid rise in the cost of living and the shortage of labor supply relative to demand. Under these circumstances a trade union helped to enable wage earners to increase their wages to an extent more closely approximating the rise in prices. The individual worker joined unions to push up his wages; the tightness in the labor market and the general level of profits enabled the union to achieve results. Organization in these instances may be regarded as predominately a market reflex.

Contrasting with these years is the second type of period, to be regarded as one of fundamental unrest. Organization of unions represented a basic dissatisfaction with the performance of the economic system and the society in general. Such were the years of Awakening (1827–1836), the Great Upheaval (1881–1886), and the New Deal (1933–1937). It is these three periods which call for special explanation.

It is well established in the analysis of economic fluctuations that modern capitalism has moved in certain long waves.[61] These long waves or Kondratieff cycles are generally regarded as approximately fifty years in length with twenty-five years of good times and twenty-five years of bad times, and are distinguished from the shorter business cycles. Professor Alvin H. Hansen's dating scheme is typical.[62]

Good Times	Bad Times
1787–1815	1815–1843
1843–1873	1873–1897
1897–1920	1920–1940
1940–	

The long wave represents a fundamental structural period in modern capitalism. The first of these waves has been designated as that of the Industrial Revolution, the second the Age of Railroads, and the third the Electrical Period.[63] The fourth may be known as that of the airplane and atomic power.

For the present purposes it is significant to note that each one of the three periods of major upheaval and fundamental unrest came at the bottom of the period of bad times in the long wave. The period of good times in the long wave is associated with a cluster of major innovations. There follows a period of generally declining prices (1815–43, 1873–97, 1920–40), during which the shorter business cycles are severe and intense. The three major periods of upheaval follow severe depressions. It is suggested that after prolonged periods of high unemployment for a substantial number in the work force and after years of downward pressure on wages exerted by price declines, labor organizations emerge which are apt to be particularly critical of the fundamental tenets of the society and the economy.

These three fundamental periods of upsurge in the labor movement must also be related to important developments in community institutions and ideas or value judgments. Thus, the first period was the Age of Jacksonian Democracy, the second the Populist, and the third the New Deal. The labor movement of 1827–1836 has been treated as an alignment of "producer classes."[64] The Knights of Labor in the period 1881–1886 has been referred to as the last great middle-class uprising. The expansion of the labor movement in the New Deal period was primarily a working class movement. The first period rallied around the slogan of free education, the second used the watch-word of shorter hours, the third was characterized by the accent on security.

Conclusion

The scaffolding may now be removed. In the distinctive pattern of growth of the labor movement in this country, one sees in outline form the way in which technology, market structure, community institutions, and the ethos factors have interacted together to yield the labor movement considered as a whole. Special types of these factors in operation in specific industries and localities account for the divergent types and forms of unionism which have developed within the generalized framework. For example, the migratory character of agricultural work and the lumber industry, together with the absence of stability of community, help to account for the type of unionism that originally emerged in this sector, illustrated by the IWW. The unions in the field of local or national government employment have become lobbying agencies by virtue of the practical prohibitions to effective collective bargaining. These specialized forms or species are variations from the main pattern of growth and development arising from special types of environments. In the same way, peculiar national characteristics shape the operation of these factors in comparing labor movements in various countries.

The framework of approach to the labor movement presented here is intended to be suggestive for a renewed interest in the writing of the history of the labor movement in general and in particular sectors. The emphasis upon the interrelations and mutual dependence of four groups of factors has served as the basis for this analysis. Not only is the analysis schematic, but it must be recognized that any simplified schemata must abstract from many complexities of behavior. The formal analysis must not leave the impression of the labor organization as primarily rationalistic. Professor Frank H. Knight has well said that there is need for "some grasp of the infinitely complex, intangible, and downright contradictory character of men's interests, conscious and unconscious, and their interaction with equally intricate mechanical, biological, neural, and mental processes in forming the pattern of behavior. The great vice is over-simplification . . . ."[65]

Endnotes

1. This chapter benefited from helpful comments by J. A. Schumpeter, A. P. Usher, and Selig Perlman.
2. Talcott Parsons, *The Structure of Social Action* (New York: McGraw-Hill Book Co., 1937), p. 698.
3. See E. Wight Bakke, *Mutual Survival, The Goal of Unions and Management* (New Haven, Conn.: Labor and Management Center, Yale University, 1946), p. 12, for a contrast between a "movement" and a "business."
4. J. B. Bury, *The Idea of Progress* (New York: Macmillan Co., 1932). See the Introduction by Charles A. Beard, pp. ix–xl.
5. Selig Perlman, *Theory of the Labor Movement* (New York: Macmillan Co.) was published in 1928. See Horace B. Davis, "The Theory of Union Growth," *Quarterly Journal of Economics*, LV (August, 1941), 611–37, and Russell Bauder, "Three Interpretations of the American Labor Movement," *Social Forces* XXII (December, 1943), 215–24.
6. Frank H. Knight, *Risk, Uncertainty, and Profit* (London: London School of Economics and Political Science, 1933), Preface to reissue.
7. Frank Tannenbaum, *The Labor Movement, Its Conservative Functions and Social Consequences* (New York: G.P. Putnam's Sons, 1921).
8. *Ibid.*, p. 29. As a statement of the origin of labor organizations, this view is to be contrasted with that of John R. Commons, "Whatever may have been its origin in other countries, the labor movement in America did not spring from factory

conditions. It arose as a protest against the merchant-capitalist system." *A Documentary History of American Industrial Society* (Glendale, Calif.: Arthur H. Clark Company, 1910), Vol. V, p. 23 (with Helen L. Sumner).

9. These lines are in italics in the original. *Op. cit.*, p. 32.

10. *Ibid.*, p. 44.

11. Sidney and Beatrice Webb, *Industrial Democracy* (New York: Longmans, Green & Co., 1897); and *History of Trade Unionism* (New York: Longmans, Green & Co., 1894). Also see Margaret Cole, *Beatrice Webb* (New York: Harcourt, Brace & Co., 1946), pp. 73–83.

12. *History of Trade Unionism* (1920 ed.), p. 1.

13. *Industrial Democracy* (1914 printing), p. 807.

14. *Ibid.*, p. 823.

15. *Ibid.*, pp. viii and 795. See note 17.

16. *Ibid.*, p. 560.

17. ". . . the whole community of wage-earners . . . may by a persistent and systematic use of the Device of the Common Rule secure an indefinite, though of course not an unlimited, rise in its Standard of Life. And in this universal and elaborate application of the Common Rule, the economist finds *a sound and consistent theory of Trade Unionism,* adapted to the conditions of modern industry: . . ." *Ibid.*, p. 795. (Italics added.)

18. Robert F. Hoxie, *Trade Unionism in the United States* (New York: D. Appleton & Co., 1921). See the Introduction by E. H. Downey.

19. *Ibid.*, p. 58.

20. *Ibid.*, p. 60.

21. *Ibid.*, p. 69.

22. E. H. Downey, Introduction to *Trade Unionism in the United States*, pp. xxiii–xxiv.

23. See the discussion under the heading of John R. Commons which follows in the text.

24. See, however, *op. cit.*, note 3, p. 59.

25. Perlman, *op. cit.*

26. *Ibid.*, p. x.

27. *Ibid.*, p. 4; also see pp. 237–53. The importance attached to job consciousness is the outcome of one of the few explicit statements on the requirements of a theory of the labor movement. "A theory of the labor movement should include a theory of the psychology of the laboring man" (p. 237).

28. Perlman disagrees with the Webbs' view that there is a tendency for unionism to give up the principle of restriction of numbers in favor of the device of the Common Rule. *Ibid.*, pp. 295–98. Also see *Labor in the New Deal Decade,* Three Lectures by Selig Perlman, . . . at the ILGWU Officers Institute, New York City, 1943–1945 (Educational Department, International Ladies' Garment Workers' Union, 1945).

29. John R. Commons, Ed., *A Documentary History of American Industrial Society,* 11 Vols. (Glendale, Calif.: Arthur H. Clark Co., 1910–11). In particular see the Introduction, Vol. V, pp. 19–37, written with Helen L. Sumner. Also John R. Commons and Associates, *History of Labor in the United States,* 2 Vols. (New York: Macmillan Co., 1918), in particular Vol. I, pp. 3–21.

30. Commons and Associates, *op. cit.*, Vol. 1, Introduction; p. 3.

31. *Ibid.*, p. 106.
32. *Ibid.*, p. 28.
33. Commons, Ed., *Documentary History* . . . . Vol. V, p. 19.
34. A. Lozovsky, *Marx and the Trade Unions* (New York: International Publishers Co., 1935), p. 15.
35. *Ibid.*, p. 16. (Italics deleted.)
36. Paul M. Sweezy, *The Theory of Capitalist Development* (New York: Oxford Univ. Press, 1942), pp. 312–13.
37. V. L. Lenin, *What Is to Be Done?*, Reprinted from *The Iskra Period* (New York: International Publishers, 1929), p. 90.
38. For a discussion of historical change refer to Melvin M. Knight, Introduction to Henri Sée, *The Economic Interpretation of History* (New York: Adelphi Co., 1929), pp. 9–37.
39. Elton Mayo, *The Social Problems of an Industrial Civilization* (Cambridge, Mass.: Harvard University Press, 1945), p. 111. Also see F. J. Roethlisberger and William J. Dickson, *Management and Morale*, Cambridge, Mass.: Harvard University Press, 1942).
40. E. Wight Bakke, "Why Workers Join Unions," *Personnel*, XXII, No. 1 (1945).
41. See Joel Seidman, *The Needle Trades* (New York: Farrar and Rinehart, 1942), pp. 81–92; also Elden La Mar, *The Clothing Workers in Philadelphia* (Philadelphia Joint Board, Amalgamated Clothing Workers, 1940), pp. 46–47.
42. Edward A. Wieck, *The American Miners' Association* (New York: Russell Sage Foundation, 1940), pp. 75–77 and 85–86.
43. J. S. Robinson, *The Amalgamated Association of Iron, Steel and Tin Workers* (Baltimore: Johns Hopkins Press, 1920), pp. 9–21.
44. Michael A. Mulcaire, *The International Brotherhood of Electrical Workers* (Washington: The Catholic University of America, Studies in the Social Sciences, Vol. V, 1923).
45. David A. McCabe, *National Collective Bargaining in the Pottery Industry* (Baltimore: Johns Hopkins Press, 1932), pp. 4–7.
46. Window Glass Cutters League of America, *A History of Trade Unions in the Window Glass Industry* . . . , reprinted from the *Glass Cutter* (March–September 1943).
47. "From Conflict to Cooperation," *Applied Anthropology*, V (Fall 1946), p. 9.
48. The interpretation of the rise of the CIO as a repudiation of the principle of craft unionism neglects the adaptations in structure to these new conditions. A fruitful research enterprise would study these effects of the Wagner Act on union structure.
49. Carleton H. Parker, *The Casual Laborer and Other Essays* (New York: Harcourt, Brace, and Howe, 1920). Also see Stuart Jamieson, *Labor Unionism in American Agriculture*, Bulletin 836 (Washington: Bureau of Labor Statistics, 1945).
50. Samuel Eliot Morrison and Henry Steele Commager, *The Growth of the American Republic*, revised and enlarged edition (New York: Oxford Univ. Press, 1937), Vol. II, p. 153.
51. See W. Lloyd Warner and J. O. Low, "The Factory in the Community," in *Industry and Society*, William F. Whyte, Ed. (New York: McGraw-Hill Book Co., 1946), pp. 21–45.

52. Arthur Meier Schlesinger, "What Then Is the American, This New Man?" reprinted from the *American Historical Review*, XLVIII (January, 1943), pp. 3–4.
53. "What qualities of the national character are attributable to this long-persistent agrarian setting? First and foremost is the habit of work." (*Ibid.*, p. 10.)
54. "The Way to Wealth," Preface to *Poor Richard Improved* (1758).
55. Merle Curti, *The Growth of American Thought* (New York: Harper & Bros., 1943), p. 656. See pp. 605–56. Also, Vernon Louis Parrington, *Main Currents in American Thought*, Vol. 3, *The Beginning of Critical Realism in America* (New York: Harcourt, Brace & Co., 1927).
56. A. L. Perry, *Political Economy*, p. 123, quoted in Francis A. Walker, *The Wage Question* (New York: Henry Holt & Co., 1886), p. 143. Compare this with the statement by the Webbs, "Down to within the last thirty years it would have been taken for granted, by every educated man, that Trade Unionism . . . was against Political Economy. . . ." *Industrial Democracy*, p. 603.
57. See George G. Higgins, *Voluntarism in Organized Labor in the United States, 1930–1940* (Washington: Catholic University of America Press, 1944).
58. Joseph A. Schumpeter, *Capitalism, Socialism and Democracy* (New York: Harper & Bros., 1942), pp. 153–54.
59. In any organization it is not always clear who should be counted as a "member". In the case of a union, depending upon the purpose, the significant figure may be those who have signed membership cards, pay dues regularly, attend meetings, vote for the union in a NLRB election, or support the union by joining a strike.
60. The titles used in Commons and Associates, *op. cit.*, have been adopted for the first four periods. The membership figures for these periods are from the same source.
61. Joseph A. Schumpeter, *Business Cycles, A Theoretical, Historical, and Statistical Analysis of the Capitalist Process* (New York: McGraw-Hill Book Co., 1939).
62. Alvin H. Hansen, *Fiscal Policy and Business Cycles* (New York: W. W. Norton & Co., 1940), p. 30.
63. Schumpeter, *Business Cycles . . .* , I, pp. 220–448.
64. At the third meeting of the Working Men's Party in New York it was not the employers who were given 5 minutes to withdraw but "persons not living by some useful occupation, such as bankers, brokers, rich men, etc." Commons, Ed., *Documentary History . . .* , V. p. 24.
65. Knight, *op. cit.*, p. xxix.

Chapter 4

INTERMEDIATE TRENDS IN INDUSTRIAL RELATIONS IN THE UNITED STATES

Dramatic and substantial changes in industrial relations appear to take place in brief climactic periods of depression, revolution, war, or crisis. In some respects these sudden manifestations of change only make evident forces that have been at work for a long time, as when a cliff crashes into the sea as a consequence of many years of erosion. In other respects, however, the specific conditions of depression, revolution, war or crisis themselves fashion the course of events and provide new tendencies for many years. The distinctive influence of these climactic periods is a major indeterminateness in all projections of trends even for intermediate periods.[1]

A discussion of such underlying tendencies may be less exciting than a bold projection of the actual course of history, and it may receive less attention than an audacious prediction of the consequences of a change in labor leadership or the effects on industrial relations of a general election. But our interest here is much more in methods of analysis and analytical frameworks than in a comparison of crystal balls. The discussion which follows is organized into four sections: (1) the major characteristics of the industrial relations system of the United States; (2) the tendencies arising within the industrial relations system that are likely to shape the intermediate term; (3) the tendencies in the larger American economy and society that are likely to have a significant impact on industrial relations through changes in

Based on unpublished paper presented to the Third World Congress, International Industrial Relations Association in London, December 1973.

the larger setting in which labor, management, and government interact in industrial relations; and (4) some concluding observations.

Major Characteristics of the U.S. Industrial
Relations System

We shall not here attempt a definitive or detailed statement of the
distinctive features of the industrial relations arrangements of the
United States or the distinctive features of its labor organizations and
workers, its managements, its governmental agencies and policies, or
their interactions.[2] But a brief statement of major characteristics is
essential as a reference point for appraising the direction and magnitude of future trends in industrial relations. This statement is cast in
a comparative setting, stressing the major respects in which industrial
relations arrangements in the United States are different from those
in other major advanced countries.[3]

The principle of exclusive jurisdiction or representation has characterized industrial relations in the United States from the outset of the
American Federation of Labor in the 1880s and from the earliest days
of governmental intervention in the representation issue in World
War I and in the railroad legislation. This practice conforms to the
American political custom of electing single representatives by majority vote. It is consonant with a labor force and labor movement that is
much less split than in other countries along political or religious lines
that reflect fundamental ideological cleavages in a society. Exclusive
representation precludes the separate or autonomous workers council.

Industrial relations rule making, and collective bargaining in particular, is highly decentralized in the United States to particular plants
and companies (only occasionally to industries), as well as to individual local and national unions. Industry-wide or confederation-wide
negotiations are generally much less significant than elsewhere. A
derived characteristic is the greater detail and wider scope for collective bargaining and a much lesser role for governmental substantive
rule making, legislative or administrative.

The role of the law in the industrial relations system of the United
States is concentrated upon establishing the relations among the participants, limiting the methods of conflict, and proscribing the collective bargaining process, often in a highly litigious setting. It is
relatively more procedural, leaving the substantive conditions of
employment and the rules of the work place (wages, benefits, hours,
and working conditions) to negotiating parties. While the governmental regulation of the substantive terms of employment has expanded

appreciably in recent years, negotiating parties probably have the widest latitude for substantive decisions while operating under the most detailed procedural constrictions specified by law. Through private arbitration and mediation, moreover, labor and management have been able to shape to their own necessities the process of the administration of agreements and even the procedures for periodic negotiations.

The industrial relations system of the United States has created relatively a much larger cadre of professionals in labor organizations, managements, and governments and private experts who devote their full time to the negotiation and administration of agreements and to industrial-relations-oriented organizations. This result is derived in large part from the decentralized character of collective bargaining, the larger scope for substantive negotiations, and the rights of exclusive representation.

These and other such fundamental characteristics of the U.S. industrial relations system are likely to remain basically unchanged in the intermediate term. The major characteristics of a national industrial relations system appear to be established at a relatively early stage in the industrial development of a country, and in the absence of a violent revolution in the larger community, a national industrial relations system appears to retain these characteristics despite subsequent evolution.[4] The future trends in industrial relations in the intermediate term may see some gradual and long-term changes within these major characteristics but no fundamental alteration in such main features of the system.

The early development and persistence of the major characteristics of an industrial relations system is not inconsistent with the view that, given longer periods of history, there is a tendency toward some confluence of the characteristics of industrial societies and their industrial relations arrangements.[5] But some basic features persist.

Tendencies within the Industrial Relations System

Labor Organizations

While membership in labor organizations may be expected to continue to grow from the 21.8 million members in 1970 with the expanding labor force (from a labor force of 85 million in 1970 to 112 million in 1990), the proportion of the labor force that is organized is unlikely to grow in this time horizon. The proportion will continue low compared with other advanced industrial countries. Indeed, strenuous efforts will be necessary to maintain the fraction of organization in the vicinity of one-quarter of the total. It is, of course, recognized that organizations akin to unions and performing some of the same functions are likely to become more pervasive among health professions, government employment, and in higher education. The fates have often seemed perverse to union growth insofar as strong unionized sectors have frequently suffered declining employment while expanding employment has taken place in industries, occupations and regions with low rates of organization.[6]

The greatest union growth is likely to come in the American analogs of general workers unions—the teamsters, retail clerks, service workers and the laborers—and in some conglomerate unions. Growth is not so likely in the industrial unions, which are tied to a single industry or to a few related industries and which often are concentrated in a few areas; nor is it likely in the pure craft unions. These general unions provide benefits, services, expert counsel, and bargaining strength throughout the country in many industries and are particularly effective and efficient in smaller size establishments.

There is likely to be a more rapid consolidation and merger of national unions in the period ahead than in the years immediately after the AFL-CIO was formed in 1955. In 1955 the new federation had 137 national union affiliates, approximately 120 in 1970, and 99 in 1983. (The decline reflected mergers.) In 1970, 137 of the 185 national unions in or out of the AFL-CIO had a membership of 100,000 or less, while there were 48 with memberships of over 100,000.[7] The smaller organizations do not appear able to service well their members or local unions or to provide quality assistance and support. But one should look more to financial stringency among the small international unions and occasional expansionist leadership of some national unions for mergers rather than to labor solidarity, ideology or rationalizing directives from a federation.

The financial assets of American unions may be expected to continue to grow at a moderate rate. These assets, including about $500 million in benefit plans financed solely by unions, totaled $2.6 billion in 1969 in comparison with $1.7 billion in 1962 and 4.0 billion in 1976. These assets are almost equally divided between local unions and national unions, indicating the very strong position of local unions in the American industrial relations system.[8] For comparative purposes it may be noted that the assets of British unions have been estimated at $300 million. While the assets of American unions are substantial in comparison with those of other union movements, they are not large in comparison with those of many other nonprofit organizations in American society. The dues income of American labor unions was $728 million in 1962, $1.3 billion in 1969, and $2.2 billion in 1976.

A significant tendency within American labor organizations likely to continue is the adoption of more professional managerial methods in the conduct of the union's business. There is likely to be an even more conscious adaptation of modern methods of planning and decision making, decentralization of administration, and use of computer and modern communication technology, research tools, and specialists. These developments follow partly from the influence of business organizations and government agencies with which the labor organizations deal and partly from the necessities and opportunities of size and scale of operations of the largest national unions.

There does not appear to be a significant tendency to alter the traditional policies of the federation and labor organizations toward political action. The American political tradition and its political organizations, do not lend themselves to close and continuing allegiance. Labor organizations have always engaged in extensive lobbying activities at local and national levels; on many occasions all labor organizations are not on the same side of an issue. Political support with financial assistance and electioneering efforts are more likely to depend on individual candidates and issues at the time than on party affiliation and class commitment. The 1972 national elections underscored the strength of the traditional position.

The relations of labor organizations to intellectuals in the society (the intellectual left) is likely to become even more strained and discordant than in the recent past. Except for the new unions in the 1930s, the mainstream of the American labor movement has always been suspicious of the intellectual left and resistant to providing any opportunity or base for influence or position. The intellectual left has been highly critical of labor organizations, particularly with regard to their economic and social objectives, their business-like methods, the life style of union leaders, their racial policies in some cases, and their failures in political action. The simple fact is that the labor organizations' view of the aspirations of workers and the role these organizations can play in American society do not comport at all with the aspirations and objectives of the intellectual left and their romanticised view of the ordinary worker and family. There seems little likelihood of any rapprochement except in some climactic development.

Management Organizations

One of the major continuing developments within American management is the explicit and formal consideration of questions of organizational behavior, human relations, personnel relations, and human resource development, or the same or related issues under a variety of other terms.[9] The philosophy, organization, procedures, and styles of management are the subject of recurrent review in large-scale management organizations. There is also intensive study of these matters in schools of business administration. The consequence of these continuing developments is that industrial relations in the large-scale enterprise are under continuing scrutiny, and the relationship between the central management functions of the enterprise and the "handling" or "participation" or "motivation" of employees has come to be more significant to top managements. Industrial relations in the broadest sense is increasingly at the center of the concerns of top management, and the full consequences of these developments have not yet been realized.

One of the major characteristics of American managements that is decisive to the industrial relations system is the relative independence of large-scale units and their unwillingness to handle industrial relations easily on an association or cartel basis. Even where labor market interdependence cannot be denied—as in rubber, automobiles, and aluminum or oil refining—there is fierce determination in managements to preserve a measure of independence of action even where settlement "patterns" come to be established. The settling down of collective bargaining in a number of major industries has not altered this basic managerial disposition, which appears to be quite different from the arrangements in many Western European countries. Association bargaining has not grown into new areas and has been weakened in old sectors. A no lesser degree of managerial independence may be forecast for the decades immediately ahead.

The sharp differences in industrial relations that previously existed between unionized and unorganized work places, particularly in the same company, have been markedly reduced in recent years, and this leveling influence, or homogenization, is likely to continue. While this comparability has often been true for wages and some benefits, only recently have third-party arbitration procedures for discharge, forms of seniority arrangements, and limitations on hours of overtime work been introduced into nonunion plants. In these and many other respects collective bargaining has come to have a direct impact on unorganized work places through management decisions. The management may prefer, for administrative reasons, greater uniformity across organized and unorganized units, or it may be largely concerned to discourage—or eliminate—an incentive for the further growth of labor organization, or it may find some of the procedures developed in its organized plants to be superior to older practices.

As Sumner Slichter, James Healy, and Robert Livernash observed, "The challenge that unions presented to management has, if viewed broadly, created superior and better balanced management, even though some exceptions must be recognized. . . .The need to compromise conflicting interests within the firm shows that collective bargaining tends to make exacting demands on management and to increase the need for wise and well-balanced executives and for effective collaboration in policy making between operating officers and staff executives."[10] In the intermediate term one of the major developments is likely to be the impact of labor organizations upon the management and performance of nonprofit institutions, local and state governmental agencies, and health and educational institutions. It is not at all certain that the judgment in the future will be as favorable as to the consequences of collective bargaining as in the case of private business enterprises. This range of issues, however, is one of the more significant for the period ahead, particularly since it is not possible to transfer literally the institutions of modern management or collective bargaining from their traditional sectors to these new areas. In any event, managements in these sectors are likely to be subject to major internal changes in the period ahead.

Interacting Tendencies

The major intermediate tendencies within the industrial relations system of the United States, including the operating of collective bargaining, derive in part from the noted changes within labor organizations and within management and in part from governments and the interaction of all three. Although the American industrial relations system has in the past been characterized by a relatively high rate of work stoppages compared with those of other countries, the severity of interruptions and the attention to strikes and lockouts is likely to continue to decline over the intermediate future. The emergency dispute is still of some concern in some transportation industries such as railroads, but such disputes are likely to be less severe and less difficult to resolve in the future. In 1952 I said "that in twenty-five years the emergency dispute will have ceased to be a serious question."[11] In part this decline in the severity of work stoppages is the result of technological developments and management practices, such as those in oil refining and communications, and in part the result of the development of private procedures by the parties, such as those in the basic steel and aluminum industries, to avoid the costs of stoppages and even the costs of uncertainty that arise with the expiration of an agreement.

Provisions for retirement benefits are likely to pose in the intermediate term a major concern for the industrial relations system. Social security and other governmental pension benefits have been increased sharply in recent years, and the problems of relating these benefits to those provided by collective bargaining agreements or by employer plans alone are certain to become more complex. Moreover, the government is likely to increase the scope of its regulation of pension funds and benefits outside the almost universal social security system. An analogous range of problems may arise in the health care area. The integration and coordination of extensive benefit plans developed and maintained under collective bargaining agreements and by employers alone with federal government retirement and health plans in likely to be particularly difficult, more so than in other countries with a different social insurance tradition.

Contrary to a good deal of popular opinion, it is unlikely that the preoccupation with job design and work reorganization attributed to the interests of a younger and better educated work force will produce very major changes in the organization and management of the work place. There are likely to be a number of experiments, and some changes will no doubt become more general in terms of flexibility in hours in some industries, more part-time workers, some greater choice for workers among fringe benefits, and some changes in a limited number of companies in employee participation in arrangements for work. But such changes are not likely to be extensive, largely because most employees do not appear to be significantly interested and because the number of managements with special interests and capacities in these areas is likely to remain limited. A good deal of the academic concern with this subject derives from an idealized view of the interests of workers.

One of the central issues within the American industrial relations system is whether significant changes in its legal framework, including the status of the parties and rules relating to their bargaining and conflict, can be changed in the course of time through consensus within the system, or whether major changes can be made only through political and legislative conflict as in the past. The legal framework of collective bargaining and many features of the formal operation of collective bargaining reflect artificial and unrealistic legislation. Many of these provisions have been ignored for practical purposes. Some of these issues, such as the structure of collective bargaining itself, the nature of the obligation to bargain, and the status of work rules (so-called featherbedding), are themselves increasingly subjects of collective bargaining between mature parties. But there exists a possibility that top leaders of labor and management may come to develop, either outside the legislative framework or through changes worked out within it, some adaptations to new needs for dispute settlement procedures, changes in the structure of bargaining, and new methods to deal even more effectively with the introduction of technological change and with growing foreign competition. The past experience of political conflict has levied its costs on both labor and management. No issue is more important for the future than the ways in which the legal framework of collective bargaining evolves.

Tendencies within the Economy and Society that Impact Industrial Relations

Aside from developments within the industrial relations system itself, there are incipient developments in the economy and within the larger society that are likely to have major impacts on industrial relations over the next several decades. First, the labor force can be expected to change in a number of respects.[12] It will be significantly larger, rising from 85.9 millions in 1970 to 112.6 millions in 1990. The proportion of women will continue to grow, from 42.8 percent in 1970 to 45.9 percent in 1990. A large growth in the 25–34 year age group in the 1970's will be followed in the decade of 1980–90 by a great expansion concentrated in the 35–44 year age group as the post-World War II baby boom grows older. The age distributions, particularly for men, will remain remarkably constant save for this "tidal wave." The racial distribution of employment and income is expected to become less adverse to minorities. These changes in the labor force do not always correlate well with the needs of the economy, and special problems arise in the development of supervision with such marked changes in age and demographic distribution in many industries. Moreover, the pressures for equal employment opportunities will continue to constitute a significant pressure on the industrial relations system, which may be expected to respond gradually to these requirements.

As the American economy and society evolves, it becomes more organized, with various groups banding together to protect or advance their interests as they perceive them. Sometimes these groups resemble and act like unions, and at other times they are quite different. They include women employees, racial minority groups, beef farmers, gasoline dealers, dentists, and tenants. The point is that the parties to traditional collective bargaining will have to confront and deal with such groups in the economic or political arenas, on some occasions they will directly complicate the bargaining process.

There can be no doubt that international competition in many sectors constitutes a new environment for industrial relations in the United States. While floating exchanges over the period may put less pressure on the industrial relations system than might otherwise have been the case, the new industrial competition from Japan and the

European Community places new and more visible constraints on
collective bargaining. The extent to which labor and management will
accept this challenge or seek protective trade legislation, unemployment and dislocation benefits, and import restraints is not yet clear.
But these questions are likely to be more prominent in the next
several decades than in the past in the industrial relations context.

The interests of the larger community in price stability will constitute a significant pressure on the industrial relations system of the
United States as well as in other western industrial countries. Lloyd
Ulman is probably correct in asserting the catnip effect, "which suggests that incomes policy is well-nigh irresistible to politicians in
office."[13] The attitudes and policies of the leaders of labor and management are a major determinant to the results of excursions into
wage and price controls, because labor disputes, the level and patterns of wage and benefit settlements, and morale and productivity
consequences are significantly affected. The extent of governmental
resort to direct controls and other measures to influence directly
wage and price decisions will prove to be a major influence from the
larger community shaping the procedures and results of the industrial
relations system in the period ahead.[14] The extent of formal incomes
policies in the future, in turn, may be expected significantly to affect
the central control or influence of national organizations in wage
decisions and collective bargaining.

Conclusion

The American industrial relations system, as that of any country, will
continue to live with a number of inner tensions, including the conflicts between local unions and their members; the different interests
of local and national unions; the balance between union democracy or
responsiveness to members, on the one hand, and the need for economic responsibility and efficiency in management, on the other
hand; the difficulties of reconciling diffused private collective bargaining and a degree of national economic planning; and conflicts among
the objectives of high employment, price stability, labor-management peace, and international goals. But the industrial relations system does accommodate and adjust to these conflicts and tensions.

Sumner Slichter, one of the wisest students of the American industrial relations scene, once said:[15]

> "By and large, I think that the United States should consider itself
> lucky. It possesses a system of industrial relations that, in its basic
> characteristics fits conditions here reasonably well. Perhaps that is why
> it represents a pretty good adaptation to conditions—it is simply the

sum total of various efforts to solve problems rather than the expression of a plan which might faithfully reflect certain principles but which, because of the fact, might not very well fit conditions . . . . We seem justified in being grateful that we have been favored by fortune and perhaps also in taking modest pride that we have pursued opportunist policies with considerable flexibility and good sense."

I believe this is still true and will likely be true in the intermediate term.

One of the most creative practitioners of public policy and collective bargaining in the United States, George W. Taylor, said in 1965 that the search for answers to the public concern with the results of collective bargaining: ". . .is to be fond ultimately, I believe, through a greater degree of cooperation between representatives of labor, management, and the government than presently seems to be possible."[16] The constructive direction of future industrial relations policy indeed lies in expanding tripartite discussion and pragmatic problem solving.

Endnotes

1. See several earlier statements in which I have sought to specify explicitly the long-term tendencies in the industrial relations system of the United States or the major results of the operation of that system: John T. Dunlop, "The American Industrial Relations System in 1975," in *U.S. Industrial Relations: The Next Twenty Years*, Jack Stieber, Ed. (Michigan State University Press, 1958), pp. 25–54; John T. Dunlop, *The Secular Outlook: Wages and Prices*, Institute of Industrial Relations (University of California, Berkeley and Los Angeles, 1957); John T. Dunlop, "Structural Changes in the American Labor Movement and Industrial Relations System," *Proceedings of the Ninth Annual Meeting, Industrial Relations Research Association* (December 1956), pp. 1–21.

2. For some statements of these major characteristics see, Derek C. Bok and John T. Dunlop, *Labor and the American Community* (New York: Simon and Schuster, 1970); Selig Perlman and Philip Taft, *History of Labor in the United States, 1896–1932*, Volume IV (New York: The Macmillan Company, 1935), pp. 1–12, "Conclusions from Past Experimentation"; Lloyd Ulman, *The Rise of the National Trade Union* (Cambridge, Mass.: Harvard University Press, 1955), pp. 23–45; Sumner H. Slichter, James J. Healy, and E. Robert Livernash, *The Impact of Collective Bargaining on Management* (Washington, D.C.: The Brookings Institution, 1960), pp. 946–961.

3. For a framework of comparison see, Clark Kerr, John T. Dunlop, Frederick H. Harbison, and Charles A. Myers, *Industrialism and Industrial Man*, The Problems of Labor and Management in Economic Growth (Cambridge, Mass.: Harvard University Press, 1960) and subsequent editions, Chs. 6–9. Also see, Benjamin Aaron, Ed., *Labor Courts and Grievance Settlement in Western Europe*, (University of California Press, Berkeley and Los Angeles, 1971), pp. vii-xx.

4. John T. Dunlop, *Industrial Relations Systems*, p. 307.

5. John T. Dunlop, "Political Systems and Industrial Relations," International Institute for Labor Studies, *Bulletin*, 9 (1972), pp. 111–13. This paper was presented at the Second World Congress of the International Industrial Relations Association. Also see, Clark Kerr, *The Future of Industrial Societies* (Cambridge, Mass.: Harvard University Press, 1983).

6. In the 1920s employment declined in the highly organized coal, railroad, and construction industries while employment expanded in the new automobile, electrical, and related mass production industries. In the past twenty years employment has grown fastest in local and state government, service industries, and wholesale and retail trade, which have been less well organized than other sectors, except for governments.

7. U.S. Department of Labor, Bureau of Labor Statistics, *Directory of National Unions and Employee Associations* (1971), Bulletin 1750, p. 90. The Bureau of National Affairs, Inc., *Directory of U.S. Labor Organizations, 1982–83, Edition*, Courtney D. Gifford, Ed. (Washington, D.C.: The Bureau of National Affairs, Inc., 1983), pp. 65–75.

8. Leo Troy, "The Financial Resources of American Labor, 1962–69," *Explorations in Economic Research*, Vol. 2, No. 2 (1975); Neil Sheflin and Leo Troy, "Finances of American Unions in the 1970s," *Journal of Labor Research* (Spring 1983), pp. 149–57.

9. George Strauss, "Organizational Behavior and Personnel Relations" in *A Review of Industrial Relations*, Vol. 1, Industrial Relations Research Association Series, (1970), pp. 145–206. For a standard text, see Paul Pigors and Charles A. Myers, *Personnel Administration* (New York: McGraw-Hill Book Company), various editions.

10. Sumner H. Slichter, James J. Healy, and E. Robert Livernash, *The Impact of Collective Bargaining on Management, loc. cit.*, pp. 951–52. As one illustration, see Ronald Berenbeim, "Nonunion Complaint Systems: A Corporate Appraisal" (New York: The Conference Board, Inc., 1980).

11. John T. Dunlop, "The Settlement of Emergency Disputes," in *Proceedings of the Fifth Annual Meeting, Industrial Relations Research Association* (December 28–29, 1952), p. 7.

12. Denis F. Johnson, "The U.S. Labor Force: Projections to 1990," *Monthly Labor Review* (July 1973), p. 3–13.

13. Lloyd Ulman, "Phase II in Context: Towards an Incomes Policy for Conservatives," in *Incomes Policy: What Can We Learn From Europe*, Walter Galenson, Ed. (New York School of Industrial and Labor Relations, 1973), p. 89.

14. In 1957 I stated the following with regard to the likely rate of inflation: "If by 1975 price increases over current levels are confined to 30 percent, I believe the record should be marked as excellent. If price levels are more than 70 percent higher than at the present, I would now regard that record as quite unsatisfactory. It is within this range that policies are likely to have their effects." I suggested that a more likely estimate would be 42.8 percent, derived from a 3 percent increase in productivity and a 5 percent annual rate of increase in compensation per hour. See John T. Dunlop, *The Secular Outlook: Wages and Prices* (University of California Institute of Industrial Relations), 1957. The cost-of-living index for the year 1972 was 44.7 percent over 1958 and the figure for June 1973 was 53.3 percent over 1958.

15. Sumner H. Slichter, "The American System of Industrial Relations: Some Contrasts with Foreign Systems," in *Potentials of the American Economy, Selected Essays of Sumner H. Slichter*, John T. Dunlop, Ed. (Cambridge, Mass.: Harvard University Press, 1961), pp. 285–86.
16. George W. Taylor, "The Public Interest: Variations on an Old Theme," *Proceedings of the Eighteenth Annual Meeting of the National Academy of Arbitrators, 1965* (Washington, D.C.: Bureau of National Affairs), p. 202.

Chapter 5

PAST AND FUTURE TENDENCIES IN AMERICAN LABOR ORGANIZATIONS

American labor organizations today reflect primarily the influence of long-term continuities with gradual changes and adaptations to evolving problems and opportunities. They are shaped much more basically by events of the past century than by the forces of recent years. Their dominant method is collective bargaining, which has grown substantially in scope and complexity in new sectors and circumstances. Legal enactment, including administrative proceedings, and participation in political elections are supportive and collaborative secondary methods which have also expanded to meet new contingencies and opportunities. The American labor movement and our industrial relations system are distinctively American, quite different from those of Europe, and even though our arrangements would not work elsewhere, they have served this society and economy well.[1]

The central directions of the past are likely to continue into the future because labor organizations and collective bargaining reflect well the character of American workers, managements, economy, and larger society. This view rejects the aspirations of those who would like to see the AFL-CIO become what is called a "genuine social movement," modeled after European labor movements, rather than the "political arm for market-unionism."[2]

It is conceivable that fundamental changes in the traditional

From *Daedalus, Journal of the American Academy of Arts and Sciences* (Winter 1978), pp. 79–96. By permission of *Daedalus*, Boston, Massachusetts.

methods of collective bargaining and legal enactment and in the directions of labor organizations could arise, however, should certain unlikely developments occur: in particular, should top labor leaders lose touch with local union officials and the rank and file of active members; should major employers operating under collective agreements launch a concerted attack on the legitimacy of unions; should the political leaders of both parties refuse to make accommodations to the aspirations of the labor organizations; or should a period of prolonged economic stagnation and inflation preclude advances in wages, benefits, and other rules of the workplace. Such drastic changes in the American environment appear remote, but should they occur they could well produce a marked shift to the ideological left and to a social movement closer to those constituting the labor movements of Western Europe.

The first three sections to follow consider structural features of American labor organizations, the method of collective bargaining, and the method of legal enactment and political action. In each instance the discussion is to portray the fundamental course of American labor organizations and to ascertain the extent of new tendencies and directions, if substantial, in the past decade or two. A fourth section on issues for the future considers the extent that new elements or new magnitudes are likely to change the course of American labor organizations and their methods. Four substantive areas are explored: workers' attitudes, participation in management, economic policies and consequences, and international interactions.

Structural Features of American Labor Organizations

American labor unions, together with employee associations such as those among police, professional athletes, nurses, and teachers that behave like unions, probably aggregated 23 million members in 1980, 25–30 percent of nonagricultural employment, almost 3 million in employee associations. Although American labor organizations approach double the absolute size of their counterparts in Great Britain and Japan, the percentage of non-agricultural employees in unions is over 50 percent in Great Britain, and 35 percent in Japan and in Germany. In Scandinavian countries the percentage probably ranges from 60 to 80 percent.[3] The percentage in labor organizations in the United States has remained relatively stable but has slipped about five points below the level of the first decade after World War II, and was adversely affected by the deep recession of 1980–83. Absolute membership continues to grow slowly save in periods of significant breakthroughs in particular sectors or regions. Union membership alone approximated 3.4 million in 1930, 8 million in 1940, 16.6 million in 1960, and 23 million in 1980.

The American labor movement is very decentralized. There are more than 175 national unions with 71,000 affiliated local unions and 35 national employee associations with almost 14,000 local chapters. More than 60 percent of the national unions are affiliated with AFL-CIO, and 85 percent of the local unions are in these national unions. The 12 largest national unions, with a half-million members or more, encompass approximately half the union members of the country,[4] the other half are distributed among more than 160 national unions.

Labor-organization membership is very unequally distributed among sectors and regions. Transportation, communications, public utilities, parts of construction, and such manufacturing industries as basic steel and automobiles are highly organized. On the other hand, finance, real estate, most retail trade, and services are very lightly organized. Government employees, who were relatively poorly organized with some notable exceptions prior to 1960, have had a significant surge to union membership since then. Approximately one-half of state and local government employees and two-thirds of civilian federal government employees now are estimated to be members of unions or similar associations. The five most highly organized states in the country are New York (45.4 percent of nonagricultural employees are members of unions or similar associations), Michigan, West Virginia, Pennsylvania, and Washington. The five least organized states are Florida, Texas, Mississippi, South Carolina, and North Carolina, with the lowest figure (9.8 percent).

The organized sector of the workforce has become increasingly white-collar and increasingly female. In 1980 organized female white-collar workers represented 15.3 percent of all white-collar workers, but they made up 34.9 percent of all organized workers, compared with only 23.8 percent in 1973. About 30.1 percent of all organized wage and salary workers were women in 1980, compared with only 23.1 percent in 1973.

American labor organizations assess their members relatively high dues compared with those applied in other countries. Membership payments are about 1 percent of the annual earnings of unionized workers,[5] who support a much larger paid staff and organization than unions do abroad; one study suggests that American unions have one paid officer to 300 members, compared with one to 3,000 members in Great Britain.[6] The decentralized collective bargaining arrangements in the United States, with private grievance handling and private arbitration rather than with labor courts or government inspectors, increase the need for union staff familiar with the workplace.

It is estimated that in 1969 American unions at all levels had income of $1.9 billion and assets of $2.6 billion compared with an estimated $300 million of assets for British unions. (These are, of course, small sums compared with those common in the corporate world.) In 1976 it is estimated American unions at all levels had income of $3.0 billion and assets of $4.0 billion. In keeping with our decentralized industrial relations arrangements, it is significant that the income and wealth of unions are almost equally divided between national unions and local organizations. The AFL-CIO raises by per capita payments approximately 1 percent of all the union dues income of its affiliates.

Each local or intermediate labor organization conducts its internal affairs and makes its decisions under its constitution and procedures, subject to applicable law, the Labor-Management Reporting and Disclosure Act of 1959. Each holds elections; arranges for appointed representatives and staff; negotiates and ratifies agreements; collects or receives dues; processes grievances; engages in job training and administers medical care plans alone or with employers under agreements; publishes papers or journals; engages in organizing activities; affiliates with other labor bodies; participates in community, educational, and social affairs; and engages in various political activities under the general guidance of the national labor organization from which it holds a charter. The autonomous national unions may in turn be affiliated with the federation, AFL-CIO. There is wide variation in the governance of local and national unions, depending on industry, collective bargaining patterns of centralization and decentralization, leadership, and internal traditions.[7]

The American Federation of Labor (AFL) was founded in the 1880s on two fundamental constitutional principles relating to its constituent unions: the autonomy of each affiliated national union and the exclusive jurisdiction of each national union specified in its charter from the federation. The principle of autonomy means that the federation is not to interfere in the internal political life, operations, or collective bargaining of its affiliates. Although the federation may render assistance when requested, it is not staffed for a major role in collective bargaining. The AFL-CIO (Congress of Industrial Organizations, founded in 1938) is not authorized to negotiate collective agreements with management groups (except for directly affiliated local branches) or incomes policies with government. Nor does it seek such authority. In the merged federation constitution of 1955 the original principle of autonomy was qualified to permit suspension of an affiliate by the Executive Council, upon a two-thirds vote, on a showing of corruption or domination by the purposes of the Communist Party or by any fascist organization or other totalitarian movement.[8] The corruption procedures have been largely preempted by the law since 1959, and there has been no occasion to use the Communist or other totalitarian proviso.

The constitutional principle of exclusive jurisdiction has been transmuted, under the necessities of government policies in the Wagner Act (1935) and the Taft-Hartley Act (1947), into the principle of constitutional respect for an "established collective bargaining relationship" and a prohibition of raiding any affiliate. This principle is enforced by an internal arbitration procedure and by appeal to the Executive Council, with the threat of all affiliates to be authorized to raid a violator guilty of noncompliance.[9] Prior to merger, the AFL held that a worker should join only the union specified by the AFL jurisdiction. Since then the internal rules of the federation comport in the main with public laws, and workers are to join only the union with an established collective-bargaining relationship with the worker's employer. "Exclusive jurisdiction" has lost its constitutional application and has been replaced by "an established bargaining relationship."

The locus of collective bargaining, organizing, and community activities in American labor organizations is lodged in national unions and their constituent local unions, with distributions of responsibility that vary widely among national unions. The federation may play a coordinating role in a few negotiations or organizing campaigns. In legislative and political questions and in international labor and public affairs, its role is greater although not preemptive.

Although the basic characteristics of U.S. labor organizations have been largely unchanged in the past several decades, a few developments are significant. The AFL-CIO merger in 1955 has continued and the internal disputes plan replacing "exclusive jurisdiction" has worked reasonably well—surprisingly well in view of the history of jurisdictional problems in the federation. Both developments are tributes to George Meany. Walter Reuther withdrew from the merger after helping to put it together, but Leonard Woodcock expressed a desire and Douglas Frazier led the United Auto Workers (UAW) to reaffiliate in the interest of a stronger national labor center. The aspirations for merger of constituent unions have not been fully realized, although more than 50 mergers of national unions or associations have taken place since 1955, most often as a consequence of financial problems. Labor organizations continued to grow slowly in absolute numbers in these two decades, until the deep recession and unemployment of 1980–83, with relatively more women and minorities as these two groups have entered more industries and occupations. The period saw a dramatic expansion of membership in the public sector, with an orderly means of recognition in many states and localities still unspecified, the role of collective bargaining in public employment largely still fluid, and management capacity grossly undeveloped.

The Method of Collective Bargaining

The American labor movement regards collective bargaining as its major business. George Meany defined collective bargaining in the following perceptive way: "On its philosophical side, collective bargaining is a means of assuring justice and fair treatment. In the economic realm it is a means of prodding management to increase efficiency and output, and of placing upon trade unions great responsibilities to limit their demands to practical realities. A failure to recognize the unique role of collective bargaining is a failure to understand the distinctive new nature of American private enterprise as it has evolved over the past seventy-five years."[10]

Collective bargaining, in common parlance, is used in this country to refer to at least three separate forms of labor-management activity: (1) periodic negotiations for a new collective agreement that may take place yearly or every two or three years depending on the duration of the agreement setting compensation and other terms and conditions of employment; (2) the day-to-day administration of the provisions of an existing agreement, including the vital steps in the grievance procedure and arbitration provisions; and (3) in some relationships, informal joint consultations and conferences that may take place outside agreement negotiations to explore common problems, to improve productivity, and to review broad questions of common interest in the industry or locality.

In the industrial-relations system of the United States the no-strike, no-lockout clause in an agreement developed concomitantly with the provision for binding arbitration over disputes arising during the term of the agreement, or more narrowly, over disputes as to the meaning and application of the agreement. The British, in contrast, generally have not made the distinction between periodic negotiations and administration, between issues of interests and rights; and accordingly almost any issue may be raised at any time on the shop floor and pressed to a work stoppage.

The collective-bargaining arrangements in this country are peculiarly the product of American unions, workers, and managers in the setting of our institutions; more recently and to a small degree, they have been constricted by legislation. The U.S. labor movement did not arise with the Wagner Act, nor were the fundamental features of collective bargaining created by government. Collective bargaining is

a highly decentralized and diversified accommodation to union structure, managerial independence, market and locality forces, and the
size of our country. Moreover, collective-bargaining institutions have
changed gradually with developments in these features. There are
probably more than 200,000 separate collective agreements, and
negotiations are designed to address the problems of each pair of
parties, including their employees (members). As Thomas R.
Donohue said, "Each of these agreements is of paramount importance to the workers involved—no matter whether it is Firestone
Rubber or a small electrical shop, whether it's New York City or
Kalispell, Montana."[11] The individual parties are not entirely free, of
course, to consider alone their preferences. The collective bargaining
processes compel them to pay attention sooner or later to the practical realities of market competition, to industrial relations developments in closely related negotiations, and to legal constraints.

For an appreciation of the decentralized quality of American collective bargaining it would be well to compare the texts of agreements
in a variety of sectors—airplane pilots, seamen, railroad engineers,
basic steel workers, construction pipefitters, insurance agents, TVA
employees. The methods of wage payment; fringe benefits; rules on
hiring, transfers, promotions, and layoffs; grievance procedures; and
arbitration—each reflects the problems of technology and markets
posed to workers and managements and their organizational histories.
No government agency could ever promulgate rules of the workplace
with such diversity or adjust them so well to changing conditions.
Within some sectors collective bargaining is relatively centralized on
a national basis, at least on key questions such as compensation, as is
the case in the basic steel industry, railroads, and motor freight trucking. In other industries, negotiations may be conducted on a regional
or locality basis as in maritime occupations, construction, and paper,
whereas in still others agreement-making is decentralized to the establishment level.

American collective bargaining is distinguished from European
and Japanese industrial relations systems in that there is generally a
single line of responsibility on the union side from the national level
to the immediate work place, local unions, and workers. In this country one agreement between management and the local or international union, or both, sets the full terms and conditions of employment. Elsewhere the works council, enterprise organization, or shop
steward constitutes a more or less independent authority. Negotiations take place in several tiers at varying levels with wage drift and
separate provisions as each level negotiates additional items.

Each agreement in the United States typically specifies a grievance
procedure, or steps in which representatives of the two sides seek to

resolve disputes or differences over the meaning or the application of the agreement that arise during its term. Agreements also tend to specify an arbitration process, including the selection of arbitrators or umpires; they may also provide that certain issues may be resolved by the controlled resort to strike or lockout, as in the case of production standards in the automobile industry. In this way the grievance procedure provides a way for responsible officers to review the operation of the agreement, to clarify the application of new provisions, and to consider questions of interpretation that had not been anticipated. The industrial jurisprudence that develops is shaped by the particular parties rather than by government agents; management supervision and workers and stewards participate in resolving most issues at the work level. In this process our industrial relations system has developed a large cadre of private arbitrators with wide understanding of plant-level issues.

One of the most significant—and often overlooked—effects of collective bargaining in the United States has been its influence on management generally as well as on unorganized or nonunion establishments, particularly of large size. Fifty years ago there were much sharper differences in wages, benefits, and conditions of work than now prevail in American industry between work places that are under collective bargaining and those that are not. In part to keep unions out and in part because multi-plant companies may have to deal with employees in both unionized and unorganized plants, these differences have been narrowed, even with regard to procedures for discharge, discipline, or layoff. "The challenge that unions presented to management has, if viewed broadly, created superior and better-balanced management, even though some exceptions must be recognized. . . . If one single statement were sought to describe the effect of unions on policy making, it would be: They have encouraged investigation and reflection."[12]

The American collective bargaining arrangements purport to perform a wide range of vital functions in the society. It is a decentralized means of setting compensation and benefits; it sets the vital rules of the work place relating to hiring, discharge, transfer, layoff, retirement, and promotion; it establishes procedures to review these decisions under collective agreements with resort to third-party neutrals; it provides means for plant-level employees and supervisors to participate in many decisions; it provides means of communication by means of the enterprise hierarchy; it constitutes a means to resolve many industrial conflicts; and it permits periodic review of rules and bargaining arrangements in the light of new technological or market conditions. These are primarily activities of local and national unions.

Although the basic features of collective bargaining have continued through the past several decades, several new features are to be noted. The scope of bargaining, in the sense of the subjects bargained about and incorporated into agreements, has grown. Health and welfare plans and pension arrangements have expanded to cover both more people and more situations. Some negotiations improve the retirement benefits of those already retired. Supplemental unemployment benefits and enhanced job security in numerous ways have been specified. Special training provisions and some modifications of the units in which seniority and rights are exercised have been developed to agree with the requirements of law respecting equal employment opportunities. The steel-workers and the basic steel industry imaginatively created an experimental agreement to avoid the costs of instability for both sides that grow out of a normal expiration date. A legal services benefit has been negotiated in a few situations. Collective agreements have grown more detailed and much longer. The greater complexity and technical nature of issues has introduced more experts and specialists on each side in some phases of the bargaining process. The negotiations process is continuing to concern itself with the greater intrusion of government into the employment relationship by means of statutes and regulations concerned with health and safety, pensions, affirmative-action programs, and the like.

But collective bargaining is not a cure-all of social and economic problems. It does not apply to a majority of work places, although its influence is widespread. It is not a principal means to eliminate poverty, to change the distribution of income, to reform the production process, to eliminate discrimination, or to reform the health-care delivery system, although it may make major contributions to all these purposes. Collective bargaining should not be demeaned because it is not an all-purpose social tool, but no one should prescribe for workers or the work places of America without knowledge and experience with collective bargaining and consultation with the parties.

The Method of Legal Enactment and Political Action

The method of legal enactment, to use the phrase of Sidney and Beatrice Webb,[13] had been used extensively by American unions from their earliest days. The principal committee of the federation at its outset in the 1880s was the Legislative Committee, later the Executive Council. A bill of grievances, formulated by a conference of national unions in 1906 and presented to President Theodore Roosevelt and leaders of Congress, called for legislation to curb immigration, to restrict the sale of products made by convict labor, to ensure maritime safety, to provide relief from injunctions in labor disputes and the antitrust laws as applied to labor, to establish a House Committee on Labor, and to enact child labor laws and suffrage for women. The pursuit of legislative objectives for union members and trade-union institutional purposes, for all workers and for broader social objectives has been a major preoccupation from the outset for both state federations and local central bodies.[14]

From their outset labor organizations in this country have debated the issue of formal political organization and mobilization of the electorate. The question arose in the early days of the federation as to whether the socialists or the Socialist Labor Party should have a special relationship to the AFL similar to the relations in Great Britain and Germany between the unions and the socialist parties. In the 1890 convention it was argued that "there is this fundamental difference between the old plutocratic [Republican and Democratic] parties and the S.L.P., that the former are notoriously the machines of the employing class, and as essential a part of the whole machinery through which they control, rob and oppress their wage-workers as is their industrial and commercial machinery; whereas the Socialist Labor Party is owned and controlled by wage-workers like yourselves. . . ."[15] But Gompers and the convention by a 3-to-1 vote would have none of it: "We hold that the trade unions of America, comprising the AFL are committed against the introduction of matters pertaining to partisan politics, to the religion of men or to their birthplace. We cannot logically admit the S.L.P. to representation, and shut the door in the face of other political organizations formed to achieve social progress." As Gompers said almost twenty-five years later, "The AFL has an independent political policy—a policy so politically independent that it is independent of the Socialist Party, too."[16] Reward your friends and punish your enemies was its formulation.

The constitution of the merged federation adopted the principle, "While preserving the independence of the labor movement from political control, to encourage workers to register and vote, to exercise their full rights and responsibilities of citizenship, and to perform their rightful part in the political life of the local, state and national communities."[17] The Committee on Political Education (COPE) is the coordinating mechanism for these activities in the federation.

The Federal Election Campaign Act has left intact the capacity of labor organizations and COPE to play a significant role in political campaigns. Although money derived from dues may not be used for contributions or expenditures for a candidate for public office, such funds may be used to communicate with union members and their families, to encourage and organize registration, and to get out the vote. In a polity in which machine organization has declined and voters appear more independent, these activities can have a significant impact. Voluntarily contributed funds can, of course, be used for direct support of a candidate.

The 1976 COPE activities surpassed earlier efforts in registration, voter participation, funds raised, and extent of activity with minorities (COPE Minorities Department and A. Philip Randolph operations) and with women's groups. COPE mobilized 120,000 volunteers in programs of registration and getting out the vote; 80 million pieces of literature were distributed to union members; 700 films were in the field by mid-September. A large number of full-time union representatives and officers were released from their regular work and were mobilized in critical states and districts in the weeks before the election. A number of national unions developed their own programs. About 80 percent of union members registered compared with about 70 percent of the voting-age population; also a higher percentage of union members voted compared with the electorate generally. In the Senate, 19 of 28 COPE-endorsed candidates were elected, and in the House of Representatives 259 of 365 COPE-endorsed candidates won. Although it is difficult to appraise precisely the independent effect of these activities, the effort is substantial and increasing over the years, and its leaders believe that it is becoming more effective.

Since the 1952 election, unlike its prior practice, the federation has generally endorsed the presidential candidate of the Democratic party; however, in 1972 the federation refrained from endorsing McGovern, and the endorsement of a number of national unions was split between the two major candidates.

Despite the considerable efforts of the federation and COPE to encourage political participation and involvement in federal elections, there remains marked diversity in the activities of the thousands of local unions in local and state politics. As Edward C. Banfield and James Q. Wilson remark, "Some unions want nothing more from city government than assurance that the police will not interfere with pickets during strikes. Others aspire to take possession of the city government and to run it as an adjunct of the union. Between these extreme positions there are many intermediate ones."[18] The rapid growth of organization among state and local government employees with their special interests in elected officials has further compounded this diversity.

Activities to influence the electorate have had their counterpart in lobbying legislative bodies and concentrated efforts to secure desired decisions from administrative agencies. From their earliest beginnings unions have advocated measures ranging from institutional concerns such as rights to join unions and limitations on suits against union funds, to issues of broad concern to all employees such as worker compensation for accidents, public works jobs, and social security, to matters of general social and national interest such as the elimination of discrimination, educational opportunities, consumer protection, and national defense. One historic illustration of these wider involvements is provided by Title VII of the Civil Rights Act of 1964. When the legislation was introduced, the Kennedy Administration had not included a title on discrimination in employment, fearing defeat of the legislation as a whole. George Meany promptly urged the inclusion of equal employment opportunity provisions, and the federation carried on a vigorous campaign for legislation. This vital role of the federation was fully recognized by the National Association for the Advancement of Colored People.[19]

The AFL-CIO is a federation of autonomous national unions, each of which not only conducts its own collective bargaining but takes its own public position on issues of major concern. The federation is at times engaged in developing a consensus, or permitting diversity, on conflicting questions such as the dispute over pipelines or railroads as a means to carry coal, or competing routes for gas lines involving sea or land. Individual unions may seek public policies for their industries, as compulsory arbitration in local and state government, only to find that the federation is unwilling to endorse such proposals on grounds of possible adverse effects on the right to strike more generally. There are likewise competing priorities for legislative programs and efforts. The federation is comprised of small unions, such as the Horseshoers with 390 members, to ones as large as the Steelworkers which approach 1.5 million; 30 unions with members in public employment and 80 with only private-sector interests; industrial unions and craft unions; unions in export industries and those adversely affected by imports; the regional concentration of members varies a great deal, as does their distribution among sectors. A federation requires consensus building and accommodation.

The federation takes positions by resolutions on major issues of domestic and foreign policies, just as state organizations do on many state and local issues. With the assistance of particularly concerned affiliates it seeks alliances in the legislative and electoral processes that may be more or less stable. Civil rights groups have often been aligned with it on questions of minimum wage, welfare, and legislation on discrimination despite tensions on some other questions. On the issue of strip mining of coal and many of the clean air issues, the federation has sided with environmentalists, whereas on nuclear power and related questions it has often taken positions close to that of industry. On many international issues it has been strong on defense and suspicious of detente. The federation has developed a very considerable familiarity with the operations of the federal bureaucracy and the legislative process.

However one appraises the effectiveness or the consequences of the method of legislative enactment and participation in political elections at national, state, and local levels, there can be no doubt that these activities are a major feature of American labor organizations. The representation of workers in their dealings with employers is the prime concern, but "social unionism, the effort to improve the general condition of their members by improving the general condition of everyone in the community,"[20] is a vital secondary function.

Issues for the Future

Sumner Slichter's judgment as to our past is correct: ". . . I think the United States should consider itself lucky. It possesses a system of industrial relations that, in its basic characteristics, fits conditions here reasonably well. The system has been developed without being planned. Perhaps that is why it represents a pretty good adaptation to conditions. . . . We seem justified in being grateful that we have been favored by fortune and perhaps also in taking modest pride that we have pursued opportunistic policies with considerable flexibility and good sense."[21]

Workers' Attitudes

Widespread attention is attracted from time to time to the view that the American work ethic has eroded, that dissatisfaction is increasing rapidly at the work place, and that union rebels are "mining a deep vein of worker discontent." After a long strike the phrasing is likely to continue, "relations between management and labor have degenerated into bitter parochial conflicts incapable of resolving the mutual discontents."[22] But the evidence is clearly that these conclusions are in the eye of the beholder and in phrase-makers of "blue collar blues" and "lunch-pail lassitude" rather than in the work place or work force. It would seem that if any events call for explanation in our times, it is not so much the occasional wildcat strike at Lordstown, Ohio as the fact that the great inflation of 1973–1974 and 1978–80 with declines in real income, and the large-scale unemployment of 1975–1976 and 1980–83, have produced so little industrial unrest or protest.

Periodic polls have asked employees, "On the whole, would you say you are satisfied or dissatisfied with the work you do?" An overall response for 1973—77 percent satisfied, 11 percent dissatisfied, and 13 percent no opinion—is rather characteristic of responses from those with paid employment over the past quarter century.[23] The study of more substantial behavioral measures such as productivity, quit rates, absenteeism, accidents, and strikes reflects that their changes over time are explained by conventional economic determinants and that there is no basis to ascribe any role to changes in worker attitudes and motivation.[24] The Survey Research Center at the University of Michigan made careful surveys for 1969 and 1973 that conclude that there were no major changes in overall job satisfaction for the labor force as a whole or for any major demographic subcategories between 1969 and 1973.[25]

There are, of course, differences among employees in different types of jobs as to their job satisfaction, whatever the term "satisfaction" may mean. Younger workers appear to reflect more dissatisfaction than older workers, but the jobs they hold as newcomers pay less well and are probably less challenging than jobs they subsequently achieve. Moreover, the proportion of the labor force below the age of 25 years has begun to decline, and absolute numbers in this age group may well decline in a few years. The evidence indicates that women are less satisfied than men with the financial rewards and challenges of their jobs, but their overall satisfaction scores do not differ significantly from those of men. Racial differences in job satisfaction appear pronounced, although differences within occupational and age groups are much less. Job dissatisfaction among racial groups and among women in part reflects resentment at discrimination.

Changes in the work place over time seem, if anything, gradually to have been favorable. Unskilled work has declined relatively, and professional, technical, and clerical positions have increased substantially.[26] Higher wages, fringe benefits, and legislation provide increased protection against risks not only of the work place but of modern life in general. An emphasis on education and retirement and changes in the schedules for working hours and increased opportunity for part-time work have tended to mitigate job dissatisfaction. Company policies in large enterprises in general have become concerned with people at the work place, reflecting in part the consequences of professional personnel functions and in part the effects of labor organizations on management. These changes are not frozen; they continue to be made in response to aspirations, pressures, and the opportunities of economic growth. Indeed, it is likely that as wages, leisure time, and educational attainment rise along with progressive income taxes, employees in the future may well seek to take a higher fraction of their rewards in improved conditions of work. These are opportunities for collective bargaining and some legislation, not the seedbed of worker rebellion or a revival of the class struggle, except as the economic environment may become hostile over a sustained period.

Participation in Management

Worker participation in industry has received widespread public attention in recent years, and European developments appear to be extending significantly worker participation in management. Participation is urged as a solution to such widespread problems of industrial society as worker alienation, low productivity, industrial conflict, and political unrest. It is also said to contribute to effective management and productive efficiency.[27]

German codetermination was adapted in 1976 from the iron and steel industry to provide nominally equal worker and management representation on the supervisory boards of companies employing more than 2,000 people. At least one of the worker members is to represent plant-level supervision; in the event of a stalemate in the board, the management chairman is to cast the deciding vote. German law also provides, as does that of many other European countries, for an elected worker council for plants, and for company-wide councils comprised of all segments of the work force to meet with management and supervision over plant-level issues. German authorities are keen on the results of codetermination and hold that it has contributed significantly to German labor peace, stability, and productivity.

The Bullock Report in Great Britain, presented to Parliament in January 1977, proposed to place worker directors in the boardrooms of enterprises with 2,000 or more people, estimated to comprise the 738 largest firms, when unions demand it and when endorsed by a vote of all the work force.[28] It is argued that this form of union participation is essential to improve the deep-seated industrial-relations malaise of Great Britain. "It is our belief that the way to release those energies, to provide greater satisfaction in the work place and to assist in raising the level of productivity and efficiency in British industry—and with it the living standards of the nation—is not by recrimination or exhortation but by putting the relationship between capital and labor on a new basis which will involve not just management but the whole work force in sharing responsibility for the success and profitability of the enterprise."[29]

The Sudreau Report of February 7, 1975 represents President Giscard's concern with *reform de l'enterprise*. The commission rejected German codetermination on the grounds that it is not suited to present-day France, where it is essential to preserve management's responsibility to direct the daily affairs of the enterprise. But there exists a need for conscious participation by all in the organization of the work. A radically different approach to participation by employees in the boards of companies is held to be necessary. It proposes that consideration be given to a one-third worker participation in supervisory boards or boards of directors with supervisory functions, a new form of participation designated cosupervision. In view of general misgivings, cosupervision should be introduced gradually. The report contains a number of other areas of company reform, including means of strengthening work councils.

In the United States, labor organizations have not only failed to show interest in codetermination but they are hostile to such ideas. They also look unkindly toward stock ownership as a means to interest workers in management. Our unions regard collective bargaining as an adequate means of influencing management. The words that follow are those of Thomas R. Donahue, but the views are widespread: "We do not seek to be a partner in management—to be, most likely, the junior partner in success and the senior partner in failure. We do not want to blur in any way the distinctions between the respective roles of management and labor in the plant. . . . And we probably bargain on as many, if not more, issues than the number we might have any impact on as members of a Board of Directors."[30] Deep recession and threatened bankruptcies may change these views in a few situations, but the mainstream views of the labor movement are not likely to change very much.

Economic Policies and Consequences

The economic consequences of labor organizations can be briefly considered under three headings: conflict, productivity, and inflation. In the period immediately after World War II, as after World War I, the concern over disruptive economic strikes reached a peak. The national emergency provisions of the Taft-Hartley Act (Title II) were enacted in 1947. The statute was seriously defective from the perspective of labor-management relations (for example, the role of the board of inquiry and the last-offer vote). Emergency disputes have ceased to be perceived as a significant problem, if they ever were one.[31] On rare occasions, however, one may continue to expect a sticky situation as in a chaotic coal organization or in public employment. Protection of the public interest in private employment is likely to be better served by bargaining of the parties, informal influence of senior labor and management leaders, imaginative mediation, and the forbearance of Congress with ad hoc legislation designed for the particular dispute as a final resort, than by the patent solutions of compulsary arbitration or the application of antitrust laws. In local and state government employment, state legislatures and courts are in the process of experimenting with a variety of procedures, and in due course the complex issues of the competing interests of taxpayers and public employees will be brought under more clearly delineated procedures.

Alfred Marshall[32] well understood, as few contemporary economists do, that labor organizations have materially increased productivity by their effect on training, morale, methods and forms of compensation, safety, support of orderly procedures, and discipline at the work place and in the work community. The favorable influence by the "prodding of management" (Meany's phrase) or "the making of exacting demands on management" (Slichter's phrase) is recognized to be very considerable by those familiar with the processes of management organizations. These influences are a continuous process and may be expected in general to continue. Moreover, in a growing number of enterprises, formal labor-management production committees outside the bargaining mechanism are operating to reduce waste, to improve quality and performance, and to tap the ideas of workers regarding the production process.[33] These joint efforts are likely to be significant in only a minority of situations with special problems, opportunities, or leadership.

The net impact of labor organizations and collective bargaining on productivity is obscured in public discussion by a few outdated work rules such as that requiring a fireman on a diesel locomotive. The elimination of obsolete practices is a continuing function of periodic bargaining, and the view has been widely accepted in American collective bargaining that such practices are a form of property right of workers to be purchased or traded in negotiations if they are realistically to be eliminated. In the interests of efficiency, American managers, with some exceptions, have done well in this process.

The inflationary potentials of collective bargaining have been obscured by the world-wide inflation in 1973–74 and 1979–80, derived in large part from food and energy. But with the leading collective bargaining settlements in negotiated agreements averaging 9 to 10 percent for 1979 and 1980, there is persistent concern with wage-cost inflation. As Arthur Okun of the Brookings Institution sees it, "A happy ending to the stagflation story *must* involve some incomes-policy or social-compact arrangement."[34] It is well that economists of both political party-persuasions now recognize that wage and price guideposts cannot be effective without full consultation with labor and management, but they have little experience, and one might add capacity, in the art of consensus building in this area.

In the United States an incomes policy or a social contract, as those terms are understood in Europe, are not a viable policy save in a dire national emergency. The decentralized federation has no capacity to commit its constituents, and they in turn have little authority or disposition to control their members on vital collective-bargaining matters. The ultimate test of any wage-restraint policy is what happens when a union strikes against the policy, as the Heath government discovered in the coal industry in England. Moreover, the use of a single yardstick (be it 3.2 percent of the Kennedy-Johnson guideposts, or 5.5 percent of the Pay Board, or 7 percent in the Carter Administration) is a crude and inappropriate measure to distinguish inflationary from noninflationary settlements. Noncompliance with these so-called voluntary standards creates strong pressures for controls. Inflationary periods distort the wage structure, and the primary task of effective stabilization as wage agreements come open is to achieve a result in which different amounts are negotiated for variously situated parties in order to restore the wage relationship and to eliminate continuing efforts to catch up or to move ahead of closely related groups. A single guidepost number is incapable of producing wage stability.[35]

The alternative policy for the United States is the identification of sectors with severe wage and price problems, to diagnose the underlying difficulties and to work with the labor organizations, managements, and government agencies involved to moderate the structural inflationary pressures, be they labor supply and training, plant capacity, collective bargaining structure, or productivity.

International Interactions

American labor unions have a long tradition of interest and involvement in international labor affairs. Gompers was a leading figure in the founding of the International Labour Office. American unions continue to participate actively in the various international trade secretariats which deal with international standards in various industries such as the transport and metal trades. The federation vigorously opposed the spread of Communist influence in the labor organizations of Western Europe after World War II; it has sought to encourage and support the growth of democratic trade unions in the developing countries. Although the federation withdrew for a period from the International Confederation of Free Trade Unions in a dispute over policies, it has expanded its activities to assist leadership development, education, technical assistance, housing, and medical and other social programs in developing countries through the American Institute for Free Labor Development (Latin America and Caribbean), the African-American Labor Center, and the Asian-American Free Labor Institute.

The labor unions of the United States could be an extremely important resource in the policy aims of the country in international relations. In Western European and some other countries, many government officials are former labor union leaders, and the complex interactions of labor unions, labor, and allied democratic parties and their governments are intertwined in ways more readily understood by those sensitive to the labor scene. Personal relations in labor forums often go back many years. Among a number of developing countries, the influence of our labor organizations, both direct and by associates in third countries, can make a contribution to the emergence of institutions more compatible with our long-term interests and values. It may not be remiss to note that among Western countries, there is none that enjoys more loyalty and security from its labor movement.

There is no more contentious issue for the future in this field than trade policy and taxes on corporate earnings abroad. Severe unemployment has exacerbated the concern in labor groups over imports and created in many communities deep hostility to the trade negotiations envisaged by the 1974 act. The magnitude and spread of adjustments required by expanded imports in the projected economic climate in such industries as clothing, shoes, electronics, automobiles, and speciality steel are certain to create strong economic and political reactions favoring bilateral restraints on imports.

It is naive to assume that workers are fungible and that one can simply add up the employment gains and losses or the gross national product effects from trade and be persuasive in a trade policy. Trade adjustment assistance in the 1974 act in the form of a measure of higher unemployment compensation, retraining grants, and moving allowances is an improvement over earlier policies. Workers affected, however, do not see why they should bear the material and psychic costs and risks of adjustment. Their labor and community leaders, particularly in the present and projected economic climate, are persuaded that the United States is simply accommodating to subtle forms of autarky abroad which encourage American firms to locate abroad and to keep out American exports, with resulting damage to American employment, while at the same time the foreign autarky subsidizes in various ways the costs and exports of its own enterprises. The state trading companies of Communist countries and government-operated enterprises elsewhere have compounded the problem. Until labor leaders are much more deeply involved in the formulation and execution of policy in this area, beyond the formalism of advisory committees, and until responsible officials are prepared to carry on a much more vigorous campaign against autarkical forms abroad, there will be little change in the present hostile policies and attitudes among labor leaders. These developments will require a long time and much new and detailed data.

A concomitant major issue concerns the increasing number of people in this country "without documents," to use the language of diplomacy, or simply illegal aliens. Various informed estimates now place the figure in the 8 to 10 million range with significant effects on competition for jobs, wages, and benefits, and welfare among the least skilled. A country of immigrants and relatives has difficulty facing the issues. Police action is ineffectual. The economic interests of some employers combine with civil rights interests against identification cards that may be used in a discriminatory manner to preclude strong legislation. Population pressures in other countries combined with large wage differentials is an invitation to movement across borders, temporarily or more permanently. It has been suggested that citizens may not be willing to perform menial jobs and that illegal aliens are essential for many activities.[36] Serious attention to this area, including further negotiations with our neighbors, is a major item on the agenda for the future likely to affect as well labor attitudes toward trade.

The American labor movement and collective bargaining are well-established institutions, deeply rooted in the character of the American worker, the economy and its structure of markets, and our political system. They have the virtue of pragmatism rather than ideology, and they respond gradually to new challenges and opportunities at the work place and in the polity.[37]

Any appraisal of the past performance or future prospects of labor organizations in this country decisively depends on the expectations that are applied. Some have expected labor unions to perform activity for which they were ill designed and never intended to accomplish, and which they abjured. Some have looked to unions for the working-class revolution. Often labor organizations have been urged to adopt the mutually inconsistent objectives of radical reform and economic responsibility; others have hoped for a new political party. Consider the following aspirations: "Labor had no more urgent job in the '60's than the focusing of its political energies on the conquest of want, illiteracy, intolerance; the building up of both health and decent housing; the realization of limitless promise of the scientific golden age. And apart from their general social necessity, these undertakings would be vastly more inspiring, to union membership and leadership alike, than the present ever more routine function of the policing of day-to-day plant grievances and the writing of mechanized contracts."[38] Labor unions will undoubtedly gradually continue to make some contributions toward some of these objectives primarily at the work place and secondarily by social and legislative activities. But in the depreciation of collective bargaining and grievance handling and in the enhancement of political methods there is a serious misreading of the nature of American workers, their organizations, and the practicalities of the American economy and society.

As memories of Viet-Nam and the 1968 and 1972 election conflicts recede, a window of opportunity emerges for a more civil and possibly productive direct dialogue between labor representatives and intellectual groups. In the university world, now almost devoid of contacts with established labor leaders, there are again students and younger faculty interested in labor union institutions and how they actually work. There is a long agenda of potential common interests— union growth in new areas, the effect of government regulation, foreign labor issues in Western countries and in developing nations. Despite the deep-seated tensions, there are some opportunities for a degree of accommodation.

Endnotes

1. Sumner H. Slichter, "The American System of Industrial Relations: Contrasts with Foreign Systems" (January 1955), reprinted in John T. Dunlop (ed.), *Potentials of the American Economy, Selected Essays of Sumner H. Slichter* (Cambridge, Mass.: Harvard University Press, 1961), pp. 285–286.

2. Daniel Bell, *The End of Ideology* (New York: The Free Press of Glencoe, 1960), p. 213. See John T. Dunlop, "The Future of the American Labor Movement," in *The Third Century, America as a Post-Industrial Society*, Seymour Martin Lipset, Ed. (Stanford, Calif.: Hoover Institution Press, 1979), pp. 183–203.

3. U.S. Department of Labor, Bureau of Labor Statistics, *Directory of National Unions and Employee Associations*, 1975. Also see Everett M. Kassalow, "International Labor Standards—Their Comparison and Implementation," unpublished paper (December 14–16, 1976): Table 1. There are numerous problems involved in such comparisons, including the handling of migratory workers and the meaning of membership. Attachment to labor organizations might be tested by voting in representation elections, regular payment of periodic dues, willingness occasionally to demonstrate, support of a long strike, or voting a labor ticket in public elections. The number of persons governed by collective agreements is still another concept which encompasses more employees than union membership. The significance of such indicia varies among countries. The figures cited in the text for the U.S. exclude Canadian membership. They also exclude a growing number of retired union members with whom many unions keep in touch by pension arrangements and political education committees. Also see, *Directory of U.S. Labor Organizations*, 1982–83 Edition, Courtney D. Gifford, Ed. (Washington, D.C.: Bureau of National Affairs, Inc., 1983).

4. In order of size in 1974 these unions were the Teamsters, Autoworkers, Steelworkers, Electricians (I.B.E.W.), Machinists, Carpenters, Retail Clerks, Labor-

ers, State, County and Municipal Workers, Service Employees, Meat Cutters, and Communcation Workers. Among associations, the largest, the National Education Association, would rank third if rated on the list of unions.

5. Leo Troy, "The Finances of American Unions, 1962–1969," in *Explorations in Economic Research* (2) (Spring 1975), p. 223. The income of the federation was about $40 million a year in 1982. See also Charles W. Hickman, "Labor Organizations' Fees and Dues," *Monthly Labor Review* (May 1977): 19–24; Neil Sheflin and Leo Troy, "Finances of American Unions in the 1970s," *Journal of Labor Research*, Spring 1983, pp. 149–57.

6. Seymour M. Lipset, "Trade Unions and Social Structure: II," *Industrial Relations* (February 1962), p. 93.

7. See Lloyd Ulman, *The Rise of the National Trade Union* (Cambridge, Mass.: Harvard University Press, 1955). Also review the history of various national unions, for instance, Mark Perlman, *The Machinist* (Cambridge, Mass.: Harvard University Press, 1961); or Martin Segal, *The Rise of the United Association, National Unionism in the Pipe Trades, 1884–1924* (Wertheim Committee, Harvard University, 1970).

8. Constitution of the AFL and CIO, 1975, Article VIII, Section 7. *Proceedings and Executive Council Reports of the AFL-CIO*, San Francisco, October 2–7, 1975 (Washington, D.C.: AFL-CIO), p. 451.

9. Article XX, Constitution of the AFL and CIO, pp. 462–466. Also see Arthur J. Goldberg, *AFL-CIO Labor United* (New York: McGraw-Hill, 1956), pp. 103–154.

10. George Meany, "What Labor Means by 'More,'" *Fortune Magazine* (March 1955), pp. 92, 93, 172, 174, 177.

11. Thomas R. Donohue, "The Future of Collective Bargaining," International Conference on Trends in Industrial and Labour Relations in Montreal, Canada on May 26, 1976, in *AFL-CIO Free Trade Union News* (September 1976); 6.

12. Sumner H. Slichter, James J. Healy, and E. Robert Livernash, *The Impact of Collective Bargaining on Management* (Washington, D.C.: The Brookings Institution, 1960), pp. 951, 952.

13. Sidney and Beatrice Webb, *Industrial Democracy* (London: Longmans, Green, 1914). The Webbs regarded the trade unionists as achieving their objectives by three main instruments or levers: collective bargaining, legal enactment, and mutual insurance (p. 150; see also pp. 247–278).

14. For the activities of the California federation, see Philip Taft, *Labor Politics American Style: The California State Federation of Labor* (Cambridge, Mass.: Harvard University Press, 1968).

15. *Proceedings of the Tenth Annual Convention of the American Federation of Labor* held at Detroit, Michigan, on December 8–13, 1890. The issue in the convention was the issuance of a charter to the Central Labor Federation of New York, which included as one constituent member the Socialist Labor Party. There was an extended and formal debate. Gompers opposed the charter.

16. Morris Hillquit, Samuel Gompers, and Max J. Hayes, *The Double Edge of Labor's Sword, Discussion and Testimony on Socialism and Trade-Unionism Before the Commission on Industrial Relations* (New York: Socialist Literature Company, 1914), pp. 134, 152.

17. Constitution of the AFL and CIO, Article II, 12.

18. Quoted in Charles M. Rehmus and Doris B. McLaughlin, *Labor and American Politics* (Ann Arbor: The University of Michigan Press, 1967), reprinted, p. 267.

19. See Derek C. Bok and John T. Dunlop, *Labor and the American Community* (New York: Simon and Schuster, 1970), p. 124; Ray Marshall, *The Negro Worker* (New York: Random House, 1967), pp. 40–41; and J. David Greenstone, *Labor in American Politics* (New York: Knopf, 1969), pp. 342–343.

20. Donohue, "The Future of Collective Bargaining," p. 5.

21. Slichter, "The American System of Industrial Relations: Contrasts with Foreign Systems," pp. 285–286.

22. Solomon Barkin, "A New Agenda for Labor," *Fortune* (November 1960).

23. George Strauss, "Workers: Attitudes and Adjustments," in Jerome M. Rosow (ed.), *The Worker and The Job, Coping With Change*, The American Assembly (Englewood Cliffs, N.J.: Prentice-Hall, 1974), pp. 74–75. There are technical difficulties with the Gallup Poll. See Robert Quinn, Thomas Mangione, and Martha Madilovitch, "Evaluating Working Conditions in America," *Monthly Labor Review* (November 1973), p. 39. Also see in the same American Assembly volume, Peter Henle, "Economic Effects: Reviewing the Evidence," pp. 119–144.

24. Robert J. Flanagan, George Strauss, and Lloyd Ulman, "Worker Discontent and Work Place Behavior," *Industrial Relations* (May 1974), pp. 101–123.

25. See Quinn, Mangione, and Mandilovitch, "Evaluating Working Conditions in America," *Loc. cit.*

26. See *Employment and Training Report of the President* (Washington, D.C.: U.S. Department of Labor, 1976), pp. 147–157 ("The Changing Nature of Work").

27. Arnold S. Tannenbaum, "Systems of Formal Participation," in George Strauss, *et al.* (eds.), *Organizational Behavior, Research, and Issues* (Madison, Wisc.: Industrial Relations Research Association, 1974), p. 78.

28. *Report of the Committee of Inquiry on Industrial Democracy*, Cmnd. 6706 (London: Her Majesty's Stationery Office, 1977); *TUC Guide to the Bullock Report on Industrial Democracy* (London: The Trade Unions Congress, February 1977); B. C. Roberts, "Participation by Agreement," *Lloyds Bank Review*, no. 125 (July 1977); 12–23; *The Economist* (November 13–19, 1976): p. 105.

29. *Report of the Committee of Inquiry on Industrial Democracy*, p. 160.

30. Donohue, "The Future of Collective Bargaining," p. 6.

31. John T. Dunlop, "The Settlement of Emergency Disputes," *Proceedings of the Fifth Annual Meeting, Industrial Relations Research Association* (December 28–29, 1952): "I believe that in twenty-five years the emergency dispute will have ceased to be a serious question."

32. Alfred Marshall, *Elements of Economics of Industry* (London: Macmillan, 1893), Chapter 13, "Trade Unions," pp. 374–411.

33. National Center for Productivity and Quality of Working Life, *Directory of Labor-Management Committees* (Washington, D.C., October 1976). For a discussion of Scanlon plans and other systems of encouraging productivity, see Paul Pigors and Charles A. Myers, *Personnel Administration* 8th ed. (New York: McGraw-Hill, 1977), pp. 356–377.

34. Arthur Okun, "Conflicting National Goals," in Eli Ginzberg (eds.), *Jobs for Americans*, The American Assembly (Englewood Cliffs, N.J.: Prentice-Hall, 1976), p. 81.

35. John T. Dunlop, "Wage and Price Controls as Seen by a Controller," Industrial Relations Research Association, *Proceedings of the 1975 Annual Spring Meeting* (May 8–10, 1975), 457–463; *The Lessons of Wage and Price Controls—The Food Sector*, John T. Dunlop and Kenneth J. Fedor, Eds. (Cambridge, Mass.: Harvard University Press, 1977), pp. 233–59. See also Committee for Economic Development, *Fighting Inflation and Promoting Growth* (August 1976), 62–77.

36. Michael J. Piore, "The New Immigration and the Presumptions of Social Policy," *Industrial Relations Research Association, Proceedings of the Twenty-Seventh Annual Winter Meeting* (December 28–29, 1974), 350–358.

37. On several occasions I have sought to outline the future course of development of American unions and collective bargaining. See John T. Dunlop, "The American Industrial Relations System in 1975," in Jack Steiber (ed.), *U.S. Industrial Relations: The Next Twenty Years* (East Lansing, Mich., 1958), pp. 1–24; "Future Trends in Industrial Relations in the United States," a paper presented to the Third World Congress, International Industrial Relations Association in London on September, 1973 (Chapter 4 this volume).

38. A. H. Raskin, "The Obsolescent Unions," *Commentary* (July 1963), 18.

Chapter 6

CONSENSUS AND NATIONAL LABOR POLICY

Our national industrial relations system suffers from excessive legislation, litigation, formal awards, and public pronouncements. The principal carriers of this disease are politicians. Our imperative need is to alter drastically our methods of policy formation to place much greater reliance upon the development of consensus.

Professor William Ernest Hocking defined the politician as the "man who deliberately faces both the certainty that men must live together, and the endless uncertainty on what terms they can live together, and who takes on himself the task of proposing the terms, and so of transforming the unsuccessful human group into the successful group." In proposing the changing terms on which government agencies, managements, and unions shall live together in an industrial relations system, our politicians have fallen far short of Professor Hocking's standards. Contrary to the wisdom of antiquity, they have separated legislation and a philosophy of collective bargaining; contrary to Holmes they have exalted a kind of legal logic over experience. They have reflected little understanding of the practical work level in an industrial society, and they have imposed rules rather than first develop a consensus among those to be affected. These same habits have characterized to a large degree the confederation levels of management and labor; thus, formalism, litigation, and unreality pervade the national industrial relations system.

Although collective bargaining, in the sense of the relationships between management and unions in the work place, enterprise, or industry, is not the topic of this chapter, I wish to express the judg-

From Presidential Address to Industrial Relations Research Association, *Proceedings of the Thirteenth Annual Meeting, Industrial Relations Research Association* (December 1960), pp. 1–14.

ment that I do not agree that the country faces a crisis in collective bargaining or that "something is seriously awry in the system of collective bargaining," at least as collective bargaining has been used to refer to the negotiation and administration of agreements. Rather, the overwhelming evidence is that, on balance, relationships never were better as judged by such standards as grievance handling, discipline, arbitration, wage structure administration, wildcat strikes, or violence. It is true that in some industries the environment has become tougher, affecting the bargaining, but that is the function of collective bargaining. It is also true that new problems are emerging which may require a new form of relationship—the conference method—among labor, management, and even government. The need for these new forms of relationships in the decades ahead does not mean that collective bargaining has failed; indeed, these new conferences are often being created by traditional collective bargaining.

This discussion of national labor policy is divided into three sections which consider in turn the formation of national labor policy by government, the decisions of the labor movement at the federation level, and finally the policy making of the confederation level of management.

The Federal Government

The management of American industrial enterprises prior to the Wagner Act by and large simply refused to recognize labor organizations. There were notable exceptions: where craftsmen were exceptionally strong, where the social pressures of isolated communities or groups of workers were particularly intense; or where some enterprises for financial reasons or through the idealistic conviction of a few managers accepted collective bargaining. But the expanding mass production industries were overwhelmingly antiunion.

On three occasions, as Sumner Slichter pointed out, a major effort was made to persuade American managers voluntarily to adopt a labor policy of recognition of trade unions and the acceptance of collective bargaining. On each occasion the attempt failed miserably. The first attempt at the turn of the century was under the leadership of the National Civic Federation, Mark Hanna, and other business leaders. The second attempt was made by President Woodrow Wilson through the Industrial Conference to perpetuate principles of labor-management relations temporarily accepted or imposed during World War I. The third attempt was made through section 7a of the NIRA, which proclaimed the rights of collective bargaining and sought to pledge employers to non-interference in the exercise by workers of self-organization.

The failure to persuade American managers without the compulsions of law to recognize labor unions is in marked contrast to the Scandinavian and British experience. In Denmark the September Agreement, made between the central confederation of employers and unions following the great lockout of 1899, shaped fundamentally the patterns of industrial relations to follow. It provided for mutual recognition and acknowledged the right of strike and lockout after appropriate notice and votes. It recognized the employer's "right to direct and distribute the work and to use what labor may in his judgment be suitable. . . ." In Sweden the 1906 "December Compromise" between the confederation levels of employers and unions recognized the full freedom of employers to hire and fire organized and unorganized workers and in exchange recognized the full freedom of workers to organize and provided for redress in case of discipline for exercising this right. In Great Britain the gradual development of its industrial relations system is well characterized by Allan Flanders, "Collective bargaining is for us essentially a voluntary process. . . . The process itself is not normally enforced or regulated by law. . . ."

While there was very considerable industrial conflict and political struggle for a period in Scandinavia and in Great Britain over the status of labor organizations, in the end the right to organize and to engage in bargaining, as well as the procedures and arrangements for bargaining, were evolved gradually by custom or by explicit agreement between organized managements and unions. They were not imposed by law.

In the early 1930s it might have appeared that the United States was headed in the general direction pioneered by Britain and Scandinavia, with the lag of a generation to which our British cousins have been prone to point. The greater size of our country, the lesser cohesiveness of our managers, the lesser class consciousness of our workers, the lesser role of export markets, and the later industrialization and greater significance of agriculture combine to explain the lag.

The Norris LaGuardia Act of 1932 only sought to remove the most serious obstacles which had been developed by the courts to labor organization and to the use of economic weapons in organizing and in bargaining with employers. This statute accorded with the dominant view of labor leaders that they only desired the government and courts to be "neutral"; they did not seek active intervention of the government in their behalf.

The Railway Labor Act of 1926 was in the same mold: It was largely shaped by the joint action of the carriers and the labor organizations.

The significant fact is that the establishment of a collective bargaining relationship between the parties and the procedures for dealing with each other were mutually determined. They had the experience of together shaping the framework of their relations and an active joint role in defining the activity of governmental agencies. This experience provides the basis for further joint activity, and when politicians deprive labor and management of this experience they eliminate a sense of responsibility for the operation of a statute and deprive the parties of a basis for further cooperation.

The Wagner Act was to constitute a major change in the development of public policy, although it was probably not so intended. On the face of it, the statute did not seem complex. It was designed simply to require employers to recognize and to bargain with labor unions where the employees desired a union. It compelled managements to do what they had resisted doing under voluntary persuasion. However, the Wagner Act was to constitute a major fork in the road of labor policy, not merely on account of what it provided, but as a consequence of the inherent implications of the legislative approach in the absence of mutual sanctions for the statute. The signs on the road necessarily pointed to the Taft-Hartley law, the Landrum-Griffin Act, and beyond because of the way in which the policies were determined under the conditions of the times.

It is not necessary here to sketch the inevitable administrative, legislative, judicial, and political steps by which the nation moved from the Wagner Act to Taft-Hartley and then to Landrum-Griffin, nor to outline the steps that are yet to come down this fork in the road. The present state of determination of governmental industrial relations policy can be briefly summarized in seven paragraphs as follows:

1. The legislative framework of collective bargaining is now regulated by a highly partisan political process. Thus, the Democratic Platform for 1960 promised the "repeal of the anti-labor excesses which have been written into our labor laws," and it accused the Republican administration of establishing a "national anti-labor policy." The Republicans pledged "diligent administration of the existing statutes with recommendations for improvements or to remove inequities."

2. The responsibility of organized management and labor in shaping the legislative framework and in the administration of the statutes is virtually nil; it is confined to making formal and highly extreme public statements. The politicians have been poor mediators.

3. The national policy encourages litigation rather than settlement. Litigation fosters unreality in the extreme. It takes a great deal of time; cases are decided years after issues are raised, violating the first

principle of industrial relations. The proceedings are highly technical, lawyers are involved in game-playing rather than in the process of practical accommodation of the parties and dispute settlement.

4. The legislative framework is more and more technical and detailed. The point has been reached where general provisions no longer make sense in many industries, and we have started in the direction of special provisions for particular industries, as Title VII of the 1959 Act indicates. Fewer and fewer members of the Congress can be equipped to understand the technical issues, and language is necessarily written hastily in late sessions and conference committees by staff lawyers far from the bargaining process. Formal compromises in words assure unending litigation.

5. It should be recognized as a first principle that no set of people are smart enough to write words through which others cannot find holes when the stakes are high. Thus, the secondary boycott provisions of Taft-Hartley helped to create hot-cargo clauses, which in turn led to new provisions in Title VII of the 1959 Act, which in turn are leading to new clauses which may well lead to more decades of litigation and then further legislation. The game-playing of the income tax law is not suitable to collective bargaining, the practical necessities of labor-management relations, and the imperatives of the times which require increased cooperation and productivity.

6. The long-term legislative framework of collective bargaining has been excessively influenced by short-term influences. The depression shaped the Wagner Act; the post-war inflation and wave of strikes influenced decisively the Taft-Hartley law; and the McClellan Committee largely determined the 1959 law. The compulsions of the immediate are hardly the most appropriate in which to set the framework in which managements and labor organizations shall live for a generation. The long view has been lacking.

7. In a democratic and pluralistic society the government is seeking to impose on parties to collective bargaining by statute and administrative rulings a set of standards of conduct which in many respects is highly unrealistic. To remove the parties from any significant responsiblity for the formation and administration of policy is destructive of the character of our society, leads to impractical and unreal policies and to mass evasion and disrespect. Such is the state of government labor policy.

The most significant research contribution that the members of the Industrial Relations Research Association can make to government labor policy is to show how it actually operates. We need less analysis of the law and the cases and much research on the experience at the work place. We need to report and to analyze what actually happens in industrial relations after the NLRB, the courts or arbitrators issue decisions and how the parties use the existence of the law. We need a greater sense of the limitations of pieces of paper.

It is unrealistic to expect any substantial turning back on the recent course to government policy, but it should be possible to resolve to proceed no further down the present course. The legislative and administrative framework of collective bargaining should be changed only after extensive consultation and mediation through neutral or government experts with organized management and labor. Labor-management legislation must be a matter of consensus to be effective. The parties should bear a measure of direct responsiblity for policy rather than leaving both sides free to criticize legislation as biased and impractical and then devote their full energies and imagination to circumventing the law. A major role should even be evolved for the parties in the administration of the present statutes and in the reduction of formal litigation. Without the consensus of the parties there can only be further litigation and political legislation. No matter how long it takes, patient mediation and the development of a consensus among top labor and management (with public and government experts) is essential to any solution to the present policy gap. (The Carter Administration and the Congress grossly violated this principle in the labor law reform struggle of 1978).

The Labor Movement

The short road to merger, to use Mr. Meany's phrase, involved putting the many unresolved problems among international unions, including their relations to a single trade union center, in the hands of the merged federation with the hope that the divisive issues could be gradually resolved. The architects of the merger rejected what Mr. Meany has called the method of perfection, which would have resolved these issues in advance of merger on the grounds this road would have taken too long even if it could have led eventually to merger.

By August 1959 it was evident that the many hard problems had not obligingly drifted away, and the Executive Council appointed a special committee to study seven areas of internal disputes. They were listed as follows:

1. The No-Raid clause in the constitution.
2. The agreement between the Industrial Union Department and the Building Trades Department.
3. The dispute between the Metal Trades Department and the Industrial Union Department.
4. The matter of boycotts.

5. The transfer to national and international affiliates of directly affiliated local unions.
6. Organizing ethics in competitive organizing campaigns.
7. Anti-contracting out provisions in trade union contracts.

The Committee was charged with the responsibility of recommending procedures for "an early and conclusive disposition of such types of disputes." The San Francisco convention in September 1959 did adopt the recommendation of the Committee that it should develop a detailed plan, to be approved at a special convention, to resolve all these types of disputes, "embodying final and binding arbitration as the terminal point in such disputes." A qualification was added that ". . . such arbitration shall be limited to the settlement of disputes only and shall not include the determination of the work or trade jurisdiction of affiliates." The promise of San Francisco was widely hailed, but by the Miami meeting of the Executive Council in February 1960 this approach to internal problems appeared to have been abandoned, and thus far there has been no detailed plan nor special convention.

The fundamental defects of the proposed arbitration approach need to be stated. There can be nothing but respect for the willingness to give up autonomy and sovereignty to the extent proposed by arbitration, but the approach is impractical. So wide a range of problems as organizing ethics, boycotts and work assignment disputes cannot readily be encompassed in a single machinery. The qualification in the resolution on jurisdiction is a reminder how far apart are those who still think in terms of "exclusive jurisdiction," the cornerstone of the AFL constitution, and those who exalt the "collective bargaining relationship," the central concept in the constitution of the merged federation. In the building trades–industrial union disputes there are more interests than the two groups of unions involved; neither contractors nor industrial plants will permit unions to arbitrate their economic destiny. No private disputes settlement can long endure when the governmental machinery yields opposite results and protects a violator of a private plan. There can be no effective enforcement machinery, and the federation has no effective sanctions except to encourage withdrawal of the strong.

These difficulties are significant, but they do not go to the heart of the problem. Arbitration was to be invoked as a way to solve problems which do not lend themselves well to stipulated issues. There must be a meeting of minds, an agreement, a consensus, on the issues listed. Arbitration cannot be a substitute for agreement-making in the areas of such disputes. The short road to merger was taken on the presumption that a number of mergers would follow among competing international unions and that many bilateral jurisdictional agreements among disputing unions would be negotiated. Arbitration cannot achieve these results, nor can it be a substitute for consent. No set of words quickly contrived can substitute for the meeting of minds that comes from extended conferences or the good faith that must be built gradually from particular cases. There may have been a short road to merger, but there is only a long road to consensus.

There is relatively little working contact, except through the head of the Federation, between the presidents of the former CIO industrial unions and the building trades and craft unions. They often do not speak the same language; they have very different concepts of jurisdiction; they have different traditions and views of the union label; they use staff assistants in quite different ways; they do not often meet. This sort of gap, which magnifies the substantive issues, cannot be bridged by formal arbitration. Agreement-making among international unions is a long and slow process; it is hard and detailed work in which persistence and imagination are major tools. An illustration is afforded in the relations between the Iron Workers and the Glaziers. Their 1957 jurisdictional agreement needed to be modernized for a variety of reasons, including the position of the glazing contractors. It took at least 15 sessions and 30 days of meetings in 1960, not to mention many other conferences with each group, to achieve the revision. In some cases more than seven years have been spent in mediating some agreements, as that between the United Association and the Sheet Metal Workers on air conditioning and kitchen equipment. The results cannot be achieved in a single session or in three or four a year. Moreover, relationships must be kept attuned to new problems, both internal and substantive.

The arbitration decisions under the no-raiding agreement and the CIO organizational disputes plan and the recommendations under Article III, Sec. 4 of the constitution, pursuant to the February 1958 action of the Executive Council, have resolved a number of particular cases. The powers of these umpires are very narrowly circumscribed, and they have increasingly confronted compliance problems; these plans have not been administered so as to achieve agreement over the underlying issues.

This is not to say that there is no place for a neutral in helping to settle these disputes or that orderly procedures are not required. But my experience and conviction is strongly that the arbitration process, particularly of the more formal type, has relatively little to contribute to the development of consensus and working relations within the federation. (In 1982 the Federation introduced an outside mediator into the internal disputes plan prior to arbitration).

Management

In his presidential address to the Industrial Relations Research Association in 1958, Professor E. Wight Bakke said, "It is not an exaggeration to say that, when collective bargaining became a part of operations of a company, managerial methods underwent a revolution greater than would have been the case if those companies had been nationalized. . . ." There have been enormous transformations in industrial management in the past generation, and along with modern technology and business schools, the rise of unionism in large scale industry has been a decisive factor creating the changes.

There have been two principal developments in industrial management related to the rise of unionism: (1) the emergence of a specialized staff solely concerned with labor relations problems, and (2) the adoption of explicit policies designed to lay down lines of action in the wide range of questions—such as discipline, transfers and promotions, compensation and grievance procedures—that arise under collective bargaining. Large-scale managements quickly learned that they needed full-time staffs to follow industrial relations developments and to engage in collective bargaining and grievance handling with union representatives who devoted full time to this specialty. Managements have been slower to learn that long-run policies and explicit administrative procedures are essential to industrial relations and that improvising and expediency may avoid an untimely strike, but they tend to lead to lack of control over costs and to whipsaw-tactics and pressure on the part of the union.

But a specialized industrial relations staff and policies are not the real source of the transformation in management. It is rather the grappling with the problems that then arise in coordinating the new staff with other policies. There is hardly an internal managerial relationship, horizontally or vertically, that is left intact, and there is scarcely a policy that is not re-examined under the impact of this new institution, literally within the cell walls of the enterprise.

It is well known that there is no uniform relation today between line and staff in industrial enterprises. In some cases the line administers all labor relations policies and the staff is purely advisory in the classical textbook fashion, while in other instances the staff has operating responsibility for all labor relations decisions including incentive rates, transfers, and all grievances. The Brookings study by professors Sumner Slichter, James Healy, and Robert Livernash concludes, on the basis of their extensive field work, that line and staff coordination, cooperation, teamwork, or mutual help is indispensable to successful industrial relations. All practitioners of industrial relations have seen instances when conflicts and frictions between line and staff at the plant level over the setting of incentive rates, the extent to which foremen may work, the application of discipline standards, or the conflicts between plant levels and the home office have been the source of many grievances and have encouraged union pressures to force a problem to the most favorable point, from its point of view, in the management hierarchy. There is no mechanistic solution to the line-staff problems within the management; there must be coordination and consensus to achieve economic objectives and stable relations with a union.

The transformation in substantive decision making is no less significant than the changes in the internal structure of management. Industrial relations policies are highly interdependent with the full range of other decisions as the following questions indicate. Shall the company make a concession in a wildcat strike to furnish orders for an important customer? What margin in capacity and in inventories shall the company establish in view of its labor relations? What shall the company say to prospective investors about labor costs and efficiency since unions and employees also have ears? What shall the company say in its public relations program about its contract differences with the union? These questions indicate that industrial relations issues ramify throughout the full range of managerial decisions. Industrial relations policies affect all other policies. Despite the reserve power to make decisions at the very top—to resolve conflict among various subordinate staffs—final decisions within the enterprise typically involve a consensus.

These adjustments in business structure and policies have tended to produce an improvement in management organization, superior in the sense that it tends to operate by reference to policies, is less addicted to slogans and platitudes, is more adaptable and geared to change in market conditions and to changes in the community, recognizes that internally and externally persuasion is more effective in the long run than the mere assertion of rights, and places top priority in management upon coordination and organization building and executive development. The unions have played no small role in the vast improvement in enterprise management in the United States. But it is still true, as Sumner Slichter said, that "By and large, the top executives of American enterprises have rather limited familiarity with problems of industrial relations. . . . Progress is being made. . . . Nevertheless, this interest is far less than it should be in view of the enormous possibilities of saving capital expenditures simply by improving employee-management relations."

These developments within the industrial enterprise are to be contrasted sharply with what has been happening at the confederation level of American management—the National Association of Manufacturers and the Chamber of Commerce. In referring specifically to the policy statements of the N.A.M. issued in 1903, 1936, and 1955, professors Douglas V. Brown and Charles A. Myers at the annual meetings in 1956 said that one would be tempted to conclude ". . . that changes, if any, in philosophy toward unionism had been relatively minor." They observed that ". . . it is still the fashion, as it was thirty or more years ago, to concede that employees have the right to organize or not to organize. It is still the fashion, as it was earlier, to deny opposition to unions as such; only 'bad unions,' 'labor monopolies,' or 'unions that abuse their power' are formally beyond the pale. It is still the fashion to insist that unions be held legally responsible for their actions."

How is one to account for the contrast between the adaptability of management in enterprises and its intransigence at the confederation level? The contrast is the more striking when it is reported that over half the directorate of the N.A.M. come from companies with collective bargaining agreements. Perhaps the explanation lies partly in the fact governments are not the only organizations which have both state departments and war departments. Perhaps, the posture has been frozen for many years and an older era is perpetuated. Perhaps these confederations attract as active members managements militant in their concern to stop the spread of unionism. These factors may play a role, but there are more fundamental reasons.

The pronouncements of the N.A.M. and Chamber are slogans; they never have to confront the reality of the industrial work place. The consequences of their statements of policy are in the political sphere rather than measured in production and in costs. They resemble the initial demands of one party in collective bargaining rather than a negotiated settlement or a realistic compromise. They are on a par with many resolutions for legislation passed at ALF-CIO conventions. If the confederation level of American managements were engaged in collective bargaining, as the SAF in Sweden, the actions of American enterprise management and policy pronouncements of the N.A.M. and Chamber might be more consonent. No enterprise is bound by the pronouncements, and so no one has to take their consequences in the practical sphere of the management of a work force.

These pronouncements do not represent the best practice of American management, nor even the average among larger industrial enterprises; rather, they are formal positions oriented toward political activity. By the practice of enterprise management in the United States, these pronouncements do not reflect any consensus of industrial relations policies. They do not even represent the self-interest of management.

The industrial relations system of the United States suffers from unreality at the confederation level of management. The vigor, imagination, and leadership of the enterprise level has no counterpart at the confederation level. I venture the view that until the confederation level of management is transformed, to reflect more faithfully the experience of industrial enterprises, management as a whole will not exercise its potential role in the industrial relations policies of the community, and the government will continue to extend further its role in the regulation of labor-management relations. Industrial management at the enterprise level has generally shown itself well capable to develop policies to protect its competitive positions and to enhance efficiency within the framework of collective bargaining. There is every reason to expect that it could do as well at the confederation level. The first requirement to achieve a national labor policy by consent is to transform the confederation level of management to reflect more faithfully the experience of enterprise management.

The Alternative of Consensus

The theme of the preceding three sections has been that our national industrial relations system suffers from the seeking of solutions to problems in terms of legislation and litigation, formal arbitration, and public pronouncements. This malady alike afflicts national governmental policy, the labor federation, and the confederation level of management. The common difficulty in its essence is a failure to develop a consensus within government, the labor movement, or management. The consequence is resort to partisan legislation and litigation and the ascendency of the politicians in national industrial relations policy. An alternative policy is reliance, to a greater degree, upon the development of consensus.

Great reliance upon consensus is particularly appropriate since the range of industrial relations problems has become increasingly technical, and uniform rules across wide reaches of the economy are impractical in many cases. Moreover, in our society rules and policies that have been formulated by those directly affected are likely to receive greater respect and compliance than those imposed by fiat. The rapidly changing circumstances of technology and markets require greater reliance on consensus since those most directly affected are more sensitive to such change, and adaptation can be more gradual than that imposed belatedly from without. Consensus develops habits of mind which encourage continuing adaptation to new circumstances.

The method of concensus is admittedly difficult to apply. It is so much easier simply to pass another law, issue another decision, or adopt another resolution. The achievement of concensus is often a frustrating process because it must triumph over inertia, suspicion, and the warpath. It is slow to build. But it is clearly the most satisfying and enduring solution to problems. It always has significant by-products in improved understanding in many other spheres than those related to the consensus.

The most fundamental feature of consensus building is that it requires or creates leadership devoted to mediating among followers, a leadership which seeks to explain problems and sell solutions rather than merely to impose a solution by sheer power or to rail against a decision from without.

An industrial society requires a considerably greater measure of consensus on industrial relations problems than we have. The present course is set toward an unending sequence of legislative regulation, litigation, and political pronouncement. The community has a right to expect more from organized labor, confederation levels of management, and government agencies. Indeed, a shift in the method of national policy making in the industrial relations area is required if labor and management are to make their potential contributions in solving the larger problems facing the community. The place to begin is to resolve that the method of consensus will be used internally in reaching decisions within the federation and confederation levels of management and in the formulation and administration of governmental policies. This is the fundamental challenge—in my view—of the next four years or the decades ahead in industrial relations in the United States.

Part Three

DISPUTE-RESOLUTION MECHANISMS

Each industrial relations system has at least one dispute-resolution mechanism, although a number of mechanisms may develop in a single system specialized to a particular class of disputes or problems. The following are examples: (1) a grievance procedure with arbitration to deal with issues arising over the meaning and application of a collective agreement; (2) a procedure, with or without a neutral chairman, to facilitate the negotiation of new agreements or to settle major questions that arise during the life of an agreement, as was the case with the role of the impartial umpire in the clothing industry; and (3) a specialized or more technical procedure to resolve disputes over pension claims, health benefit claims, incentive pay plans, premium pay rates as in handling specialized cargoes in longshoring, safety issues, or jurisdictional disputes. Any dispute resolution mechanism needs to be understood in terms of the larger industrial relations system of which it is an integral part and of the level at which it operates, nationally or locally.

A comprehensive treatment of dispute resolution mechanisms might well begin with grievance procedures and related arbitration. But these procedures are rather well known and their legal status relatively well defined. The annual proceedings of the National Academy of Arbitrators contain descriptions of various types of grievance and arbitration procedures, describe their differing styles, and discuss contemporary issues between the parties and the status of arbitration awards in relation to the law.

The chapters that follow, after an initial one on the function of the strike, consider three specialized types of disputes and the mechanisms designed to deal with them: (1) emergency disputes that are said potentially to endanger the nation's health or safety, (2) jurisdictional disputes in construction, and (3) disputes over the terms of collective agreements in state and local government. Each of these chapters on the procedures for dispute resolution is preceded by one devoted to a discussion of the basic problem or the distinctive characteristics of the industrial relations system in which the dispute resolution mechanism has arisen, so as to place each dispute resolution mechanism in its appropriate setting. In this way the adequacy and appropriateness of machinery for dispute resolution can be related to the organizations and contexts among which the disputes arise.

Chapter 7

THE FUNCTION OF THE STRIKE

The strike has had many meanings at different times and places. It has been seen by friend and foe alike as leading to an uprising by the working class against a capitalist society.[1] Carleton Parker saw the strike as the pugnacity to be expected psychologically from economic suffering and social humiliation. The International Workers of the World sang:

> *Tie 'em up! Tie 'em up; that's the way to win.*
> *Don't notify the bosses till hostilities begin.*

In colonial areas of the world the strike was used to demonstrate against the foreigner and to promote independence. The strike has been represented as an expression of a fundamental constitutional right: to work or to refuse to work in concert with one's peers. The strike is also described as an extension of a free market, a normal development when buyers and sellers fail to agree. Still others envisage the strike as an amoral instrument in collective bargaining, to be used as a last resort to facilitate agreement: "It is a means by which each party may impose a cost of disagreement on the other."[2] The social theory and social history of the strike, however, is beyond the scope of this chapter. The present concern is rather the function of the strike, or more precisely of a few types of strike, in the industrial relations system of the United States.

A variety of work stoppages by strike or lockout do not belong in this study of new methods of dispute settlement in collective bargaining: strikes over organizational rights, strikes that constitute jurisdictional disputes or arise from rival organizing campaigns, most secondary boycotts, demonstrations or protests, and most wildcat stoppages.

Frontiers of Collective Bargaining, John T. Dunlop and Neil W. Chamberlain, Eds. (New York: Harper & Row, Publishers, 1967), pp. 103–21. By permission of Harper & Row, Publishers, Inc.

It is not that such work stoppages are unimportant or that there is little need to perfect machinery to facilitate settlement or to provide an effective alternative to conflict. Rather, the purposes of this study are best fulfilled by concentrating on two groups of work stoppage: disputes over the terms of reopened or expiring collective bargaining agreements, and limited or controlled use of the work stoppage to settle disputes during the term of an agreement.

Work stoppages over the terms of reopened or expiring agreements are widely regarded as the most deliberate use of economic and political power in industrial conflict. They are also considered controversies for which there is the least adequate settlement machinery—private or public—in the United States as compared with other advanced countries. Such disputes probably provide the greatest scope for the development of new procedures in collective bargaining and mediation. Moreover, the initiative of the private parties and constructive mediation, private or public, are probably less constricted by governmental regulation than they are in the case of other types of work stoppage. Over 40 percent of work stoppages and 80 percent of the worker-days idle in recent years have involved renegotiation of agreements arising from expirations or reopenings.[3]

The number of work stoppages in the United States reached a post-WW II peak of 5,117 in 1952 with 3.5 million workers involved and 59.1 million days idle, or .48 percent of the total working time. The year 1959 was also a year of extensive work stoppage activity. Lost time from work stoppages reached a post-war period low in the first half of the 1960s at .13 percent of the total working time, although the last half of the 1970s and early 1980s were only slightly above that level in the percentage of the total working time lost in work stoppages.

A work stoppage was included in the bureau's reports if it involved six or more workers and lost a full day or shift or more. These data do not measure the indirect or secondary effects of a work stoppage on other establishments whose employees are made idle as a result of any material or service shortage. And such statistics, including tabulations by major issues and contract status, reveal little about the function of the strike and the contribution it makes to settlement of a dispute.

Strikes have a variety of forms. A complete shutdown of operations is most common. But there may be a refusal to work overtime, sporadic and irregular attendance, a slowdown or a deliberate reduction in the pace of work or in the quality of performance, a skipping of work operations—such as failure to perform an operation on every tenth item on an assembly line—or a sitdown, or even conduct described as sabotage. Indeed, there are few limits to the ingenuity of workers and their organizations in bringing pressure to bear on managements through affecting the presence of workers or their performance.[4]

One of the major accomplishments of collective bargaining has been to provide rules of conflict and to eliminate certain forms of interruption of work operations and artificial barriers to efficiency. It is not unusual on the eve of a strike to find agreements between management and union prescribing fire protection or maintenance of sensitive equipment in a plant, or operation of pumps in a coal mine; provision of essential services or supplies to the military; or delivery of essential services to hospitals. The strike and the lockout among experienced parties are conducted in accordance with rules as formal as those of the Marquis of Queensberry.

Strikes Classified by Function

The strike can play many roles even when our concern has been narrowed to disputes arising over the terms of reopened or expiring agreements. It is not sufficient to say that the strike (or lockout) is a means of imposing a cost of disagreement or a means of changing a position in negotiations to achieve a settlement. A review of a number of strikes over contract terms suggests that it may be useful to distinguish four types according to function or purpose, as follows. (It is unfortunate that we do not have a body of detailed case studies of particular work stoppages in recent years to use in the analysis of strikes and in the study of mediation.[5])

Strikes to Change the Structure of Bargaining (Type 1)

The central purpose of a number of significant strikes and lockouts in recent years appears to be the desire by one party to change the structure of bargaining: to change the organization holding the leadership role on one side or the other, the geographical scope of the negotiations, or the level of negotiations—national or local—at which various issues are settled. If a traditional arrangement of bargaining is unsatisfactory to some party, a strike may be used to try to achieve a transformation. The objective is not to reach agreement within the existing structure of negotiations but rather to change that structure itself. Sometimes the purpose is achieved; sometimes the old resists change; and in other cases the old system is destroyed, but no stable new arrangement is found.

While a number of strikes have been nominally directed against management, their major objective has been to change relationships with other unions. A review of the major stoppages in each recent year, published by the Bureau of Labor Statistics,[6] suggests that an attempt to change the structure of bargaining in some ways was primarily involved in an appreciable number of these work stoppages. It is a significant category. These stoppages appear to arise frequently in the maritime, printing, and construction industries.[7]

The 114-day New York newspaper strike of 1962–1963, for instance, was fought by Bertram Powers and the "Big Six" of the Printers largely to change a structure of bargaining under which a pattern of wage settlements was made between the publishers and the Newspaper Guild and then extended to other groups. The contract expiration dates that resulted from the strike "cancelled the five-week lead the Guild had previously enjoyed and thus eliminated its ability to clamp an industrywide mold on all the other unions before they ever got to the bargaining table." The strike enabled Powers "to break a follow-the-leader pattern that had stripped his union of any effective right to negotiate its own wage agreements."[8] The 1965 negotiations in which a $10.50 a week settlement by other crafts yielded to a $12.53 settlement with Powers, established his new leadership in the structure of bargaining.

The 1966 Boston newspaper strike by the Printers' local, which shut down the papers for 31 days, produced a change in the structure of bargaining to permit some printing unions to elect an increase comprised of health and welfare and pension benefits and others to elect instead a wage rate increase; previously the group of ten unions had had the same level of benefits in a common fund since the early 1950s. There was no dispute about the money package in the strike, and the employers would have been willing in the main to accept any uniform allocation settlement the group of unions could agree upon. The settlement required the modification of five agreements that had already been signed. The printers and certain other crafts elected to put the money into the wage rate, while five other crafts elected the higher level of benefits that had initially been agreed upon as common policy. In the opinion of the mediator, "The strike settlement provided a greater freedom to separate union bargaining by the establishment of two levels of benefits in the funds. . . . The fund flexibility is a real plus as to future bargaining."[9]

The strike that shut down virtually all construction work in Cleveland in 1964 arose from a bargaining structure that had existed for fifteen years or more and could not adapt to an insistent demand for a change in wage relations. The general contractors had traditionally bargained with a committee of the crafts and the local building-trades council to establish a dollar-and-cents pattern which was then applied in separate craft negotiations. In 1964 the committee agreed on a three-year settlement approximating 75 cents, but the Iron Workers had announced in advance of negotiations that, as a result of wage increases for Iron Workers in other cities, they would not accept the committee-negotiated figure. After the strike the separate settlements ranged from 95 cents to $1.05, and trades that had settled for 75 cents insisted on and secured comparable increases. The strike did not create any new structure of bargaining, nor did it change wage relations among crafts, which was the problem in Cleveland as in other localities; but it did mutilate the old bargaining arrangements.

The rubber industry experienced a number of work stoppages in the late 1960s and 1970s where a central problem involved the issue of wages and conditions to apply to non-tire plants of a company, or the exclusion of non-tire plants from the master company-union agreement and negotiations at these plants on a plant-by-plant basis. In the late 1970s the desire of basic steel companies to exclude certain operations, such as warehouses, from the basic agreement on account of high wage rates became a factor in negotiations over the renewal of the Experimental Negotiations Agreement. The structural problems of intercraft differentials and commuter railroads have continued into the 1980s to be major factors in railroad disputes.

The National Labor Relations Board has limited influence in disputes over the structure of bargaining.[10] The certification of bargaining units, which I prefer to designate as election districts, has an influence on bargaining structure in multi-plant firms and craft severance situations, particularly where rival unionism is acute. Multiple-employer bargaining units confront a confusion in the law with regard to the obligation to bargain and the use of the strike to compel a settlement against a single firm; the rules relating to withdrawal from a multiple-employer bargaining unit are also uncertain. The question may be raised whether the role of the National Labor Relations Board in disputes over the structure of bargaining should be strengthened as a means to reduce such stoppages. On the record to date, my judgment would be in the negative, in part because the Board has appeared to be concerned to develop generalized rules which have little place in structure of bargaining issues in different industries.

Strikes to Change the Relations Between Principal Negotiator and Constituents in Unions or Managements (Type 2)

The relations between union leadership and members, and company or association negotiators and principals, are typically complex and vary from case to case. This is intimate and relatively unexplored terrain. There is a class of strikes that are aimed primarily at affecting these relations on one side or both.

In some cases a strike may be designed to solidify and to unite a union or an association, to strengthen the internal leadership both in dealing with the opposite side and in accommodating conflicting interests within the group. In rival union situations or where there are active competitors for internal power, a strike may demonstrate to external rivals strength, militancy, and virility, or it may arise because bargaining compromises with management are incompatible with internal political survival. It has been said, for example, that the racial composition of new employees of the Transit Authority in New York City and the problems of control they posed for Mike Quill significantly enhanced the need for a large settlement and even a strike on January 1, 1966. The basic steel interim settlement in the spring of 1965 involved an accommodation without a strike to internal political uncertainty in a union election year.

Other strikes may arise, despite the better judgment of the leader or top negotiator on either side, because there appears to be no other way to secure a change in view among the membership on the union side or among one's principals or association members in management. The strike serves to bring the constituents around after a period to the more realistic judgments of one or the other or both the principal negotiators.

Strikes to Change the Budgetary Allotment or Policy of a Government Agency (Type 3)

Strikes among some government employees at times have been directed less against the immediate government employing agency than toward securing for that agency appropriations or grants from the politically responsible executive or legislative body—that is, funds that are outside the resources of the agency. The strikes in New York City of teachers and of transport workers involved this factor, compelling the mayor and the governor to develop resources to meet the requirements of an acceptable settlement. The timing of budget making and collective negotiations in government employment is central to settlement of disputes; indeed, the failure of such coordination has been a major factor in some strikes of government employees. "It is a fundamental principle in government employment that collective negotiations and the resort to procedures to resolve an impasse be appropriately related to the legislative and budget-making process."[11]

In cases of government procurement the direct employer is often a private contractor. A strike against such an employer may be directed primarily to change some of the procurement policies prescribed by the government contracting agency. The dispute may be less with the immediate employer than with the constraints imposed upon him by the agency. The government procurement agency, for instance, may divide a construction project into a number of separate contracts, which result in a mixed union and nonunion labor policy on the same site even at the same work stations. A strike against a contractor may be designed to secure policy commitments from the agency to preclude such a condition. As a member of the President's Missile Sites Labor Commission, I reported, "The fundamental fact is that the procurement policies in effect at Cape Kennedy are inconsistent with labor relations policies which would secure a higher degree of uninterrupted operations."[12]

Some strikes may constitute a rejection of governmental stabilization policy. The parties might well be in disagreement about the government's policy of constraint. The Machinists' strike in 1966 against five airlines despite the recommendations of an emergency board headed by Senator Morse involved this factor.[13] So did the 1973 strike by Local 1099 in New York City against voluntary hospitals. As governments seek to implement wage and price stabilization policies, this type of work stoppage may be expected to increase, at least in the absence of a no-strike pledge as in wartime.

Strikes to Change a Bargaining Position of the Other Side (Type 4)

The most frequent type of strike or lockout over the terms of reopened or expiring agreements is presumably one whose purpose is simply to change a bargaining position of the other side. There is no problem with the structure of bargaining; it continues as in the past. The negotiators and their constituency are as one, or at least their relations are not a factor. The government is not involved. In these circumstances the strike or the lockout is a means to compel a change in position of the other side toward the position of the party exerting the pressure.

The issues separating the parties may be relatively simple and analogous to those faced in earlier negotiations, or they may be highly complex or novel. They may concern wages and fringe benefits, for example, or they may include methods of wage payment, seniority systems, subcontracting, manning schedules, wage differentials among job classifications, adjustments to significant technological changes, plant closings, training, grievances procedures and the arbitration system, and union security.

The above-described four types of work stoppage, over the terms of reopened or expiring agreements, are described to encourage an analytical approach to work stoppages. Such differences are significant to the development of procedures to facilitate the settlement of disputes over terms of agreements.

Since the types of strikes are specialized by function, even over the terms of expiring agreements, so should be procedures to prevent such work stoppages. Substitutes for a work stoppage need to be designed in accordance with the diverse functions and specialized purposes of the strike.

The use of joint study committees, for example, may be expected to be most significant to disputes that may result in strikes or lockouts to change the structure of bargaining (type 1), or to change a bargaining position on a complex issue or range of problems (type 4), or in some cases to assist in changing the relations between negotiators and constituents or principals (type 2), particularly when issues are complex. Disputes of these types are most likely to lead to prolonged work stoppages, because they involve the most difficult problems of adaptation. A study committee would not ordinarily be effective in cases involving efforts to change the relations between the principal negotiator and constituents (type 2) unless it was used as a long-term educational device; this problem is internal and political. A study committee in cases involving procurement policy (type 3) cannot be an effective alternative to the strike unless some continuing sessions include government agency representatives.

The Decline of the Strike

Arthur Ross and Paul Hartman observed:[14]

> *We find a pronounced decline in strike activity throughout the world. . . . The fact is that the textbook or dictionary definition of the strike is fully applicable only in the United States and Canada. Only in these two countries—which really comprise a single system of industrial relations—is the strike still sufficiently frequent to constitute a significant method of determining conditions of employment and, at the same time, sufficiently long to test the staying power of workers and employers.*

The statistical study of work stoppages does reveal a marked long-term decline of the strike, certainly in advanced Western countries including the United States. In the United States, the percentage of estimated total working time in work stoppages was .25 in 1951–60; .194 in 1961–70; and .177 in 1971–80. It is also clear that the extent of violence in labor disputes has declined, although it has not disappeared. Compare with the present, for instance, the period January

1, 1902 to September 30, 1904, when it is estimated that 198 persons were killed and 1,966 injured in strikes and lockouts.

The gross statistics are not adequate for the analysis of disputes over the terms of collective agreements since they reflect all types of stoppage. The total strike figures are also significantly influenced by a number of major "centers of conflict"[15] such as basic steel and coal, which may have a cycle of their own. Strike activity also may be related to levels of business activity and the initial impact of unionization in newly organized sectors of the economy, in public employment in the 1960s. But the available statistics bear out the view that in the United States work stoppages among established parties over the terms of collective bargaining agreements have been gradually declining, although it would be an exaggeration to state that this country was experiencing a "withering away of the strike."

What has caused this decline? Has the strike proved an ineffectual tool in an increasing number of bargaining situations? Has management learned better how to operate during a strike by virtue of the use of supervisors and inventories? Has technological change shifted industry to more continuous operations that can readily be sustained through a strike? Have workers with greater affluence and installment debt become less willing to engage in strikes? Have collective bargaining procedures and institutions and leaders become more permissive? Do the same old issues confront the parties over and over again? Have more viable and adaptable solutions been worked out over the years? Or has mediation become more expert and successful? All these factors, and others may have contributed to the decline of the strike, but their relative importance is not easy to assess.

I suggest that the following factors have been most significant in eroding the role of the strike in disputes over the terms of collective bargaining agreements among established parties:

1. *The capacity to shut down operations by the collective withdrawal of production and maintenance workers has been limited in a number of industries by the technological characteristics of new industries and changes in older ones.* The growth of supervisory and technical employees, outside of union organization, has made it possible to operate certain plants with newer technologies for long periods without a complement of regular production and maintenance employees. The legislation of 1947 which constricts the secondary boycott has facilitated the delivery of output produced under these circumstances. The experiences of oil refineries and chemical plants with stoppages lasting as long as a year are abundant proof of these developments. The telephone, utilities, and communication industries also provide illustrations.

It is important to note that the decline of the effectiveness of the strike, in these cases contrary to much popular discussion, is not simply a result of technological change. A significant role is played by the large number of supervisors, the failure of the unions to organize them, their willingness to cross picket lines and their relative unconcern with union opprobrium. At the same time, legal and technological changes have permitted the delivery of raw materials and the dispatch of output. These prolonged conflicts are, of course, not without cost to management even though it may still operate: maintenance becomes increasingly difficult; there is the additional danger of fire or explosion; supervisors tend to resent living for periods of time in a plant under a long siege; the community may become hostile; and there may well be long-term costs in morale and productivity after the strike.

2. *The responses of customers to repeated strikes in some sectors of the economy have increased the costs of a stoppage to both parties and made the strike and the lockout less attractive.* The adoption of alternate sources of fuel by steam-generating plants—even if they did not entirely switch to oil or gas—adversely affected markets and employment for coal following the strikes of the 1940s. In basic steel even the threat of a stoppage now leads to a considerable accumulation of inventories by customers. This distortion of production patterns is expensive for both parties in the increase in overtime costs and storage facilities, in supplementary unemployment benefit costs, in disruption of vacation schedules, in disturbing employment regularity which both parties have sought to stabilize. In the maritime industry the threat of a strike, even months ahead, may lead shippers to change routes or mode of transport and has thereby a serious economic effect upon both parties. Moreover, a strike in steel and other industries has led customers to develop new permanent sources of supply, including imports. Bus transportation and newspaper strikes also provide many illustrations of this point.

3. *Some sections of the economy where labor organizations have recently spread are particularly sensitive to public opinion, and a strike may even be legally prohibited and penalized, as it is in public employment.* In the area of critical military procurement, including related transportation and construction, strong pressures develop on all parties to resolve disputes without a stoppage. The threat to strike may succeed in bringing a union problem to the attention of government agencies, but an actual stoppage may involve wide criticism, subtle retaliations, and on a case-by-case basis private opposition from the leaders of the labor movement who have consistently supported the national security objectives in this country.

Whatever may be the legal right to strike all the railroads in the country, it is clear that the community and the government are not likely to tolerate such a stoppage. The legal right to strike or to lock out all the railroads at once appears to exist only provided it is not exercised. Under these circumstances neither the strike nor the lockout is an effective instrument to resolve issues in dispute.

A strike in public employment involves considerable hazards in this country, despite the numbers that have taken place. The traditional government unions, such as those for Postal employees and the Fire Fighters, have formally restricted the strike. No court or legislature has found such strikes to be legal. There are strong feelings in the community and legislative bodies against them, which are widely disseminated through news media. The object of the strike pressure is not always easy to focus on in view of the diversity of legislative and executive responsibility.

4. *A number of the issues in collective bargaining are so complex and require such detailed and intimate study that, after the legal period of sixty days' notice, the strike or the lockout cannot effectively produce a settlement.* The problems of revising methods of wage payment, seniority systems, wage differentials among job classifications, and manning schedules require the balancing of different interests of many workers and management and also prolonged mutual study. A midnight settlement under pressure may not be sufficient.

In a more profound sense the solutions to some of these problems can be achieved only by consensus, and a strike or a lockout may be unble to produce the required mutual consent. Indeed, the necessary co-operation for dealing with such complex and delicate problems may not be possible after resort to coercion. Mature parties may come to recognize that only persuasion can solve some issues. The strike or the lockout may produce some compromises or formal resolutions but may also preclude more desirable solutions. Attitudes, morale, and co-operation may produce results in terms of efficiency, costs, earnings, and security.

5. *The resort to a strike or a lockout may lead to long-run retaliations on each side and thus escalate the conflict.* A variety of strikes seeking to play one employer off against another encouraged the enlargement and clarification of management's legal right to lock out. The same tactics helped to develop strike insurance in the airlines and the railroads. One party that economic force has compelled to make a settlement it regards as bitter and distasteful is likely to harbor resentments and await favorable circumstances when it may get even and impose its will on the other in turn. An industrial conflict may set the "loser" to work to marshal resources and plans for the next time; his energies are pointed to the next battlefield. Escalation of conflict and retaliation is not the necessary, or even the typical, response to

the strike or the lockout, but it is one of the dangers and the limitations of resort to economic conflict in established collective bargaining relations.

6. *Although their role may be difficult to assess, private and public agencies in the industrial relations area have contributed to the increase in settlements of disputes over the terms of collective bargaining agreements.* There are more and better trained federal and state mediators; a few localities also have developed municipal staffs to facilitate dispute settlement. Private mediation has grown as parties have become acquainted with private arbitrators. Industrial relations institutes at many universities have carried on a variety of educational programs with labor and management representatives. Many organizations of management and affiliates of the labor movement have conducted numerous community forums and programs to educate the parties in improved collective bargaining procedures. Professional staffs advising the parties have had some influence. The experience and the *expertise* of negotiators have increased.

Arbitration has not, however, been a significant factor in the settlement of disputes over the terms of agreements. Indeed, the general impression is that while arbitration was never a major factor in contract settlements, the resort to contract arbitration has probably declined over the past decade. A further reduction in work stoppages in disputes over terms of agreements depends upon improved negotiation and study procedures, including national referrals in local industries, rather than upon resort to contract arbitration by outside neutrals.

The six points above are not presented as a full explanation for the apparent decline in the resort to the strike and the lockout in disputes over the terms of reopened or expiring agreements. I have not referred to the changing skills of negotiators, the disposition of employees (members) to strike or of managements to lock out, the permissiveness of the economic environment, the effectiveness of alternative means of dispute resolution, or other factors—all of which probably have had some influence. It would be interesting to study and to assess in detail the role of each. The observations above do suggest, however, that the work stoppage has declined as an effective means to achieve agreement in negotiations among many established parties.

Two cautions against unwarranted inferences are in order. First, nothing in this section should be interpreted as encouraging further legal limitations of the right to strike. The factors noted here act on the parties directly, producing a decline in the resort to economic force; in the main they do not arise from legislation and they do not necessarily warrant further legislative restrictions. Second, interest in the factors leading to a decline of the strike should not conceal the fact that some sectors are likely to have become more vulnerable to the strike. Some occupational groups have become more strategic in the productive and distributive processes. In a few sectors the decline of the strike and the lockout may even reflect growing disparities in bargaining power, where resort to economic conflict appears entirely futile and leads to assent to imposed conditions.

The Controlled Use of the Strike During the Agreement Term

The function of the strike in disputes over the terms of an expiring agreement may be contrasted fruitfully with the deliberate and limited use of the strike to resolve certain disputes, after specified procedures have been utilized, during the term of the agreement. In the automobile industry, for example, collective bargaining agreements have explicitly excluded from arbitration certain disputes over production standards, health and safety, and wage rates on new jobs.[16] The agreements provide for procedures for resolving such disputes to be followed at local plants and then by the national department of the union and the central industrial relations office of the company. If no agreement is reached, written notice permitting a strike, only within a sixty-day period, may be filed with the central industrial relations office at the company. The Ford-UAW agreement provides:

> *Failing to reach agreement as herein provided, the Union shall have the right to strike over such dispute; provided such strike is properly authorized in accordance with the provisions of the International Union's Constitution and by-laws.*

The same agreement further provides:

> *It is expressly understood and agreed that no grievance, complaint, issue, or matter other than the strikeable issue involved will be discussed or negotiated in connection with disputes to which this Section is applicable, and the Union shall not request or insist upon the discussion or negotiation of any extraneous issues either before the authorization of a strike or after the occurrence of a strike.*

The strike, or the threat of strike, during the term of an agreement is used in the automobile industry as a special-purpose instrument. The issues on which a strike may arise are narrowly specified; detailed procedures are prescribed for both local and national levels; the powers of arbitrators are expressly limited to exclude these items; the strike may take place only after notice and within a specified period; and responsibility for the strike is controlled by the national negotiators of the agreement. It is said that the strike in these circumstances is a more appropriate instrument than arbitration for resolving a dispute and reaching agreement over a production standard established by management. The strike, or its threat, places pressure on local management to establish reasonable standards, and on local union leaders to secure acceptance of these standards, and on both parties to reach an agreement. The same pressures operate at the national level. It would have to be a major question before the national union would authorize a strike involving a whole plant or before company management would decide to shut down a whole plant. The strike, or its threat, has proved an effective pressure in the resolution of disputes over the past. As the contract language cited above indicates, there is danger that the possibility of the strike on a limited issue may be used for bargaining about other issues. It is not easy to isolate the strikable issue.

In the over-the-road trucking industry the strike or the lockout may apparently be used to resolve any grievance that is unresolved by the grievance procedure or by *ad hoc* agreement to arbitrate. The contract provides:

> *It is agreed that all matters pertaining to the interpretation of any provisions of this contract may be referred, at the request of any party at any time, for final decision to the Joint Area Committee after first being heard by the Joint State Committee, and in event of referral, the Joint State Committee's decision shall not become effective.*
>
> *Deadlocked cases may be submitted to umpire handling if a majority of the Joint Area Committee determines to submit such matter to an umpire for decision. Otherwise either party shall be permitted all legal or economic recourse.*

The system has the advantage that it compels the parties to resolve their own disputes; it results in better solutions; and it saves the costs and delays of arbitration; and it avoids referring disputes to outsiders unfamiliar with the industry.

This "open end" grievance procedure, with resort to economic power, has been described[17] as a tool of internal political control, as a means to discriminate and play favorites among companies and employees. The Jameses state: "Most labor leaders strongly favor arbitration as the final stage of the grievance procedure for it helps ensure that justice rather than power is the basis for settlement and relieves their obligation to call a work stoppage over a grievance involving only one individual."[18] These authors appear not to be familiar with other "open end" grievance procedures in this country and with the absence of final steps for many plant-level problems in Great Britain and Western Europe. Their preoccupation with power has diverted them from a more dispassionate review of the function of the strike in this grievance procedure.

The national agreement between General Electric and the International Union of Electrical, Radio and Machine Workers provides another illustration of the possible use of economic power to resolve certain grievances arising during the term of an agreement:

> (i) *Some types of grievance disputes which may arise during the term of this Agreement shall be subject to arbitration as a matter of right, enforceable in court, at the demand of either party.*
> (ii) *Other types of disputes shall be subject only to voluntary arbitration, i.e., can be arbitrated only if both parties agree in writing, in the case of each dispute, to do so.*

The agreement then defines matters in each category. The strikes and lockout article precludes such action ". . . unless and until all of the respective provisions of the successive steps of the grievance procedure . . . shall have been compiled with by the local and the Union, or if the matter is submitted to arbitration. . . . ." Thus, if a matter is not a mandatory subject of arbitration and has not been submitted to voluntary arbitration, it becomes a subject for economic action after the grievance procedure has been utilized.

A limited and controlled use of the strike was incorporated in the Boeing-Machinists agreement relating to the difficult issue of seniority-ability control. Note the specialized conditions under which resort to the strike is permissable.

> *A strike by the Union after midnight March 31, 1966, shall not be deemed a violation of Article XIV of the collective bargaining agreement executed as of the date hereof if (a) the parties have not by that time been able to reach mutual agreement as to the terms and conditions of the collective bargaining agreement in regard to the subject . . . of seniority-ability control; and (b) the Union by written notice to the Company within 30 days after that date gives written notice to the Company of its intentions to open the collective bargaining agreement on the subject of seniority-ability control; and (c) the strike is Company-wide (except as to the Vertol Division) and is solely for the purpose of supporting Union demands regarding the subject of seniority-ability control; and (d) the strike begins before the end of the 30 day period specified in (b) above and continues without interruption until ended. Any strike that does not meet all of these conditions shall be deemed a violation of Article XIV of the collective bargaining agreement.*

The General Electric-IUE agreement provides more scope for a strike during the term of an agreement than do the automobile industry agreements or the Boeing contract but much less scope for the strike than under the Teamster agreement. Under the General Electric-IUE agreement the problem may arise of isolating an issue that is subject to strike from those other issues that are subject not to strike but to arbitration. As in the automobile industry, the parties may tend in discussion to tie cases together: thus they threaten to strike on one issue in order to resolve in fact an issue which may be clearly arbitrable but which the union may not wish to take to arbitration. It may also be difficult to define unequivocally the dividing lines between precise questions that are subject to arbitration as a matter of right and those that may be the subject of economic conflict during the term of an agreement.

The significant point is that in the four collective bargaining agreements cited, the parties have themselves designed a function for the strike during the term of the agreement. They have sought to prescribe a limited and special purpose for the strike; they have designed procedures and constraints specifically to meet their problems and circumstances, and these provisions are not transferrable or generally applicable elsewhere. These instances of the controlled use of the strike during the agreement suggest the possibility of greater control of the use of the strike or the lockout in disputes over the terms of expiring agreements.

Summary and Conclusion

Any analysis or policy concern over strikes and lockouts should commence with a recognition of the wide variety of strikes and of their different functions, for these factors affect the procedures for their resolution. There has been a secular decline in the resort to the strike and the lockout and a marked decline of violence in industrial strife. Part of the reason for the secular decline is that some types of work stoppage—organizing, jurisdictional, secondary boycotts—have become subject to public machinery designed to resolve the dispute or prohibit the stoppage.

The major concern of this chapter has been strikes or lockouts over the terms of reopened or expiring agreements. These stoppages have involved approximately 80 percent of the worker-days idle in recent years. The private or public machinery for the settlement of such disputes is probably less well developed in the United States than in other advanced countries. Moreover, such disputes probably offer the greatest scope for the development of new procedures by private parties through joint negotiations, joint study committees, and improved mediation.

This chapter distinguishes four major functions of strikes over agreements among established parties: to change the structure of bargaining, to change the relations between the principal negotiators and their constituents in unions and managements, to change the budget allotment or policy of a government agency, and simply to change a bargaining position of the other side. Such an analytical view of strikes and lockouts is requisite to the design of machinery to facilitate the settlement of disputes over the terms of collective bargaining agreements.

I have also identified a number of reasons for the secular decline of economic conflict as a means to settle disputes over contract terms: the capacity to shut down operations in many industries has been reduced; the costs of a stoppage to both parties have been increased by the reactions of customers through inventories and substitutions; the expansion of government employment and sensitive sectors has made the strike less effective; some issues in negotiations cannot be resolved as well by traditional bargaining procedures with resort to strike or lockout; negotiation and mediation skills and resources are probably more highly developed.

The parties to collective bargaining agreements in some situations use the strike during the term of an agreement to induce settlement, as in agreements in the automobile industry, in the over-the-road trucking industry, between Boeing and the Machinists, and between General Electric and the International Union of Electrical Workers.

The parties to collective bargaining may be reasonably expected to experiment more and to devote their attention to the design and perfection of procedures and machinery to resolve disputes over the terms of collective agreements. Such procedures are intended to fulfill the range of functions now performed by the strike. As general use of the strike or the lockout in such negotiations declines further, a more special purpose and limited use of the strike may be expected to continue.

Endnotes

1. Karl Marx in *The Communist Manifesto:* "In depicting the most general phases of the development of the proletariat, we traced the more or less veiled civil war, raging within existing society, up to the point where that war breaks out into open revolution and where the violent overthrow of the bourgeoisie lays the foundation for the way of the proletariat."

2. Carl Stevens, "Is Compulsory Arbitration Compatible with Bargaining?" *Industrial Relations* (February 1966), p. 10.

3. These figures exclude work stoppages arising from negotiations of a first agreement. Approximately 18 per cent of work stoppages and 7 per cent of man-days idle involve such initial agreements. See Bureau of Labor Statistics, *BLS Handbook of Methods,* Bulletin 1910 (1976), 195–202. Beginning in 1982 the Bureau of Labor Statistics, as an economy measure, ceased to collect and publish data on work stoppages smaller than those involving one thousand workers.

4. David McCalmont, "The Semi-Strike," *Industrial and Labor Relations Review*

(January 1962), pp. 191–208. Also see National Labor Relations Board cases involving the scope of protected "concerted activities for the purpose of collective bargaining or other mutual aid or protection" (Section 7).

5. See, however, the excellent study of the national shipbuilding and engineering dispute in Great Britain in 1957: H. A. Clegg and Rex Adams, *The Employer's Challenge* (Oxford: Basil Blackwell, 1957). See also, Bernard Karsh, *Diary of a Strike* (Urbana: University of Illinois Press, 1958).

6. *Work Stoppages in 1965* (Washington, D.C.: Bureau of Labor Statistics, January 11, 1966).

7. The stoppages in the automobile and other industries on local issues at contract negotiation periods are also of this type.

8. A.H. Raskin, "The Great Manhattan Newspaper Duel," *Saturday Review of Literature* (May 8, 1965), p. 58.

9. Dan Hurley, "1966 Boston Newspaper Case" (unpublished memorandum, April 20, 1966).

10. I am indebted to Professor Clyde W. Summers for emphasizing the issue of the role of the NLRB in bargaining structure. See Arnold R. Weber, ed., *The Structure of Collective Bargaining* (New York: The Free Press of Glencoe, Inc., 1961). Also see Derek C. Bok and John T. Dunlop, *Labor and the American Community* (New York: Simon and Shuster, 1970), pp. 229–59.

11. Governor's Committee on Public Employee Relations (State of New York, March 31, 1966), p. 33.

12. *Memorandum to the Commission* (April 19, 1965).

13. *Report to the President by the Emergency Board* No. 166 (June 5, 1966).

14. Arthur M. Ross and Paul T. Hartman, *Changing Patterns of Industrial Conflict* (New York: John Wiley and Sons, Inc., 1960), pp. 3, 5.

15. Arthur M. Ross, "The Prospects for Industrial Conflict," *Industrial Relations* (October, 1961), pp. 57–74.

16. The discussion follows the Ford Motor Company and the UAW-AFL-CIO agreement.

17. Ralph and Estelle James, Hoffa and the Teamsters, *A Study in Union Power* (New York: D. Van Nostrand Company, Inc., 1965), pp. 167–185.

18. *Ibid.*, p. 167.

Chapter 8

THE SETTLEMENT OF EMERGENCY DISPUTES

The advantage of trying to treat a large subject in a small space is that it compels attention to fundamentals. The disadvantage of such compression is that many subtleties and nuances are missed, and the impression of dogmatism is difficult to avoid. I apologize in advance. Let us consider a list of nine propositions or conclusions which center attention on the major problems of our subject. The last two are the most important.

1. Full agreement on an approach to emergency disputes is not likely even—or should I say particularly—in a group such as the Industrial Relations Research Association. At one end of the spectrum is the view that no legislation is necessary and that for a period in the future we ought to rely exclusively on collective bargaining, mediation, and "playing it by ear." This view suggests that we had few national emergency disputes before we had national emergency legislation. At the other end of the spectrum is the group dedicated to apply the antitrust laws to the emergency dispute. From this viewpoint we could both reduce the concentration of economic power in the unions and prevent emergency disputes all for the price of one.

In between these two views is an almost infinite combination of positions. If there is any central tendency it is perhaps the "armory of protective weapons"[1] idea in which the chief executive would choose from a wide variety of measures, such as fact-finding with or without recommendations and seizure with or without injunction, depending on the particular case. But there are a great many advocates of particular gadgets on which many of us have patents pending. Some would have special procedures to determine whether an emergency really

From *Proceedings of the Fifth Annual Meeting, Industrial Relations Research Association* (December 28–29), 1952, pp. 1–7.

existed. Some would use a public hearing to have the parties show cause why they should not arbitrate the dispute. Some would resort to a variety of seizure plans designed to make the prospects appear equally unattractive to unions and managements. Some would bring the Congress more actively into the process. The relations between wage stabilization and strikes designed to change these policies is a Pandora's box by itself. A consensus here is not likely on these issues.

2. There can be no solution to what the program for this session calls "the problem" of emergency disputes. There can be no final resort to end emergency disputes. But there is also no way convincingly to still the insistent question. "Then what?" If mediation fails, then what? If fact-finding and recommendations do not produce settlement, then what? If seizure and injunction fail, then what? If the use of the armed forces or putting workers in the militia fail, then what? If you put the leaders in jail and there is still no settlement, then what? The quest for the end of this road is a dangerous illusion. Yet it is a common and popular reaction in the search for guarantees and certainty that essential health and services be not impaired. There can be no such guarantees.

3. It is important to see American experience in the context of developments abroad. In this setting our record is pretty good. The comparison is not made to flatter nor to belittle the major issues which emergency disputes raise. The purpose is rather to provide perspective.

We have not, as in Australia, had to ration gas for a few hours a day while coal barges awaited unloading. They were only unloaded when a bonus was paid from an emergency government fund by the prime minister over the strong objection of the arbitration court. We have not, as in England, had to use troops to unload essential cargoes from ships. We have not, as in France, had to send troops into the mines to prevent flooding of mines and the destruction of property. We have not, as in Denmark, as a routine matter, settled emergency disputes by enacting into statute the recommendations of a mediator. Neither have we resorted in the private sector in peacetime to compulsory arbitration in name or substance outside of the railroads. This context should help to stimulate a little more detached view of American experience.

The perspective of our own history shows that recent strikes have had almost none of the violence of an earlier generation. We have had a greater outpouring of words but almost no blood.

4. It is a basic principle that each labor dispute, and particularly an emergency dispute, is unique to a degree. In some degree the procedures should be tailor-made to the case if settlement be the objective. In some cases the parties may want the government to come in while

in others they may want no part of the government. One side may take quite a different position from the other, depending on weakness or strength. In some cases the parties may want to be taken off the hook. In some cases the ideology of the union may be a factor. There may be varying degrees of control by the leaders of each side over constituent members. The issues in dispute may vary widely in their complexity. In some cases there has been in fact no previous bargaining, while in others there has been a great deal. Some cases may involve a few parties, others a great many. To develop a single standardized legislative prescription for all situations—past and conceivable in the future—is certain to result in procedures that are ill adapted to many emergency disputes.

5. No machinery to settle disputes can remain the same over time. Use changes it. All three parties in these emergency disputes are continuously adapting their positions to moves of the other parties. A grievance machinery set up in a contract five years ago works much differently today than it did at first. The railway labor act and the emergency boards appointed under the act in fact operated differently today as the parties have adjusted their tactics and approach to the existence of these boards. Some observers have severely criticized these changes in practice as a breakdown of the emergency board system and have sought to find various sinister and political causes. But the simple fact is that disputes machinery cannot operate over time and be unchanged. It must adjust to the changing desires and tactics of the parties. I know that the jurisdictional machinery established five years ago, while having many of the same forms, operates quite differently in fact.

This principle is no less true even when the parties using the machinery change or when use is infrequent. John L. Lewis and the United Mine Workers were fined for contempt of an injunction. On the second go-round Judge Keech found no violation. This experience has not been missed by other unions which might elect the same policies. Each side will take the existence of such emergency disputes machinery into account and will adjust its tactics accordingly. This in turn will compel changes in the way the machinery actually operates.

6. The nature of an emergency dispute depends greatly upon whether the country is at peace, in partial mobilization, or in full war. The definition of an emergency will substantially depend upon just where the country lies between the poles of peace and war. Yet there may be great difficulty in getting any consensus on our national position since any judgment involves assumptions about the future and the enemy. Our best information may be highly classified and competing public views are likely to be tinged with partisan political colorations, or at least widely alleged to be. The day-to-day changes

in the international scene will change the seriousness with which a stoppage in a particular plant or industry may be viewed. Moreover, there is a natural tendency for directors of a military procurement program to view with dismay any interference with their schedule and plans. The task of weighing the increased risk to national security of a stoppage and delayed production against the dangers of government interference in collective bargaining does not lend itself to any ready standards. How can anyone weigh these intangibles? What is the risk involved in a delay of one week or one month in the completion of a facility? Subordinates can indicate cases of more or less risk, but it seems to me that only the chief executive should exercise this type of discretion. No one else can be given the full range of information and no one else has the responsibility.

The type of international situation will also determine the type of disputes machinery. In a full war, presumably a continuing board or agency is required. In time of full peace *ad hoc* boards would generally be conceded to be adequate. The issue naturally arises at what point in increased international tension the shift should be made from one to the other. Was the shift made too early in May 1951? Or were the views of the international emergency held by the Administration and industry too different?

7. In the handling of emergency disputes there are two questions which must be distinguished: first, how do you keep essential production or services going, and second how do you settle the dispute between the parties from which the threatened cessation arises? It is true that a settlement of the dispute may normally be expected to restore production. But production may be needed to continue before the dispute has been settled.

There are a number of ways of securing needed production. The threatened stoppage may be postponed for a period, minimum production for vital needs may be provided during a strike, an injunction may be secured and be respected, seizure may be used. There is a sense in which seizure is the last resort at present in this country. It works, in part, because the government may then secure an injunction to prevent a strike, but more because of the current moral sanction that "you don't strike against the government." In a different context this moral sanction might not work.

There are a number of ways of stimulating a settlement of a dispute: mediation, fact-finding and recommendations, and more mediation. But there is only one last resort at present in this country to settle a dispute: agreement between the parties. There is no other way. Agreements differ. Some are signed with a smile and others with a grimace. Some are entered into willingly and others with great reluctance. Whatever its real nature, only an agreement will settle a dispute.

While some measures may be required to keep vital production going, the central objective is to produce agreement which both keeps production going and settles the dispute.

8. The most fundamental question in the field of labor legislation confronting the country is not the emergency dispute nor the revision of the Taft-Hartley law. It is rather the question of the *process* by which laws affecting collective bargaining are to be enacted. We face two broad alternatives. The first would make the legal framework of collective bargaining primarily a product of the political process. The details of a labor law depend narrowly upon the mustering of votes in the Congress on particular amendments. The second approach would bring the parties—labor and management—more actively into the process of shaping the legal framework of collective bargaining. I cannot help but add that this approach would also bring the parties more actively into the administration of the legal framework of collective bargaining. As a country we are far down the road on the first approach. It is my considered judgment that this is a most dangerous road. The present occasion in our national life is timely to pause and to reconsider our policy.

If collective bargaining is to be the cornerstone of our national labor policy, the legal framework of collective bargaining cannot remain a partisan political matter. Neither industry nor labor can tolerate a world in which the legal status of collective bargaining is changed every two or four years, depending upon the latest election returns. Stable and constructive industrial relations cannot be built on such shifting foundations.

Labor and industry must share actively in the development of a new and substitute law for the Taft-Hartley act. The parties most directly affected should assume some responsibility for jointly proposing the legal framework of collective bargaining. The usual Congressional process of hearings is not enough, for there people state only their formal positions. There must be in advance joint consultations, certainly informal, between union and management representatives, with the assistance of neutrals. The next labor law must not be thrust down the throat of either side; the parties together must take, and must even be made to take, some measure of responsibility for a stable legal framework for collective bargaining.

9. It seems to me certain that there will be some statutory provisions for dealing with emergency disputes on the books for some time to come. Despite my convictions just expressed, I fear these provisions are likely to be more influenced by the politicians than the

parties to collective bargaining. It has occurred to me that there is an approach to the emergency dispute which deserves some attention.

There were ten occasions up to 1952, and 31 occasions up to 1983, on which the emergency provisions of the Taft-Hartley law have been invoked. There are a limited number of sections of the economy in which emergency disputes can arise. The most important are, no doubt, railroads, atomic energy, coal, maritime and steel. On a national basis instances may arise in other sectors, but they are likely to be most rare.

In looking over this area of most potential trouble it is interesting to observe that special machinery is in existence for the railroads and atomic energy. In my judgment emergency disputes have been most adequately handled in these two sectors. This is so, in my view, because the machinery in both cases was substantially designed by the parties alone or with their full support and cooperation.

It is proposed that every attempt be made in those sectors where there is no specialized machinery—coal, maritime, steel—to encourage the parties to develop their own procedures to mitigate emergency stoppages. The interposition of further private machinery or quasi-public machinery is desirable between the initial breakdown of collective bargaining and emergency dispute procedures. The parties can help to develop "another place to go" before resort to generalized emergency procedure. If you must have more legislation, pass a law requesting the parties in these industries to submit to the Congress in a year their suggestions for mitigating emergency dispute stoppages in these industries. I have great confidence in the ingenuity of the parties to develop such procedures. They can develop their own conciliation steps. They may decide to limit stoppages to some fraction of the total production of the industry; they may mutually select new wage leaders more apt to reach agreement; they may declare in advance their willingness to handle any vital cargo or production. In brief, the subject of emergency disputes should itself become a subject of bargaining between the parties in the particular industries in which these issues arise at the request of the government. The Federal Mediation and Conciliation Service should take the lead in assisting the parties in these directions.

The proposal is that the parties be encouraged to interpose a layer of private devices to settle disputes or to insure essential production and services before the general emergency dispute provisions be invoked. These procedures would be designed and tailor-made, of course, to suit the special problems of the particular industry.

I believe that, as collective bargaining develops, the emergency dispute will cease to be a serious question. The public will have insisted that something be done about serious stoppages in vital areas. Under this pressure the parties in the several industries will develop their own procedures. I am suggesting that this approach be stimulated and hastened as a matter of public policy.

Endnote

1. The phrase is that of Peter Seitz in *Proceedings of the Fourth Annual Conference on Industrial Relations* (April 18, 1952), University of Buffalo, p. 24.

Chapter 9

PROCEDURES FOR THE
SETTLEMENT
OF EMERGENCY DISPUTES

A comparative view of national industrial relations systems,[1] or one feature such as the procedures for the settlement of emergency disputes, is always highly rewarding intellectually. But there are severe practical limitations to the transplant of statutory measures or institutions from one country to another. Among advanced countries the more diverse the societies and economies the greater the difficulty with any transposition.

Some of the difficulties and subtleties involved in making comparisons in industrial relations among advanced countries are simply illustrated by the title of this chapter. The term "emergency disputes" has meaning in the context of the industrial relations arrangements of the United States. It has very little meaning, and in any event a different meaning, in other countries.[2] The term "emergency disputes" conjures up in the mind of anyone familiar with the industrial relations system of the United States the experience with Section 10 of the Railway Labor Act, Section 201 of the same statute as applied to the airlines, and Sections 206-10 of the Taft-Hartley statute. It is not the idiosyncrasy of machinery or statutory language which is incommensurate so much as the underlying concepts and governmental approaches to labor and management.

A simpler and even more fundamental illustration is provided by the terms "worker" and "employee," which cannot readily be trans-

From *International Conference on Automation, Full Employment and a Balanced Economy* in Rome, Italy, The American Foundation on Automation and Employment, Inc. (1967), pp. 3–10.

posed from one industrial relations system to another without artful shadings in meaning. Thus, *arbeiter* and *angestellter* in Germany (F.R.) and *radnici* and *sluzbenici* in Yugoslavia convey differences in groupings of people in groups of jobs and even a degree of social differentiation that our blandness in the use of *worker* and *employee* does not convey. There is need to be ever alert to the inherent difficulties of translating the experience, the institutions, and even the language of one industrial relations system into another. On this account I have confined explicitly the first three sections of this chapter to the experience of the United States. Some comparisons are attempted in a final section.

The *first* section is descriptive and presents a brief summary of the two major types and three specialized procedures in use in the United States to resolve disputes between labor organizations and managements in sectors particularly sensitive to the public interest. This brief summary of various machinery cannot be definitive; it is primarily designed for our friends from other countries who understandably may not be at home with our peculiar institutions. The *second* section discusses analytically the major issues involved in discussions over the design and revision of such procedures in the United States. The *third* section states briefly my own conclusions and proposals. The *fourth* and final section seeks to place the experience with the emergency dispute in the United States in the larger setting of industrial relations in other Western countries.

The Emergency Dispute Machinery

The Railway Labor Act

This act became law in 1926 and was extended to the airlines industry in 1936. It provides for an emergency procedure if the private parties are unable to settle by collective bargaining or through mediation a dispute arising out of notices filed by one or both parties to change the terms of a collective bargaining agreement. The rejection of the ritualistic proffer of arbitration, made by the Railroad Mediation Board—and this proffer is almost invariably rejected by the unions— is the signal to authorize legally a work stoppage at the end of 30 days and to presage the intervention of the President. If an unresolved dispute,". . . in the judgment of the National Mediation Board, threatens substantially to interrupt interstate commerce to a degree such as to deprive any section of the country of essential transportation service, the Mediation Board shall notify the President, who may thereupon, in his discretion, create a board to investigate and report respecting such dispute." This *ad hoc* emergency board has 30 days to hear the dispute and submit its report, and by custom its recommendations, although the time may be extended for practical purposes by mutual consent of the parties. ". . . for thirty days after such board has made its report to the President, no change, except by agreement, shall be made by the parties to the controversy in the conditions out of which the dispute arose." Under this statute a strike or lockout is legal after 30 days following the report of the emergency board. In practical terms, the carriers may also impose changes in rules rather than lockout after the 30 days.

The emergency procedures of Section 10 and 201 of the Railway Labor Act have been invoked in an aggregate of 209 cases (plus 3 cases under the Rail Passenger Service Act of 1982) since 1926 in railroads and since 1936 in airlines. The total is comprised of 175 cases in railroads and 34 cases in airlines. In the twenty-year period 1947–67, the statute was used on 127 occasions, while in the period 1967–83, these emergency procedures were utilized in 72 cases.

For practical purposes not only nationwide disputes but most disputes relating to major individual carriers have resulted in resort to this practice. [There were more than 190 class I carriers and terminal switching companies involved in a national railroad case in the 1960s. There were 13 domestic truck and international air carriers and another 13 local service lines under the machinery, and their cases ordinarily arose individually by carrier and craft union.] In assessing the significance of these numbers it may be well to remember that labor organization in both industries is on a craft basis, with crafts negotiating singly or in groups with the carriers. There are more than 20 standard railroad labor organizations and half that many in the airlines industry. (See Chapter 2 for a brief description of other features of the industrial relations system and the railroads.)

Some appreciation of the volume of disputes processed through the machinery of the Railway Labor Act (I use "processed" to reflect a production operation) is reflected in the experience of the participants in this session. David L. Cole served as a member of board number 66 in 1948, number 94 in 1951, and 98 in 1952; and I have scars to exhibit from board numbers 109 in 1955, 130 in 1960, and 167 in 1966. The average rate of output appears to be a little more than five a year, although there was one six-year period, 1945–50, when the railroad industry alone managed 73 boards.

This is not the occasion to undertake a detailed evaluation of the operation of these emergency procedures.[3] It may be noted that most of the parties in the railroad industry, their lawyers, and consultants "seem to feel that the procedures before emergency boards are eminently sensible and fair; these practices have the familiarity and the

sanctity of tradition, which rules this industry as it does no other."
The carriers in recent years, however, have advocated the enactment
of a statute providing for finality through arbitration in all disputes not
resolved by collective bargaining and mediation in the railroad industry. It is the neutrals who have served on the emergency boards in
recent years, however, who have been most outspoken in their criticism of the machinery and the way the parties have used, or abused,
it. First, they point out that at least since World War II, little bargaining takes place between the parties until after the emergency board
report and recommendations. Instead of constituting a means to close
a narrow gap between the parties it must hear all the formal proposals, few of which the parties take seriously themselves. Second, the
procedures have often been criticized on the ground "that their
mechanical rigidity tends to chill normal collective bargaining and
make mediation difficult," and another board compared not unfavor-
ably the emergency board performance to a kabuki theatre.

The Labor-Management Relations Act

Passed in 1947 and providing for an emergency procedure in Sections
206–210, this provision applies outside of the railroads and airlines.
"Whenever in the opinion of the President of the United States, a
threatened strike or lockout affecting an entire industry or a substantial part thereof engaged in trade, commerce, transportation, transmission, or communication among the several states or with foreign
nations, or engaged in the production of goods for commerce, will, if
permitted to occur or to continue, imperil the national health or
safety, he may appoint a board of inquiry into the issues in dispute
and to make a written report to him. . . ." The report shall contain no
recommendations. On receiving the report the government seeks
from the courts an injunction against the strike or lockout to run for a
period of 80 days. The procedures further provide that at the end of
60 days the board of inquiry shall report to the President the current
position of the parties, and they further provide for a secret ballot of
the employees conducted by the National Labor Relations Board on
the question of whether they wish to accept the final offer of settlement made by management. At the end of the 80-day period a strike
or lockout is legal. The President is required to submit to the Congress a report on the dispute "together with such recommendations as
he may see fit to make for consideration and appropriate action."

The emergency procedures of Taft-Hartley have been invoked 31
times in 35 disputes in the years since 1947, an average annual rate of
almost one compared with more than five a year under the Railway
Labor Act. Strikes have occurred on the expiration of the 80-day

statutory moratorium in only seven disputes, and all of these cases were in the longshore and maritime industries.[4] Some indication of the rate of flow of these cases is again reflected in the experience of the participants in this panel; David Cole and I served together on the 8th board of inquiry in the bituminous coal dispute of 1950 and the 25th board in the General Electric Evandale plant dispute of 1966. Mr. Cole also served on three other of the 31 boards of inquiry, the clear leader in the field of this specialized occupation.

While no extended evaluation of the Taft-Hartley procedures is here possible,[5] there are several statutory provisions that are widely regarded as uncommonly inept. The function provided for the board of inquiry in the statute is sterile and purely ministerial enroute to an injunction. It is true, however, that on a few occasions circumstances have permitted a board to break away from this prescribed role and make a contribution toward settlement through mediation. The suggestion has often been made that a board of inquiry should be empowered, at the outset or on petition to the President,[6] to make substantive recommendation for the settlement of the dispute. The statutory provisions for the required vote on the employer's last offer is simply silly; it fails to understand the complexities of the bargaining process, with last-minute changes in positions, and the normal relations between union negotiations and their members.

There is one feature of the Taft-Hartley procedures which has not been widely appreciated; the requirement that at the end of the 80-day period the President is required to submit a report to the Congress with recommendation for appropriate action. This procedure in effect makes a continuing dispute a matter for Presidential report and legislative action or inaction. A private labor-management dispute is thus transmitted into a political and public policy issue. Any further postponement or restriction on the private rights of strike or lockout in the public interest, and the designation of any further procedures for the resolution of a dispute, become a matter for mutual accommodation between the President and the Congress, the elected representatives of the nation as a whole.

From the prospective of hindsight, the Taft-Hartley procedures—despite their serious technical flaws—have worked out better than might well have been expected. The statutory provisions surely could have been improved. But the ingenuity of public officials in designing mediation and special fact-finding procedures has often compensated for the formal deficiencies of the law. The uncertainty of legislative action at the end of 80 days has been a factor. The change in the competitive position and the climate of labor-management relations in several vital industries such as coal, steel, and atomic energy facilities have also played a role. This assessment of the record should give pause to us experts who generally made other assessments, publically and in private, when the statute became law. The language of President Truman's veto message, as it related to emergency disputes, now sounds a little shrill. "This procedure would be certain to do more harm than good, and to increase rather than diminish widespread industrial disturbances. . . . I find that the so-called 'emergency procedure' would be ineffective. . . . I cannot conceive that this procedure would aid in the settlement of disputes."[7]

Other Settlement Arrangements

In addition to the two major procedures for the settlement of emergency disputes, there are several specialized arrangements to be noted briefly: the Atomic Energy Labor Relations Panel, first established in 1948; the President's Missile Sites Labor Commission, established in 1961; and the growing number of procedures for handling disputes involving employers of Federal, state, and local government agencies. This latter category is mentioned, but not discussed, to recognize the sector as one in which economic conflict is not regarded as a suitable instrument to settle disputes over the terms of agreements. There is rapid development in the United States of procedures to facilitate the establishment of collective bargaining and to resolve disputes in the public employment sector.

The Atomic Energy Labor Relations Panel was established in 1948 with a no-strike, no-lockout pledge on the part of labor and management and with the initiative of government when collective bargaining began to be established in atomic energy production facilities. The public panel was designed to provide specialized mediation and to make recommendations for the resolution of disputes.[8] After 1953 the Panel continued without benefit of the no-strike, no-lockout pledge. Indeed, the Taft-Hartley procedures were used in three disputes at atomic energy installations thereafter.

The President's Missile Sites Labor Commission was established by Executive Order 10946 in 1961. It was a tripartite body with the Secretary of Labor as chairman and the director of the Federal Mediation and Conciliation Service as vice-chairman. It also started with a pledge of top labor and management representatives to use the procedure of the Commission to resolve disputes rather than to strike or lockout. The Commission operated largely through separate tripartite panels, one for construction and another for industrial operations. The Commission operated as a special mediating agency with the authority to issue recommendations not only to the parties but also to government procurement agencies.[9]

The Significant Issues in the Design of Machinery

There are a number of key questions around which the discussion among specialists centers on the procedures for the settlement of emergency disputes in the United States.[10] This section is designed to list these issues and to portray some of the major contending views. The design and revision in our procedures involves critical choices at these points.

Legislation with Labor-Management Consent or by Combat

It has often been said that the 1926 Railway Labor Act was substantially shaped by discussions between representatives, including lawyers, of railway labor and management. The procedures to settle all disputes in World War II were agreed upon in a labor-management conference. The Taft-Hartley machinery, on the other hand, was bitterly opposed by labor and enacted over the veto of President Truman. It is a critical question in the design or revision of emergency disputes procedures whether responsible spokesmen for organized labor and management are able to agree to a procedure or whether statutory machinery is enacted by Congress over the violent objection of one side or the other.

The failure of labor and management in the United States to agree in establishing and revising the legal framework of collective bargaining, including emergency disputes procedures, constitutes a major characteristic of our industrial relations and contrasts with some other countries. One consequence is that emergency disputes procedures in the Taft-Hartley law and discussions of major revision have been highly political and charged with partisanship. The acceptability and the effectiveness of emergency disputes machinery is clearly influenced by the process by which it was established.[11]

The Enigma of Legislative Timing

In the absence of a crisis there is great difficulty in focusing diffused and divided public and legislative opinion on emergency disputes procedures, particularly when there is no broad agreement between organized labor and management on the desirable procedures. In times of a crisis, however, there is danger of intemperate and even punitive legislation. There is also the periodic return of the election year, every other year, to complicate the legislative timing.

When Secretary of Labor Arthur Goldberg called together a group of experts to consider legislative proposals, one of them said, "I think very strongly that we should not go to Congress for changes at this time. I shudder to think what Congress might come out with if it were to be approached." The situation is still certainly no more promising. There appears to be no ideal or reliable time, and legislation for the long view may be shaped grotesquely by the strike or lockout of the moment.

The legislative result at any time, moreover, tends to be influenced in our political system significantly by a key committee chairman or by the views of influential and strategically placed members of Congress. The amendment process in committee, on the floor, or in a conference committee may produce most unpredictable legislation as compared to a parliamentary system.

Fixed Versus Ad Hoc Procedures

A central issue in the design of emergency disputes procedures concerns the respects in which the machinery and its operation is fixed and may not be altered by the President and the degree to which the procedures may be shaped to fit the features of the particular dispute, the issues, and the parties. In general, the argument for relatively predetermined procedures is that the parties should know in advance the rules of the game with governmental intervention; fixed procedures tend to minimize the use of a serious labor-management dispute for the political advantage of an incumbent administration. The Taft-Hartley procedures were in part designed as a reaction to the view that wartime and post-war fact-finding boards had favored the labor side.

The case for the more flexible procedure is that no two of these disputes is the same, and the President should be empowered to match the procedures to the special characteristics of the dispute. It may be appropriate to vary the size and composition of a board, its stated assignment and responsibilities, the period of its operation, its relations to other governmental agencies, and the extent of public attention focused on its work. The different styles of neutrals may also produce different approaches to the parties. Variations from past procedures used with the same parties may contribute, or may not, to the settlement of a dispute. There is merit in the view that all procedures, used in the same way, in labor-management disputes tend sooner or later to lose their effectiveness or tend to wear out. At the present time there is a sense in which the procedures are *ad hoc* after all the specified steps have been exhausted. The type of action which the Congress may take, if any, in a dispute which exhausts the procedures of the Railway Labor Act or Taft-Hartley without settlement is uncertain, and in this sense the ultimate steps in any procedure are not fixed.

The Determination of What Constitutes an Emergency

One view on the design of machinery for emergency disputes is that a separate step should include explicit consideration of whether any emergency really exists, whether there is in fact any peril to the "national health or safety." An opposing view is that such a determination is for practical purposes the prerogative of the chief executive of the country. Perhaps a judgment on this matter is influenced in part by the authority and severity of the machinery invoked. Thus, if the machinery ultimately should lead to an imposed final solution without further action of the Congress, one might be more concerned to provide a review of the determination that an emergency existed than with machinery that could only postpone a work stoppage without even authority to make recommendations, as in the present Taft-Hartley procedures.

Some interruptions of production or service may be thought to produce an emergency almost immediately. Perhaps a nationwide railroad or power stoppage is of this nature. In many other situations, however, illustrated by coal and steel, inventories permit the continuation of a flow of vital supplies for a period after a cessation of operations. Indeed, the prospects of a serious dispute or work stoppage tends in itself to encourage the holding of larger inventories in the hands of both producers and consumers to cushion the impact of any actual stoppage. The specification of the point of an emergency in these circumstances is not simple.

The most difficult questions of definition of an emergency, however, under present legislation concern public opinion and political reactions. It is often not so much the objective impact of a stoppage on the nation's health or safety, as those words are literally understood, which creates pressure on the President for action. The reaction of community interests locally, regionally, or nationally—expressed through newspapers, mayors, and governors, congressional representatives, industry leaders, the labor movement, and the like—constitutes the mechanism through which forces impinge on the President. The convenience of the public and the business and employment of many third parties may be affected by an airlines shutdown or a stoppage of regional rail transportation. It is these pressures which generate demands for limitations on a threatened or actual shutdown. As one reviews the occasions on which emergency dispute procedures have been evoked, there are probably few cases of actual immediate threat to the national health or safety, narrowly defined. The cases have more often involved the realm of community reaction to inconvenience, irritation, loss of business and employment, political divisiveness, and the like. The degree of tolerance by major groups within the community to shutdowns, or the priority these groups attach to collective bargaining without governmental intervention relative to other objectives, may well be changing. These changing moods are likely to be reflected in the resort to emergency disputes machinery by political leaders.

Brief mention should also be made of the problem of defining an emergency in cases involving single plants producing a significant fraction of the output of an item of military significance in time of international tension or war. The Taft-Hartley machinery is limited to "an entire industry or a substantial part thereof. . . ." A plant producing a significant proportion of the engines for a type of military aircraft is not a substantial proportion of the transportation equipment industry, or the aircraft manufacturing industry, or even the aircraft engine industry. But if the industry is defined narrowly enough, such as the military jet engine industry, the statute can be literally applied. The courts have supported such narrow definitions of the affected industry in cases involving output of significance to the military or to atomic energy. In the year 1966–67 the four cases in which the Taft-Hartley procedures were used were cases of single plants or shipyards in one port with an impact on military procurement.

Dispute Settlement Versus Other Objectives Such as Stabilization

The emergency disputes procedures of the Railway Labor Act and the Taft-Hartley law are exclusively concerned with preventing an interruption of vital goods or services and in advancing a settlement between the parties. There is no explicit reference in either legislation to a public interest in the substantive terms of the settlement. An issue of growing significance in discussions of emergency disputes procedures, as with collective bargaining generally, is whether this passive posture should be continued or whether the proposed settlements should explicitly take into account other objectives of public policy than the avoidance of strikes or lockouts, such as economic stabilization, the guideposts, or an "incomes policy," to use the preferred language of Western Europe.

In major disputes there has been more concern in the past with national economic policy than might be imagined. Any nationwide wage case almost invariably includes in its record a discussion of inflation, impacts on other settlements, productivity, and international competition. In a world of rising wages, management representatives tend to introduce a discussion of the larger consequences of the union proposals, and the union representatives often are impelled to argue respecting the economy-wide contentions of management. The existence of government stabilization policies or guideposts are often introduced into the proceedings. Moreover, in one of the emergency disputes procedures identified earlier, the Missile Sites Labor Commission is empowered to make recommendations "to assure efficient and economical completion of missile programs." The Commission on occasion found provisions of agreements to operate uneconomically and provided that they should not be used for purposes of computing reasonable costs—that is, it actually set aside or modified provisions of existing collective bargaining agreements.

The issue raised here is whether, as an explicit matter, emergency disputes procedures should appropriately be expected to include a requirement to conform to the objectives and pronouncements of national economic policy or whether such a question is only to be considered in connection with wage and price controls and general constraints on collective bargaining. [12]

Novel Measures to Put Strong Pressure for Settlement on Each Side

There has been considerable discussion over whether it is possible to design procedures to make direct voluntary settlement between the parties relatively more attractive—in other words, to make the costs of non-settlement and continuing resort to the government in the settlement of disputes the more costly or unpalatable to both parties. A great deal of ingenuity is displayed in various proposals. One proposal would require an arbitrator to adopt the final offer of either side but not to adopt any intermediate position. The rationale of the proposal is to encourage both sides to make concessions and reach agreement in order to avoid the risk that the arbitrator would choose the position of the other party.

The non-stoppage strike[13] or statutory strike proposal provides that vital operations would be continued but that profits of the enterprise would be reduced and some wages or possible retroactive payments to employees would be withheld. The reduction in profits might take place through government seizure of the property[14] with a provision for just compensation to the owners which would presumably be less than current profits. It would be possible theoretically to apply varying degrees of pressure on each side, depending on how much profit and how much wages are withdrawn from each side and how the schedule of such withdrawals is distributed over time or how uncertainty over such costs is arranged. The question naturally arises as to the mechanism or the body to make these decisions on the arrangements for the nonstoppage strike. It is interesting to note that in the railroad shopcraft dispute of 1967, the Senate considered but rejected by formal vote a proposal of this nature.

The issue raised here in the design of emergency dispute machinery is whether such novel proposals have any place in the range of procedures and in what types of disputes or under what circumstances are they likely to be most fruitfully used. In the continuing experimentation with procedures, are there ways of introducing such new approaches or other new ideas?

The Relative Responsibilities of the President and Congress

In the event that a dispute has not been settled by resort to the established machinery of the Railway Labor Act or the Taft-Hartley law, the question arises as to what further steps shall be taken, if any, and the relative responsibilities of the President and the Congress for such steps. If there is no settlement 30 days after the report of an emergency board under the Railway Labor Act or no settlement after the 80-day injunction has been dissolved under Taft-Hartley, what is to happen and what are the responsibilities of the Congress and the President? These may be fixed or *ad hoc* procedures. If there is no further specified machinery, as at present, then one option is to do nothing and to allow at least for a period of a strike or a lockout. If some further procedures are deemed necessary, as in the 1967 railroad shopcraft dispute,[15] the issue arises as to the relative initiative and roles of the President and Congress.

This is not a simple relationship on a difficult and sensitive problem. On some occasions—for example, the machinist strike on five airlines in 1966—the President may prefer to leave the initiative with the Congress. On other occasions—as in the railroad shopcraft dispute of 1967—the initiative may clearly lie with the President. On other occasions the President may make one proposal and the Congress may adopt a different solution acceptable to the President in the end, as in the railway work rules dispute of 1963.[16] It is understandable that members of Congress may desire to place on the President any onus for a course of action in these circumstances, and the President in turn may prefer to leave the question to Congress, with suggested alternatives. In the end the responsibilities have to be shared, since any special legislation requires the concurrence of both.

These relations are further complicated by the proximity to national elections.

The consideration by the President and the Congress of further legislation after the established machinery has failed to resolve a dispute is itself a major factor influencing any continuing negotiations or mediation. In the 1966 airlines case, the threat of legislation—indeed its imminence—was a factor stimulating settlement. In other situations, as in the 1967 railroad shopcraft case, the prospects of legislation tended to freeze positions and make negotiations futile.

Conclusions and Proposals

We have considered briefly the emergency disputes procedures of the United States and identified the major issues involved in the discussion among specialists concerned with the design or revision of our present machineries. Let me now summarize my views on procedures for the settlement of emergency disputes in the United States. These conclusions and proposals are fair game for critical review. It is hoped that serious criticism would include a statement of preferred alternative procedures.

1. A generalized and ideological discussion of emergency disputes procedures will not prove very productive. A ringing declaration of the virtues of free collective bargaining, or of the evils of compulsory arbitration, or of the sacredness of the right to strike or to lockout, or that any government intervention as an opening wedge will lead inevitably to full government controls or socialism is not likely to provide a basis for serious discourse. The fact is that collective bargaining is increasingly under public scrutiny in the United States and that the public interest in the results of collective bargaining is clearly on the ascendancy. My concern is that in the future there may be a serious collision between a public which does not well understand collective bargaining, particularly when it brings some serious inconvenience or perceived threat to vital interests. The area of decision now, however, is some minor adjustments in the governmental procedures for treating emergency disputes and some serious review by the parties in certain critical industries of their bargaining arrangements.

The right to strike is not, and has never been, an absolute right in the United States.[17] The I.W.W. was the only labor group to insist consistently on no limitations on the resort to strike; on this ground they opposed collective bargaining agreements. For a long time unions used the strike as a weapon to secure recognition. The unions supported the governmental election machinery as a device to eliminate strikes over recognition. The strike was widely used at one time to secure compliance with the provisions of a collective bargaining agreement before the modern views of a grievance machinery and contract arbitration prevailed. While the strike is still used, subject to very detailed contract regulation, to settle disputes during the life of some agreements on some issues, the right to strike over grievances during an agreement term has been generally eliminated; it probably could not be generally reintroduced. The right to strike in jurisdictional disputes and in certain defined secondary boycotts has been eliminated by statute. The strike or lockout may be postponed under existing emergency disputes procedures. Aside from the issue of rights, there are a number of sectors of the economy in which the parties to collective bargaining have concluded—-on account of automated equipment, extensive supervision, or hostile public reaction— that resort to economic force is not an effective way to resolve disputes over the terms of an agreement. The parties have sought to develop substitutes.

Compulsory and formal arbitration is not the only or most appropriate substitute for the strike. A major difficulty with the advanced private commitment to arbitrate or to publicly prescribed arbitration is the effect which this procedure has upon the collective bargaining process over the terms of new agreements. It often appears to stultify bargaining and increases repetitive use of arbitration. The resort to formal procedures, with lawyers and technical consultants, tends to expand the area of controversy to the full range of formal demands rather than to concentrate upon the few key issues which may really separate the parties. The development of substitutes for the strike, aside from compulsory arbitration, is a subtle and dynamic process calling for considerable ingenuity and imagination among the parties. Among private parties there have been shown to be possibilities of joint study committees, private mediators, development of contract standards or formulae such as prevailing wage data and tests, early reopenings, and specialized fact-finding with recommendations. In the development of emergency disputes procedures, at least in specific cases, there is opportunity for the same sort of creativity.

2. In the United States we now must probably admit that we have apparently come upon a procedure to be followed when the more stereotyped procedures of the Railway Labor Act or the Taft-Hartley Act have been exhausted without settlement. It is, of course, possible for these procedures to be exhausted and a strike or lockout to develop. In cases in which the President and the Congress both conclude that the private interests of the parties must yield to the public interest in uninterrupted operations, the *ad hoc* legislation has been enacted providing for an imposed settlement in the absence of a

private agreement. This is a pragmatic solution and may take a wide variety of forms, involving varying degrees of compulsion. The Congress could prescribe substantive terms of employment as it did with the eight-hour day for train service employees in railroads through the Adamson Act in 1916. It could prescribe formal arbitration as it did in the railway work rules dispute in 1963; or it could provide for a "show cause" hearing on a mediation proposal as proposed in S. J. Res. 81 in the railroad shopcraft dispute in 1967. In 1983 the Congress enacted the substantive recommendations of an emergency board in a national dispute involving locomotive engineers. There are a wide variety of other possibilities that may be developed in future disputes that reach this stage.

In my view this approach is sufficient for the present. We need to examine the results of these experiments before embarking upon any generalized new machinery to resolve disputes that have not been settled through the Taft-Hartley law or the Railway Labor Act. The widespread demand in some industries, in many newspaper editorials, and some political circles for a final solution to the "emergency dispute problem" is unwarranted. There is no undiscovered formula or magic solution. (This view is not designed to preclude a number of technical revisions of both statutes if politically feasible in the legislative process. But this seems highly doubtful.) It may be that so many cases arise on an *ad hoc* basis that the Congress will rebel from this approach, and it may require far too much time of the chief executive. A generalized compulsory arbitration statute in transportation or railroads, it appears to me, is not appropriate, and the process of experimenting with various critical cases is likely to prove very useful should we have to face a more generalized solution.

3. Legislation could fruitfully be used to impel or to require the parties in the industries with the most serious industrial relations problems to review together their procedures for bargaining and to report at the end of a year or eighteen months on proposals to improve the performance of their collective bargaining.[18] The staff facilities of the Department of Labor should be available to these parties, and the Secretary should be authorized to develop with the relevant parties the plans for review, including the use of public or private experts. The list of industries I have had in mind is somewhat broader than those which have created the most frequent emergency disputes, but it would certainly include these sectors. The most urgent industries for this joint review are railroads, airlines, maritime, newspapers, and construction. This approach is designed to place responsibility publicly on parties in these industries to improve their bargaining arrangements and performance. If further *ad hoc* intervention is necessary in these sectors, the parties will have been placed on notice of the public concern with their sector.

It is my view that a great deal of the difficulty in the sectors designated above arises not from classic conflicts between labor and management over issues of principle. Rather the difficulty often lies in the structure of bargaining arrangements and the internal government of the labor organizations and associations of employers. The more specific questions concern the distribution of responsibility between local and national levels of bargaining, the rivalry among labor organizations, the differences in interests among different groups of employers, the bargaining and ratification procedures, the size of wage differentials among different occupations, and the effects of cents-per-hour wage changes over many years on groups of rank-and-file workers. These bargaining structure defects are accentuated by the need to respond to rapid technological changes, to new forms of competition and to an economy of full employment. These problems of adaptation in bargaining structure vary greatly among industries; they are not readily amenable to legislation.

4. The parties to collective bargaining generally, and in sectors prone to emergency disputes in particular, might well be encouraged to develop provisions in their agreements to be followed when the agreements are open for further negotiation or cancellation. In the United States the parties have not devoted much attention to this question. Our procedures for administering the agreement are very detailed, and on the whole they work well. But there is no reason why each major agreement should not specify a variety of steps the parties agree to take to seek to resolve any dispute over the contract renewal. In this respect our industrial relations arrangements have a great deal to learn from the experience of Western Europe, despite the difficulties of direct transfer.

Some Comparisons with Other Countries

In view of the international composition of this conference, it may be appropriate to try to relate the emergency disputes procedures of the United States to the larger experience of Western countries. These comparisons and contrasts are advanced most tentatively.

1. As far as I am aware, there is no other country in the group with a highly developed and specialized procedure designed to handle a specialized type of disputes labeled as "emergency" disputes. This is not to say that specialized procedures have not been developed or invoked elsewhere for some major disputes, but a separate class of disputes and procedures is distinctive to our experience. This fact calls for explanation, and a full understanding of the reasons for these unusual procedures would provide significant insight into the industrial relations system of the United States.

One of the operative factors probably is the relative weakness on the confederation level of our labor movement in matters of collective bargaining, even when there are significant impacts on the public and threats of possible legislative enactment that would affect adversely the whole labor movement. The federation has difficulty exercising influence in the bargaining arena, certainly against the wishes of an important affiliate. The same independence of national organizations is exhibited on the management side. Another contributing factor is the absence of the same degree of sensitivity to national political considerations that exists with a labor party. In brief, the large national unions and large companies have been less subject to influence by confederation leaders; as a consequence, other governmental procedures have been designed to deal with emergency disputes. Further, our labor organizations have operated with a relatively greater economic orientation. They have the resources to support long strikes. The resort to demonstration strikes of a day or two occurs very infrequently.

2. There are a few developments in some other countries that deserve brief mention. In Canada, special procedures for railroads were begun in 1903, and after World War II they were generalized for other industries. "Canada's major experiment in intervention started with public-interest disputes. Ultimately the technique worked out was enlarged in scope until it became a procedure of general application. In the process public interest disputes were swallowed up in a sea of general disputes."[19]

The enactment by the Canadian Parliament of *ad hoc* legislation since 1950 on several occasions to provide for arbitration within specified limits in disputes on the railways is clearly more parallel to our own recent experience. After conciliation reports had failed to resolve the difference in these instances the Parliament required the continuation of operations and the return to work of men on strike where a strike was in process, and a settlement of the disputes by compulsory arbitration.

The *ad hoc* approach is also illustrated by the Danish experience since 1933. On a number of occasions since then the Parliament of Denmark has enacted special legislation in particular disputes either giving the force of law to the recommendations of the mediator or providing for compulsory arbitration.[20] In 1965 in a case involving radio-telegraphers, the Parliament prohibited a strike and provided for a settlement through compulsory arbitration.

3. In the United States it might be said that we have procedures for ordinary disputes which only involve a role for government through mediation, and procedures for a class of emergency disputes, and, finally, *ad hoc* action of the Congress in some cases when the

emergency procedures have not settled the dispute. In most other Western countries, in this perspective, there appear to be only two classes of disputes, one which can be handled by ordinary procedures including recommendations by a government body or an appointed board, and the special cases which may produce *ad hoc* legislation. In some countries such legislation has not been necessary. The essential difference is that the role of government intervention is more narrowly circumscribed in the United States. In most of the rest of the Western world it would be taken as normal that the government would make proposals or recommendations for settlement in a dispute of any significance. A special class of cases does not exist in these countries designed as emergency disputes where a stoppage would threaten the nation's health or safety.

It is interesting to speculate that the economies, and the industrial relations systems as well, of the United States and many Western countries are becoming more similar. If these developments are taking place—and there is some evidence to this effect—then the emergency dispute problem might not be so distinctive to us in the future. There is a tendency for our mediation service to make more recommendations, both informally and formally, than in the past. In this respect our experience may be congenial to the experience of other Western countries. But the absence of more responsibility for bargaining or for interruption of essential services in central labor and management organizations in the United States, coupled with the special legislation, is likely to continue the emergency disputes procedures as a distinctive feature of our industrial relations system. As has been noted, the procedures have evolved with the addition of the *ad hoc* legislation.

"The ingredients of industrial peace and stabilized labor-management relations are numerous and complex. They may well vary from age to age and from industry to industry. What would be needful one decade might be anathema the next." (United States Supreme Court)

Endnotes

1. See John T. Dunlop, *Industrial Relations Systems* (New York: Henry Holt and Company, 1958).
2. Despite many differences, perhaps, the Canadian experience is least alien to our own.
3. See Irving Bernstein, Harold L. Enarson, and R. W. Fleming, eds., *Emergency Disputes and National Policy,* Industrial Relations Research Association Series (New York: Harper & Brothers Publishers, 1955).
4. See *National Emergency Disputes Under the Labor Management Relations*

(Taft-Hartley) Act, 1947–65, U.S. Department of Labor, Bureau of Labor Statistics, Bulletin No. 1482 (March 1966).

5. See James E. Jones, Jr., "The National Emergency Disputes Provisions of the Taft-Hartley Act: A View from a Legislative Draftsman's Desk, *Western Reserve Law School* (October 1965), pp. 133–256.

6. *Collective Bargaining*, A Report by the President's Advisory Committee on Labor-Management Policy (May 1, 1962).

7. National Labor Relations Board, *Legislative History of the Labor-Management Relations Act, 1947* (Washington, D.C., 1948), Vol. I, p. 919.

8. See *Report of the Secretary of Labor's Advisory Committee on Labor-Management Relations in Atomic Energy Installations* (Washington, D.C., 1957).

9. See Wayne E. Howard, *The Missile Sites Labor Commission, 1961 thru 1967*, Federal Mediation and Conciliation Service, Washington, D.C., 1969.

10. This formulation is designed to exclude extreme proposals advanced in some political circles, such as the break-up of industrywide bargaining or the general use of compulsory arbitration or labor courts. The issues under review here are those seriously discussed among specialists.

11. See David L. Cole, *The Quest for Industrial Peace* (New York: McGraw-Hill Book Company, 1963), pp. 33–36.

12. See John T. Dunlop, "Guideposts, Wages, and Collective Bargaining," *Guidelines, Informal Controls, and the Market Place, Policy Choices in a Full Employment Economy*, George P. Shultz and Robert Z. Aliber, eds. (Chicago: The University of Chicago Press, 1966), pp. 81–96.

13. See Neil W. Chamberlain, *Social Responsibility and Strikes* (New York: Harper and Brothers, 1953), pp. 279–86.

14. For the definitive study of seizure in labor-management disputes, see John Blackman, *Presidential Seizure in Labor Disputes* (Cambridge, Mass.: Harvard University Press, 1967). The study is a review of the 71 instances of Presidential seizure.

15. See Hearings before the Subcommittee on Labor of the Committee on Labor and Public Welfare, United States Senate, 90 Cong., 1st Sess., on S. J. Res. 81, *Railroad Shopcraft Dispute*, May 10–24, 1967 (Washington, D.C., 1967).

16. Public Law 88-108, 88th Cong., S. J. 102 (August 28, 1963).

17. See George W. Taylor, "The Public Interest—Variations on an Old Theme," *Proceedings of the Eighteenth Annual Meeting of the National Academy of Arbitrators*, January 27–29, 1965 (Washington, D.C.: B.N.A. Inc.), pp. 191–202.

18. John T. Dunlop, "The Social Utility of Collective Bargaining," *Challenges to Collective Bargaining*, The American Assembly, Lloyd Ulman, ed. (Englewood Cliffs, N.J.: Prentice-Hall, Inc., 1967), pp. 168–80.

19. H. D. Woods, "Canadian Policy Experiments with Public-Interest Disputes," Industrial Relations Research Association, *Proceedings of the Spring Meeting* (May 6–7, 1963), p. 745.

20. Walter Galenson, *The Danish System of Labor Relations* (Cambridge, Mass.: Harvard University Press, 1952), pp. 130–38.

Chapter 10

THE INDUSTRIAL RELATIONS SYSTEM IN CONSTRUCTION

The building and construction industry is a large and diversified sector of the economy. Four million workers are employed by hundreds of thousands of contractors, ranging from organizations that operate a world-wide business to self-employed persons sometimes working for a price per unit and at other times working for an hourly wage. Construction operations on a single site range in duration from several hours to, for a few projects, many years. There are a variety of branches of the construction sector: commercial, industrial plants and utilities, home building, military and defense installations, highway and heavy construction, and cross-country pipelines and transmission lines. Each of these has its special features. The industry encompasses new construction, modernization, repairs and alterations, periodic turnaround work, and continuing maintenance by contract. The output of the industry is purchased by governments, commercial and industrial businesses, and households.

The manual workers are substantially organized into about twenty international unions of varying size and strength, although some sectors or localities are largely non-union or open shop. The contractors are likewise organized into as many national associations, although there are many unaffiliated local contractor associations and many other contractors are not affiliated with any association. Some contractors hire only one craft, while others employ the full range of craft skills. Despite this great diversity, there is an inner unity and logic to the relations among workers and their organizations, contractors and their organizations, and public agencies that warrants the reference

From *The Structure of Collective Bargaining*, Arnold R. Weber, Ed. (New York: The Free Press, 1961), pp. 255–78.

to the industrial relations system of the building and construction industry.

This chapter is divided into four sections. The first sets forth very briefly the major characteristics of the industrial relations system in construction under collective agreements. The second section summarizes the major facts concerning the scope of bargaining in the industry. The third seeks to interpret and to explain these facts, and a final section indicates some of the wider implications of the industrial relations experience of the construction industry.

The Major Features of the Construction System

The industrial relations system of the construction industry in the United States constitutes a distinctive set of arrangements. Their principal features include:[1]

1. *Area-wide Determinations.* Wages and conditions of work are determined on an area-wide basis generally in advance of any employment on a project. Indeed, these determinations are essential before a contractor normally bids for work. The scope of the area of determination of wages and other conditions of work is not uniform among crafts or even among terms of employment for one craft.

2. *Jurisdiction.* Work operations are assigned on the basis of craft jurisdiction, which is also related to the subcontracting or specialty contractor arrangements in the industry.

3. *Area Pool of Labor.* An area pool of labor is shifted among projects. While some contractors maintain some key workers on a steady basis, there is considerable movement among contractors and branches of the industry in the labor force. The area pool concentrates attention upon hiring procedures and travel arrangements.

4. *Apprenticeship and Training.* The training of apprentices and the upgrading of the skills of existing journeymen is a major activity of contractor associations, labor organizations, and governmental agencies. Two-thirds of the work force is classified as skilled labor, and well over half of all registered apprentices in the country are found in this industry.

5. *Diversity and Uniformity among Branches.* There is continuing conflict and competition over the question of whether area wage and benefits and jurisdiction should apply uniformly across all branches of construction or whether distinctive rules shall apply to commercial, heavy and highway, home building, and pipeline construction and some other major sectors of the larger industry. Labor is typically mobile across these lines, but there are often markedly different conditions of competition in the product market for these various

types of construction services. In some localities, such as San Francisco, construction is divided into separate wage contours only by craft, while in most localities some of the various branches of the industry such as heavy and highway or pipeline construction also constitute separate wage contours by craft.

These major distinguishing features of construction industrial relations can be understood in a framework applicable to any industrial relations system.[2] These features are related to and derived from: (1) the technical conditions under which construction takes place; (2) the character of the markets for construction services and for building trades labor; (3) the status of relationships among contractor organizations, labor organizations, and governmental agencies directly affecting the field; and (4) the commonly shared ideas, beliefs, and values within the industry. This framework seeks to explain the five principal features noted above and to account for the fact that industrial relations arrangements are significantly different from those in manufacturing plants, the transportation field, government offices, or other major industrial relations systems. The discussion briefly applies each one of the elements of the analytical framework to the facts of the construction industry, to show how the distinguishing industrial relations features have arisen and how they are related to fundamental features of the industry.

Technical Context

The work place of construction is highly variable; the sites of work frequently change and no two projects are identical. A number of projects also involve for some workers a shift of living accommodations. The work force on a single project is highly variable, typically building up to a peak and falling, and the variability for any one craft or contractor on a project is even sharper. The size of the work group on a project may vary from one or two men to many thousands. The technology and variation in operations among projects requires that a very high proportion (two-thirds) of the work force of the industry be skilled. The variation among projects and technical change through time place a premium on men skilled in a range of duties in a craft rather than trained solely in narrow specialties. The on-site operations provide employment largely for men only, at times under hazardous conditions, and the work is often out of doors, with weather a factor in the availability of employment.

These technical conditions place great stress on organization-building in management, since contractors must be continuously expanding or contracting a work force (often with a nucleus of key men) and adapting an organization to new conditions. Construction in-

volves assembly of components, and the precise timing and flow of
operations is essential to efficient operations. These conditions place a
great premium on a flexible and skilled work force, on continuously
matching jobs and available men, on shifting the work force around
among different contractors, and on uninterrupted operations. The
significance of the area pool of labor, with hiring procedures and
travel arrangements, and the central role of apprenticeship and training are directly related to the technological context of construction.

Market Context

By many of the criteria used to classify product markets, construction
is a competitive industry. There are a great many enterprises selling
construction services; there is widespread freedom of entry, and even
specialized branches of the industry confront competition from contractors that move from one branch to another. Thus home builders
may expand into school and commercial construction, and mechanical
specialty contractors in commercial work may shift into industrial
construction. Moreover, contractors confront the competition of
"force account work" in government, construction work by industrial
plants, and various do-it-yourself arrangements. There is considerable specialization among contractors; many operations are seasonal,
and the bidding system lends itself to peddling of contracts and subcontracts. Prices are not fixed for a season or otherwise administered;
typically a new price is bid on each project. Competition is not only
among similar types of contractors; general and specialty contractors,
national contractors, and joint ventures vie with each other over
whether work will be kept in one contract or subcontracted to others.
There is keen competition between contractors with union agreements and those operating non-union or open shops in many areas
and branches of the industry. At the same time, however, the product is not standardized, specifications are complex, and quality of
service and dates of completion are very significant elements of competition. The uncertainty of many construction conditions and the
importance of responsibility and experience lead to many continuing
relationships between owners and contractors and to protected markets. The bidding conventions in a branch of the industry, if organized, place little pressure on wage rate negotiations, although competition from outside the branch of the industry may have a
significant effect. There are vast differences in the character of competition from one branch or specialization of the industry to the next.[3]

These features of the product market have a decisive influence on
the industrial relations system of construction. The traditional function of collective bargaining, as elaborated by the Webbs, is to place
highly competitive enterprises on the same wage rate basis in pur-

chasing labor services. This is the function of the area rate. It has not always been so well recognized that the prohibitions against piecework or lumping in the industry and uniform jurisdictional rules are part of the same concern. If workers or self-employed persons were to accept variable price quotations in individual bargaining to perform specified amounts of work (that is, so much to install studding, or so much to apply a bundle of shingles), the uniform area wage rate would be eroded. Piece rates would be much more difficult to police in the industry than time rates. Similarly, uniform jurisdictional rules in a locality are essential to the bidding system and to protect the area rate and to assure competition among contractors on other than the price of labor services. If one highway contractor were to bid on the basis of using laborers for an operation, a second to calculate by employing the wage rates and performance of teamsters, and a third to estimate on the basis of using operating engineers, there would be little standardization of wage rates for a craft. The area rate and jurisdictional rules[4] are both aspects of the standardization of the price of labor among contractors. They still, of course, compete in labor costs on the basis of efficiency of operations and managerial competence in running the project.

The divergent product market conditions among different branches of the industry—such as commercial, highway and heavy, pipelines, and home building—have decisive consequences in determining whether area rates and jurisdiction are uniform across all branches or whether separate area wage rates and jurisdictional practices are established for some of these separate markets creating distinctive wage contours. The policy choices made by the unions in these respects are often decisive in determining whether the work is performed under union conditions in all branches of the industry or whether segments of the industry are open shop. A differentiated wage and work rule policy is often difficult for local unions with members working on various types of projects and even the same member working in different branches of the industry from time to time. The history of the industry demonstrates that international unions are much more likely to accept different conditions in various branches of the industry in order to control the work.

Relationships Among Association Contractors, Labor Organizations, and Governmental Agencies

The status of these interrelationships in the construction industry are in many respects quite different from those in industry generally. These relationships have centered upon problems reflecting the major features of the construction system noted earlier.

The Davis-Bacon statute and its administration under the Secretary of Labor is a major factor in the recognition and defense of area rates. There are analogous determinations under some state laws. On federally financed construction in contracts over a specified dollar limit, the Secretary of Labor predetermines the wage rates and benefits for each classification of labor. These determinations are significant to many features of the industrial relations arrangements. They may help to stabilize rates in an area of mixed labor policy; they may help to give recognition to separate conditions for commercial as compared to heavy and highway work; they influence the recognition of particular job classifications within a craft or labor organization; and on federal work they affect the dividing line between work performed by contractors and building tradesmen and work performed by industrial plants and their unions, as in atomic energy and missile installations.

Although a few isolated elections have been held, by and large the collective bargaining relationships have been established without NLRB elections and without certifications. The labor organizations traditionally have been interested as much, if not more so, in organizing contractors as organizing workers on a particular project. The project is of short duration and men often have to be organized again on another job. But the signing of a contractor to an agreement means that in the future, work will be bid, started, and performed under union conditions and that workers will be hired through the hiring procedures established under the agreement. The approach to individual workers is seen as a separate problem from signing up contractors.

The government has played a considerable role in the programs for the development of apprentices and the retraining of journeymen in the industry. The work of the Bureau of Apprenticeship of the Department of Labor is noteworthy in this connection. The programs involve a complex interrelation of government, vocational schools, unions, and contractor associations.

Any review of the large volume of cases and problems in this industry confronting the NLRB since 1947 clearly reflects the relationships among contractors, unions, and the government and the attempt by statute to redefine these relationships. The central problems have concerned procedures for hiring, occasional jurisdictional disputes that have escaped the private machinery established in 1948, and the secondary boycott problem reflecting traditional organizing methods at a common situs.

The relations among government agencies, contractor associations, and unions in this industry are significantly different from those in industry generally. This is illustrated by the Davis-Bacon statute, apprenticeship activity, the wartime stabilization programs, the administration of section 10(k) of the Taft-Hartley law, the special provisions respecting construction in the 1959 legislation, and the effort of the labor organizations to overturn by legislation the Denver Building Trades case and to permit situs picketing. Moreover, these relations have been focused upon the same major features of construction industrial relations noted at the outset of this section.

Common Ideas and Values

There are common ideas and values distinctive to the construction industrial relations system that help to bind the system together. Historically, they grew out of the common environment and now reinforce the system. The workers are more individualistic than others; they shift from job to job, and often from locality to locality. A considerable number move from journeyman to foreman and to supervisory positions and back again. They tend to be tied more to the craft and the union than to a single work place or enterprise. They exalt skill and technical knowledge of the craft and industry. They think in terms of craft jurisdiction. Compared with other workers they tend to accept layoffs and discharges as inherent in the operation of the construction labor market. They tend to be relatively conservative on economic and social issues; their differences with contractors or superintendents, many of whom have come from the ranks, are confined largely to compensation. They tend to believe that all employees in the same craft or classification should receive the same compensation regardless of the branch of the industry; this often complicates the task of organizing and makes difficult the relations between the labor organizations and contractor associations. Contractors and workers and their organizations oppose seniority; they seldom resort to third-party arbitration; they oppose industrial unionism, and they continue to believe in traditional jurisdictional concepts.

We have pointed to five major features that together characterize construction industrial relations: area-wide wage and benefit determinations, jurisdiction, area pools of labor, apprenticeship and training, and the problems raised by diversity across major branches of the industry. The discussion has sought to relate these features of the construction industrial relations system to a general framework of analysis that puts emphasis on the technological and market contexts; on the relationships among contractors, labor organizations, and governmental agencies; and on the common ideas and values shared by those within this system. Although the major features of the construction industrial relations system in the United States have been only sketchily drawn, they are essential to an understanding of the geographical scope of collective bargaining in this industry.

Classification of the Geographical Scope of Bargaining

The geographical area encompassed by a collective bargaining agreement in the construction industry varies from nation- and industry-wide to a single project with a single craft and contractor, depending upon the subject matter and the parties involved. The simple classification of local or national bargaining is inapplicable and neglects significant features of this industrial relations system. Collective bargaining in the industry reflects complex interrelations that have created a vast network of agreements of varying geographical scope, applicable to differing sectors or branches of the industry. The following listing provides a classification of the *geographical scope* and the *industrial breadth* of collective bargaining in the industry, with illustrations of each type.

Nationwide for All Major Branches

The 1948 agreement creating the National Joint Board for the Settlement of Jurisdictional Disputes was entered into between the Building and Construction Trades Department, representing its nineteen affiliates as of that date, and the major national contractor associations. This agreement established machinery and procedures for the settlement of jurisdictional disputes (see the next chapter for a discussion of this machinery). It was drafted after consultation with the National Labor Relations Board. Another illustration of the industry's comprehensive approach to its problems was the statement of policy of April 7, 1959, issued by all the international unions and the major national contractor associations. They joined in creating the Construction Industry Joint Conference for promoting the industry and providing a common forum to work together on a range of mutual problems.

The OPM agreement of July 22, 1941 was made between the Building and Construction Trades Department and the major procurement agencies of the government.[5] Among other terms, it provided for uniform overtime and shift arrangements, for the preservation of customary subcontracting practices, for a no-strike provision, and for a board of review to administer the agreement. It was designed to facilitate wartime construction. The Stabilization Agreement of May 22, 1942,[6] provided for a program of wage stabilization in advance of industry generally, and wage controls by agreement were extended after V-J Day until early 1947.

The Nuclear Power Construction Stabilization Agreement of 1977 between the Building and Construction Trades Department and its international unions and the large powerplant builders, with the cooperation of the electric power utilities, is an illustration of a nation-wide agreement with all crafts for a single type of construction.

Nationwide for Particular Branches

There are a variety of both procedural and substantive agreements in this category. Several sectors of the industry have agreements providing for national machinery to settle disputes over the terms of new or expired collective bargaining agreements that cannot be settled directly between local unions of an international union and local chapters of a national association of contractors. Perhaps the most well-known is the Industrial Relations Council created in 1919 by agreement between the International Brotherhood of Electrical Workers and the National Electrical Contractors Association. This Council is operative in almost all localities and for most local affiliates of these organizations. There is no resort to a third-party neutral. Similar plans are applicable in the plumbing and piping, sheetmetal, bricklaying and tile branches of the industry and are practiced more informally in other sectors.

Then there are agreements made between international unions and national contractor groups, creating promotional bodies and trade boards to advance the interests of a particular branch of the industry. The activity of the Masonry Institute and the Lathing and Plastering Bureau and similar endeavors in the painting and decorating and sheet metal branches of the industry are illustrative. In other branches there are less formal arrangements, and national associations of contractors meet with international union officers from time to time to consider common problems.

There are agreements national in scope and applicable to a branch of the industry that are designed to promote and to administer apprenticeship programs. National joint committees, with the assistance of the Bureau of Apprenticeship, design the standards for apprenticeship and the programs of instruction, encourage and supervise local committees, and direct national and local full-time staffs. In recent years several branches of the industry—the plumbing and pipe-fitting, for instance—have provided through collective bargaining, for a national fund to be administered by joint trustees, to provide an improved quality of apprenticeship and to improve the skill of the existing journeymen. The Educational Trust Fund created by the United Association and the National Constructors Association provides for the contractors to pay into such a fund according to each hour of work by a journeyman.[7] Only if a national contractor is a member of a local association, participates in the local negotiations for a similar fund, and pays an equal or greater amount into a local fund is he relieved of the obligation to pay into the national fund.

Another group of agreements, national in scope and applicable to a whole branch of the industry, more nearly resembles ordinary collective bargaining agreements, because it contains a wide range of conditions and terms of compensation. The agreement between the National Union of Elevator Constructors and the National Elevator Manufacturing Industry, Inc. is one of these. The agreement contains the following provision on wages:

> At a meeting held in Atlantic City, July 11–16, 1921, between the representatives of Elevator Manufacturers and members of the Executive Board of the International Union of Elevator Constructors, it was agreed that the average wage rate of the five highest of the following principal building trades, namely, (1) bricklayers, (2) plasterers, (3) carpenters, (4) electricians, (5) sheetmetal workers, (6) plumbers and steamfitters, and (7) ironworkers, be accepted as the wage rate for the Elevator Constructor Mechanics. . . .

The agreement between the United Association and the National Constructors Association mentioned above provides for recognition, a definition of trade or work jurisdiction, union security, hiring procedures, shifts, reporting pay, union representatives' access to jobs, subcontracting, fabrication, grievance procedure, and other general subjects. The agreement provides for minimum wages, but higher wage rates or overtime rates negotiated locally in area agreements shall prevail. The agreements in the pipeline branch of the industry are of the same character; indeed, they provide wage scales on the basis of zones. The federal regulation of union security and hiring practices has been a factor tending to promote such substantive national agreements on these matters in some branches of the industry.

In the post-war period, so-called "national agreements" between international unions and individual contractors operating in more than one area have grown greatly in popularity. Most international unions have such standard agreement forms. These agreements traditionally provided for recognition by the contractor and for the employment of union men regardless of the area of operations, in accordance with the wages and other provisions of local agreements. This arrangement was of advantage to the international union, since the union did not then have to organize the contractor in each new area. It was an advantage to the contractor in that he had access to the local labor pool of skilled and experienced union men in any area and recourse to the international office in the event of difficulty with the local union.

But these international agreements have also created a number of problems for local contractor associations and local unions. The relations are often less than cordial between local contractors and a national contractor who has won a bid against their local competition.

And the national agreement may permit the national contractor to work during a strike against local contractors over the terms of a new agreement. It is understood that the national contractor will pay the new agreed-upon wage scale, either to the date of the strike or the date the new scale is effective on other jobs in the locality. The national agreement may be used by the contractor from out-of-town or out-of-state to seek relief through the international office from some established local practices. Or the national contractor may fear that the terms of the local agreement may not be administered as favorably in his case or that he may not receive as competent men as local contractors. Despite the various potential frictions inherent in national agreements between local and national contractors and unions, they have become even more firmly established and are a major feature of the network of relationships in the industry. The NLRB policies on hiring procedures have required revision of these provisions in national agreements and have no doubt further extended their use.

Certain national working rules have been established historically by some international unions for at least some segments of the industry. These rules have the effect of setting conditions of work, even though they are incorporated in union working rules and generally recognized by contractors rather than being incorporated into a collective bargaining agreement. The national working rules of the Iron Workers relating to structural steel erection is one example. They contained a wide range of rulings governing conditions of work—crew sizes, overtime or premium rates, and safety rules.

Area- or Locality-wide for All Major Branches

There have been a few localities in the country where all the local unions affiliated with the international unions in the Building and Construction Trades Department have negotiated agreements with a group of contractors representing all branches of the industry. The arrangements in Seattle on occasion were of this sort. This form of bargaining has the advantage of simultaneous settlement of new agreements, but the separate unions and contractor groups necessarily lose some of their individual scope of action. There are a few such agreements with a single employer, such as between the TVA and a TVA valley-wide council. But such agreements are relatively rare, and area or locality agreements normally are negotiated separately for each major segment of the industry.

Area- or Locality-wide for Particular Branches

Agreements among separate labor organizations and general and specialty contractor associations are developed for designated localities or areas. They typically apply to the commercial and industrial branches of the industry. It is these area or locality agreements that have led many observers to categorize the industry as one engaged in local bargaining. In some few areas, such as California, these same agreements have been also applied to heavy and highway construction, home building, pipelines and other branches; but the more usual arrangement is that separate agreements are negotiated to apply to heavy and highway construction and pipelines. In some localities other branches of the industry, such as home building, have agreements that differ in some respects from the principal locality or area agreement applicable to commercial and industrial construction.

One significant feature of these area or locality agreements for commercial and industrial construction is the persistent differences in their geographical scope for different crafts. The agreements for some crafts apply to a very constricted area or locality; for other crafts the area may be as broad as a state; and for still others the agreement may apply over a number of states. The geographical scope of the agreements historically applicable to San Francisco has been selected as an illustration. We have listed these agreements in rough order from those with the widest scope to those with the narrowest. The territory is here only roughly defined in terms of number of counties or other general indication, although the text of the agreements name the precise counties. (The same listing of the number of counties does not necessarily mean the territory is identical.) The geographical territory beyond the scope of the cited agreement is not only subject to a different agreement but the wage rates are different and tend to change at a different time.

Wide Area

Boilermakers	Eight western states including Alaska
Asbestos Workers	Northern California and most of Nevada
Operating Engineers	Northern California and most of Nevada
Iron Workers	All of California and 11 counties in Nevada
Marble Setters	Northern California and most of Nevada

Medium Area

Pile Drivers	Northern California
Cement Masons	Northern California
Elevator Constructors	Northern California
Teamsters	Northern California—but separate rates for 2 counties
Laborers	Northern California—but separate rate for 1 county
Tile Setters	17 counties
Bricklayers and Stone- masons	12 counties
Painters	10 counties
Sprinkler Fitters	9 counties

Narrow Area

Carpenters	4 counties
Glaziers	4 counties
Electricians	4 counties each with separate agreement
Plumbers	4 counties
Steam Fitters	4 counties
Roofers	2 counties
Sheet Metal Workers	2 counties
Lathers	San Francisco and part of San Mateo
Plasterers	San Francisco

These groupings are not in all respects typical of the country at large. In particular, the Laborer and Teamster classifications here prevail over an area relatively broader in scope than in the country generally, because of the uniformity of heavy and highway and commercial agreements. The Sheet Metal Workers, on the other hand, appear to be narrower in scope than generally is the case. In addition to the above area zones for commercial, home building, and heavy and highway work, for San Francisco there are separate agreements and zones applicable for some crafts in dredging work (operating engineers) and transmission line construction (electricians). In most areas of the country there would be separate rates and classifications and other zones for heavy and highway work, for pipeline construction, and in some localities for home building. But within commercial and industrial work there would be a similar and consistent pattern of variation in the area, subject to the respective area or locality collective bargaining agreements setting wage rates and fringe benefits. These systematic patterns of variations are evident in the wage determinations of the Secretary of Labor on federally financed construction, which reflect the actual wage rates paid.

Project-wide for All Branches or Single Crafts

Project-wide agreements applicable to all crafts have been negotiated on a few very large and relatively isolated projects, between the contractor or group of contractors on the project and the international unions or the Building and Construction Trades Department, authorized to represent the international unions. These have included the Hungry Horse Dam, the Portsmouth, Ohio atomic energy project, the Taconite project in northern Minnesota, and a few oil, chemical, and power plant jobs. These agreements were designed to deal with special problems of travel expenses, travel time, isolation pay, or particularly difficult and unruly local labor conditions. Project agreements became very much more common in the late 1960s and 1970s. The widespread resort to project agreements with terms at variance from the relevant locality or area agreements tend to create problems for both local contractors and unions and often magnify the stress between local and national organizations on both sides.

The agreements providing for continuing contract maintenance, patterned after the 1955 Tidewater project agreement, are signed between the international unions and a single contractor engaged in continuing maintenance work. The agreement provides for time and a half rather than double time, and the agreement precludes travel expenses. The agreement applies only to a given plant or project and may provide for a lower rate such as 80 percent of the construction scale.

The geographical scope of bargaining thus reflects a wide variety of arrangements—from at one extreme, nationwide bargaining with all branches and sectors of the industry to, at the other, locality agreements with a local contractor association and local union, or a project agreement. The geographical scope of bargaining varies not alone with the issues but also varies systematically among crafts and sectors and among branches.

Significant Developments in the Scope of Bargaining

There have been four major developments in the structure of collective bargaining in the construction industry: (1) there has been some tendency for the geographical scope of agreements to widen, but there are still persistent differences in the geographical scope of agreements applicable to the various crafts; (2) national agreements between international unions and individual contractors and associations of contractors have become more important, and there is a marked tendency for these agreements to incorporate more substantive terms; (3) there is a tendency in some branches of the industry and for some crafts to develop an increasing number of classifications with separate wage rates for each—for example, the operating engineers, laborers, and teamsters on heavy and highway work, who are using increasingly more mechanization and new equipment; and (4) there is growing recognition of differentiation in wages and other conditions among some major branches of the construction industry. The agreements in heavy and highway and pipeline construction may be cited.

The persistence of variations in the geographical scope of agreements among crafts requires explanation. Why are agreements between boilermakers and their contractors, as has been noted, typically multi-state, and carpenter agreements with their contractors among the narrowest in scope? Although a number of factors contribute to such persistent differences among crafts, the two basic factors operative are the volume of work of the craft available on a continuing basis in a locality relative to the number of journeymen, and the related area over which a number of local contractors typically travel to bid for work. In some types of work a number of men may be required in a locality while a job is in process; but after that, continuing work will not be available there, and the men will have to travel to secure continuing jobs. The work of boilermakers on tanks and power houses is of this sort. The Boilermakers international union may also have been influenced in the policy for wide areas by its participation in the railroad and shipbuilding industries. In the case of the carpenters, at the other extreme, there is a large volume of continuing work even within a locality of modest size, and traveling is not so essential for many workers to secure continuing employment.

When a contractor employs operating engineers—particularly on heavy and highway work—he may require a large territory to find such projects and in which to keep expensive machinery in continual use. The factor of the relative amount of continuing work in a locality operates on both the contractors and the workers.

The hard realities of financing local labor organizations also play a role. A certain size of membership at a given dues structure is required to finance a local union and a full-time union representative. Crafts and trades with a relatively small membership in a locality (when all work in the jurisdiction in the locality is organized) are required to extend the geographical limits of a local union to secure the requisite membership to support a full-time representative. Many international unions are concerned with establishing local unions with territorial jurisdictions in which they may be self-supporting.

The greater ease of transportation and communications in recent years for both workers and contractors has been the major factor extending the geographical scope of a single rate. The geographical dimensions of wage contours have widened as a consequence of technical and market changes, at least within a single major branch of the industry such as commercial or heavy and highway work. Additional aspects of these technical and market developments have been the growth of suburbs, the growth of the highway system and the use of automobiles, the development of major projects—particularly in defense industry—in rural and more remote areas, and the resultant need to import skilled labor.

The most striking instances of the growth in new classifications are related to mechanization in the work of operating engineers on heavy and highway work. The San Francisco schedule, for instance, contains 96 classifications divided into 13 wage brackets. The higher rate for the more complex machines no doubt reflects the familiar features of wage determination, in which greater skill or responsibility and higher productivity affect wage rates for individual classifications. There is some tendency for the emergence of additional classifications in other crafts, as a consequence of further specialization. This is a persistent tendency in the wide range of work operations of the carpenters, particularly in the homebuilding branch of the industry. While a number of specialties are recognized in many areas, such as hard floor layers, shinglers, dry wall erectors, scaffold erectors, acoustical appliers, form builders, cabinetmakers, and millwrights, the international union tends to a degree to constrain these developments in the interests of more broadly trained men and as a protection against the changing fortunes of narrow specialists. Moreover, rate differentials among these specialties may not be large; a number may carry the same rate as the journeyman carpenter.[8] Similar developments have occurred in the bricklayers with specialties of stonemason, tuck pointers, caulkers and cleaners, and blocklayers. Other crafts reflect similar developments.

The impact of widely differentiated product markets in various branches of the industry—for example, heavy and highway compared with commercial work—has resulted in most localities in different wage scales and conditions of work for the major branches of the industry. The failure of local unions to recognize such differentiated product market conditions often has meant that the labor organizations were unable to organize or to keep organized the heavy and highway branch of the industry on the basis of the wage scales and working conditions that were developed for commercial work. The outstanding organizing success of the Pact of Four (operating engineers, laborers, carpenters, and teamsters) in heavy and highway construction emphasized the importance of the separate agreements for this branch of the industry.

The greater role of national agreements must in part be related to the greater role of government activity in the industry—for example, the concern with hiring practices and union security. The large size of many projects—the billion-dollar job—and the geographical diversification of work, often involving remote areas, have also played a role in the development of national agreements in particular branches of the industry. Periods of high employment and labor shortages, as in the late 1960s and early 1970s tend to extend the scope of high wage rates and benefits while periods of protracted unemployment, as in the early 1980s tend to restrict the scope of area rates.

The significant developments in the bargaining arrangements in the industry are: an expansion in the geographical scope of agreements, the greater role of the national agreement, the increasing number of classifications and specialties in some crafts and branches of the industry, and the development of separate agreements for major branches of the industry. These developments can be related directly to the changes in technology and markets and the changing public policies affecting the construction industrial relations system.

Implications Beyond Construction

Although this chapter has been concerned with collective bargaining in the building and construction industry, with its distinctive features, compared with the more familiar arrangements in industrial plants, there are a number of other implications for a more general analysis and appraisal of collective bargaining, as follows.

1. *No single major feature of collective bargaining in this industry, such as the geographical scope of bargaining and area-wide agreements, or jurisdiction, or hiring arrangements, can be understood apart from the construction industrial relations system as a whole.* These separate features are not accidental; they are parts of an interdependent whole that is understood most fully in terms of an explicit frame of reference. This frame of reference includes the technological context, the market environment, and the status of labor organizations, contractor associations and government agencies, as defined by the community and reflected in a common body of ideas and values. Moreover, long-term changes in these features of construction are related to changes in these fundamentals of any industrial relations system. The method of analysis can be applied generally, and the industrial relations arrangements in any industry or country can be illuminated by this framework.

2. *The geographical scope of collective bargaining varies with the problem or issue.* In construction some questions have been settled by agreements applicable to all international unions and national contractor associations. At the other extreme, some questions have been settled by agreements between local contractors and local unions for a locality or even for a project. It is a gross oversimplification to classify collective bargaining as local or national. Indeed, great mischief has been done by seeking to settle some questions locally that, given the fundamentals of a system, can only be effectively settled nationally. Conversely, other questions have been assigned to national settlement that in the nature of the system require local settlement. The simple fact is that the geographical scope of collective bargaining is necessarily related to an issue or subject matter.[9] Moreover, this relationship is not fixed forever; fundamental developments in the

structure of an industrial relations system tend to expand or to narrow the geographical scope of bargaining on a particular subject matter.

3. *Public policy under labor-management legislation from the Wagner Act on has contributed to unreality in a number of ways.* In the unique industrial relations system of the United States, the government determines an election district in which employees vote for or against representation by a labor organization. The government has designated the election district as the collective bargaining unit. The election district and the scope of the parties represented at the collective bargaining table do not necessarily have any relationship to each other. The true bargaining unit is often not the election district. Further, the area of direct and immediate application of any agreement is often broader than the parties actually represented or directly participating in the bargaining sessions. It is imperative that we separate these three concepts—the election district, the actual negotiating unit on the specific issue, and the area of direct impact of any settlement—recognizing that indirect ripples of a major settlement may be very wide. In the steel industry, for example, certification of election districts is the production and maintenance workers of a single plant; the scope of negotiations on general wage changes has been eleven or twelve companies; and the area of direct impact is the basic steel industry. The public regulation or determination of the election district in the United States has only indirect bearing on the actual scope of bargaining.

4. *The actual scope of the direct impact of an agreement on one issue or group of problems in collective bargaining also is relatively independent of the scope of the parties directly engaged in the bargaining across the table.* It makes only little difference for the area of impact whether there is a formal association, an inner steering committee, a few leaders, or a single wage and industrial relations leader. The form of the bargaining is relatively unimportant. The terms and the level of the settlement may be affected to a degree, but the area of impact depends on more fundamental features of the industrial relations system. The most decisive factors are the nature of the related product and labor markets.

5. *Persons with experience in collective bargaining find it congenial to recognize that the area of direct impact of a settlement is affected significantly by the character of product market competition, over and above labor market considerations.* The product market is one dimension defining a wage contour.[10] Thus in construction, as noted above, for identical classifications performing commercial construction and heavy and highway or pipeline construction, separate rates prevail for most localities in the United States. This is no passing or temporary aberration in the markets, although in some localities

long-run changes in these differentials may occur, including even their elimination. There are many instances of the decisive role of product markets in defining the limits or scope of a settlement. The local trucking field, with different rates for various branches of the industry, is another illustration.

6. *The analysis of the scope of bargaining and the area of impact of settlements suggests an inherent inconsistency between the realities of product and labor markets and the public determination of election districts in which workers freely choose their bargaining representatives.* It may be intemperate to say so, but there are many situations in which the announced policy of the Wagner Act does not fit the facts of life. When a multi-plant company dealing with a single union establishes a new plant, the company is often most anxious that the free choice of the new workers be of a certain kind.[11] So is the union. The company does not want to educate a new national union about its problems, its method of wage payment, or its internal wage structure and benefit plans, or to face conflicts of principle over these questions with a new union that approaches the issues with a different policy. The old union does not wish to face competition at a new and strategic plant. Within the law there are a variety of ways in which the parties may control the situation. The practice in the construction industry of organizing contractors and workers separately without benefit of elections represents basically the same view that the election process may yield results intolerable to the realities of product and labor markets and the policies of enterprises and labor organizations. The policy of governmental determination of election districts and free choice by workers continues to pose many difficult problems—problems on the one hand for multi-plant companies and associations and on the other hand for labor organizations seeking to develop a private means of settling no-raiding disputes or seeking to revive the concepts of traditional jurisdiction.

7. *There is a growing body of writers who believe that public policy should intervene in determining the actual scope of negotiations.* The following view of Professor Edward H. Chamberlin is illustrative: ". . . it appears to me as a matter of principle that the size of unions and the size of bargaining units in different areas of the economy—in short, the structure of labor organization—should be dictated by the public interest rather than by the desires of the laborers concerned."[12] This view fails to understand the distinction between the government determination of the scope of bargaining on an issue and the area of direct impact. The scope of bargaining is determined by much more than "the desires of the laborers concerned." The structure of labor organizations and the scope of bargaining are not uniquely related, and the scope of bargaining varies

widely by issue. Moreover, the notion that there is an operational test or that there are definable guideposts by which to judge the public interest in this matter—by legislation, the courts, or administrative agencies—appears to me unwarranted. Those who would advocate the public determination of the geographical scope of bargaining must some day reply to the repeated challenges to come forth with a specific range of proposals.

8. *Any discussion of the scope of bargaining highlights the difficulties and conflicts inherent in relating the choices of workers and their aspirations to the constraints of product and labor markets.* An organization of employees must seek to reconcile the often inconsistent desires of a large group of diverse workers. The establishment of priorities and hard choices among a group of workers is one of the most important functions of a labor organization and the collective bargaining process in the American community. This function has not received adequate recognition. At the same time, these conflicting preferences of groups of workers must be related in bargaining to the evolving technology, changing market constraints, and changing community expectations and values.

Endnotes

1. See John T. Dunlop, "Labor-Management Relations," in *Design and the Production of Homes*, Burnham Kelley and Associates (New York: McGraw-Hill Book Co., 1959), pp. 259–301; William Haber and Harold M. Levinson, *Labor Relations and Productivity in the Building Trades* (Ann Arbor: University of Michigan, Bureau of Industrial Relations, 1956); Gordon W. Bertram and Sherman J. Maisel, *Industrial Relations in the Construction Industry, The Northern California Experience* (Berkeley: University of California, 1955). Also see Daniel Q. Mills, *Industrial Relations and Manpower in Construction* (Cambridge, Mass.: M.I.T. Press, 1972); U.S. Department of Labor, Labor-Management Services Administration, *The Bargaining Structure in Construction: Problems and Prospects*, 1980.

2. John T. Dunlop, *Industrial Relations Systems* (New York: Henry Holt & Co., 1958). See, particularly, Chapters 1–3 and 6.

3. Economists have largely neglected the product market structure and nature of competitive and monopoly elements in contract construction.

4. A complete explanation of jurisdiction would indicate a role for craft unionism that is ordinarily made to bear the full explanation. Jurisdiction is substantially a reflection of both product market and labor market factors, and jurisdictional disputes arise no less on account of conflicts among contractors than as the result of union craft rivalries.

5. For the text of the agreement, see John T. Dunlop and Arthur Hill, *The Wage Adjustment Board, Wartime Stabilization in the Building and Construction Industry* (Cambridge, Mass.: Harvard University Press, 1949), p. 138.

6. For the text, see *Ibid.*, p. 141.

7. Article 8 of the July 1, 1958 agreement.

8. See Walter Galenson, *The United Brotherhood of Carpenters, The First Hundred Years* (Cambridge, Mass.: Harvard University Press, 1983).

9. In many western European countries there are different labor organizations for industry-wide and plant-level negotiations. The role of the works council deserves more study.

10. See John T. Dunlop, "The Task of Contemporary Wage Theory," in *New Concepts in Wage Determination*, eds., George W. Taylor and Frank C. Pierson (New York: McGraw-Hill Book Co., 1957), pp. 131–34.

11. There are, of course, some companies that prefer and may pursue policies designed to encourage diverse representation in their plants or no representation.

12. E. H. Chamberlin, "Labor Union Power and the Public Interest," in *The Public Stake in Union Power*, ed. Philip D. Bradley (Charlottesville, Va.: University of Virginia Press, 1959), p. 20.

Chapter 11

RESOLUTION OF JURISDICTIONAL DISPUTES IN CONSTRUCTION

In the construction industrial relations setting analyzed in the last chapter, an endemic and peculiar class of disputes concerns work assignments and craft jurisdiction.[1] An understanding of the way in which labor unions, contractors, and government have grappled with machinery appropriate to these disputes should provide insight into problems of dispute resolution as they are embedded in this distinctive setting.

On June 23, 1947 Congress overrode President Harry Truman's veto of the Taft-Hartley bill and the Labor Management Relations Act of 1947 was to become law. President Truman had requested legislation to prevent work stoppages over jurisdictional disputes. Under the new law it was an unfair labor practice for a labor organization:

> . . .*to engage in or to induce or encourage employees . . . to engage in a strike . . . or to threaten, coerce or restrain . . . where an object is:*
>
> *(D) forcing or requiring any employer to assign particular work to employees in a particular labor organization or in a particular trade, craft, or class rather than to employees in another labor organization or in another trade, craft, or class, unless such employer is failing to conform to an order or certification of the Board determining the bargaining representative for employees performing such work." Section 8(B) (4)D*

The Taft-Hartley amendments also provided that the General Counsel of the NLRB, at his discretion, could seek an injunction in the federal district courts to terminate any such work stoppage. Further, under Section 10 (k) of the statute the NLRB:

". . . is empowered and directed to hear and determine the dispute out
of which such unfair labor practice shall have arisen, unless, within ten
days after notice that such charge has been filed, the parties to such
dispute submit to the Board satisfactory evidence that they have adjusted, or agreed upon methods for the voluntary adjustment of the
dispute. . . ."

Following enactment of the prohibition against strikes in disputes
over work assignments, which had been targeted in legislative discussion on construction, the leaders of the Building and Construction
Trades Department and the leaders of the major national contractor
associations approached me to assist in developing an effective private
machinery which the statute appeared explicitly to encourage. I had
worked with these national representatives as a public member of the
Wage Adjustment Board, the wartime construction stabilization and
dispute settling agency under the aegis of the War Labor Board.[2]

The agreement creating the National Joint Board for the Settlement of Jurisdictional Disputes in the Building and Construction
Industry, reorganized as the Impartial Jurisdictional Disputes Board
in 1973, was developed with the active support of the Chairman of
the NLRB and detailed assistance of the General Counsel, a new
office in the agency.[3] The Board and General Counsel were anxious
to avoid involvement in this complex area in an industry in which it
has no experience, since the National Labor Relations Act was not
applied as a matter of policy to construction in the years 1935–47. In
these circumstances, I accepted the post of impartial chairman of the
National Joint Board, starting April 1, 1948, on a day-a-week basis,
and was to remain for almost 10 years. Later I served for 3 years as
chairman of an appeals board, a new post in the machinery. The
National Joint Board was equally divided between labor and contractor representatives and in turn equally divided between representatives of the general and specialty contractors and the basic and specialty trades, reflecting the fundamental structure of organization of
labor and management in the industry. After 1973 the Impartial
Jurisdictional Disputes Board was comprised solely of three "impartial members who are knowledgeable or experienced in construction."

Exclusive Jurisdiction and Work Assignments

The constitution of the AFL from the 1880s until merger with the
CIO in 1955 provided for the principle of exclusive jurisdiction
among constituent national unions. Each national union was to have a
clear grant of jurisdiction and one—and only one—union was to have
title to particular work. The constitution provided:

*No charter shall be granted by the American Federation of Labor to
any National, International, Trade, or Federal Labor Unions without a
positive and clear definition of trade jurisdiction claimed by the appli-
cant, and the charter shall not be granted if the jurisdiction claimed is a
trespass on the jurisdiction of existing affiliated unions, without the
written consent of such unions. . . . (Article IX, Section 11)*

Jurisdiction was understood as a property right; the reference to
"trespass" in the constitution underscores the analogy to property.
Jurisdiction was exchanged among national unions[4] or recognized to
be the property of one union rather than another, for a term of years.[5]

A continuing problem for the AFL with the concept of jurisdiction,
prior to 1935 and the Wagner Act, was enforcement and compliance
with decisions of the Federation. The ultimate decisions in the AFL
on jurisdiction were made by the Executive Council and the convention, and the ultimate instrument of compliance was expulsion from
the Federation for non-compliance, not a very satisfactory remedy for
a voluntary federation, particularly when used against a large affiliate
with considerable market power.[6]

The passage of the Wagner Act in 1935 granted to the NLRB the
authority throughout industry to determine bargaining units—more
accurately, election districts. Before the Wagner Act the AFL asserted the authority to determine the union a worker should join in
each job territory; thereafter the government through the NLRB had
the authority to specify election districts, craft or industrial, for instance, and workers voted on representation questions regardless of
the AFL's views on union jurisdiction. Carpenters might be represented by a rubber union or plumbers by a cement union rather than
the union which had been granted exclusionary jurisdiction.[7] The
split within the labor movement in the period 1938–55, with the
resulting open competition and rivalry, ended for most of industry
the determination of jurisdiction within the labor movement. The
merged federation, AFL-CIO, adopted as its central constitutional
provision relating to constituent national unions, that each affiliate
shall respect the "established collective bargaining relationship" of all
other affiliates, and further provided in Article 20 for internal machinery to prevent raiding among affiliates. The basic constitutional
provisions of the federation and its internal machinery after 1955 thus
were again congruent with federal law.[8]

In the construction industry under collective bargaining the developments were quite different.[9] With the tacit agreement of construction unions and contractors the NLRB as a matter of policy did not
hold elections in construction under the Wagner Act.[10] The CIO did
not make significant inroads into construction, and the unions, the
contractors, and the government continued the policies of the past

(except for the wartime relationship) until the passage of the Taft-Hartley amendments in 1947. The latter led to the creation of the National Joint Board by national agreement and to the processing of cases under unfair labor practices provisions of the statute.

The national contractor associations welcomed making jurisdictional strikes an unfair labor practice, but they were anxious in 1947 to develop an effective private jurisdictional dispute machinery for the industry. They had no experience with the NLRB and were concerned over potential substantive decisions the government might make under Section 10(k) procedures. The time required for the government to act—certainly to make a decision—would be longer than private machinery. There was a history of contractor participation in national private machinery to resolve jurisdictional disputes[11] and in local plans in Chicago and New York. The period of constructive cooperation in wartime, moreover, was a recent experience.

The differences among types of contractors is a major factor contributing to work assignment and jurisdictional disputes. General contractors and specialty contractors are in competition with each other, and national contractors are in competition with both. Local contractors often resent visiting contractors coming into an area and bidding jobs away from them. A number of contractors on a single project create somewhat artificial boundary lines between the work to be performed by each. Different assignments by different contractors for identical work on the same project is likely to create serious disputes. Superintendents and contractors often have come out of particular crafts and may even maintain union membership; accordingly they may be regarded as less than dispassionate in making work assignments among competing trades. The fact that some unions work exclusively, as a matter of policy or custom, for particular contractors, and that particular contractors tend to hire a single craft tends to convert competition among contractors into jurisdictional disputes among unions. Some of the most serious disputes involve a contractor with an associated union contending against a different contractor and an associated union. One illustration is the dispute between a general contractor and the Carpenters, on one side against a specialty contractor and the Iron Workers, in the other, over the installation of metal windows. The specifications and boundary lines in the package of bids developed by the architect and the owner often further complicate such controversies by providing subcontracts at variance with established jurisdictional lines. Thus, supporting iron, the jurisdiction of iron workers, might be included in an electrical subcontract.

Work assignments and practices do in fact vary widely across the country from community to community on many work items. The degree of specialization will vary with the size of operations and the amount of construction activity. Contractors may be influenced at a particular time by financial stringency. Local unions of an international union differ in their organization and policies across the country. Jurisdictional issues may be intertwined with myriad other industrial relations and bargaining issues.

The fact that jurisdictional disputes so frequently result in work stoppages needs attention. The limited duration of construction jobs contributes to work stoppages. If the work is not stopped, in the eyes of the complaining union, there may be no work left to be done. Contractors shut down work or switch assignments that are in controversy to avoid difficulties on a project. The time factor in construction is central to all procedures for settling jurisdictional disputes. Strategically placed crafts, at different stages of construction of a project, are able to exert maximum pressure on a contractor.

It is surprising that the literature on jurisdictional disputes in construction has regarded jurisdictional disputes solely as conflicts among unions, not recognizing the deep involvement and conflicts among types of contractors that contribute fundamentally to the class of disputes.[12] The statutory prohibition proceeds from this same assumption that jurisdictional disputes are a union creation. But nothing is farther from reality. Contractors are inextricably involved in the generation of these disputes (some types of jurisdictional disputes more than others), and they need to be involved in any viable and practical procedures to resolve them. It would be impractical for unions to resolve these disputes themselves. National leaders of the contractor associations have generally recognized this involvement and have been anxious to have a role in jurisdictional dispute settlement when they are governed by collective agreements. Indeed, jurisdictional disputes are an inherent and integral part of labor-management relations in construction under collective bargaining, and machinery for resolution of disputes is a necessary part of national negotiations in the industry.

The Operations of the National Joint Board

The agreement creating the Plan for Settling Jurisdictional Disputes in 1948 envisaged four functions for the National Joint Board and its impartial chairman: (1) restoration of work operations on a project shut down by a union or a contractor in a jurisdictional dispute, (2) a job decision on disputed work on a particular project with particular contractors, (3) the mediation of national agreements resolving continuing disputes between national unions with the participation of national contractor associations, as appropriate, or the establishment of a hearings panel to render a national decision on a recurrent disputed issue, and (4) the maintenance of close working relations with the General Counsel of the NLRB so as to settle disputes to the maximum degree possible and thus to avoid litigation and precedents adverse to the private machinery.

The National Joint Board codified, initially on October 20, 1949, its Procedural Rules[13] clearly specifying the responsibility of contractors to make work assignments, the standards for assignments, and the relative responsibility of various contractors on a project. These rules also defined the responsibility of various contractors on a project. These rules also defined the responsibility of local and national unions to maintain members at work, to forbid strikes and picketing, and to process cases before the National Joint Board; they also prescribed the procedures used by the National Joint Board in its operations. These Procedural Rules, amended from time to time in the light of further experience, have contributed significantly over the years to the standardization of procedures for work assignment problems in an industry previously without such standards.

In its early work the National Joint Board developed a viable compromise between the traditional principle that jurisdiction and work assignment are national and uniform as represented by national decisions or recognized national trade practice or by national agreements and the fact that on many work tasks there are wide differences in craft assignments among localities. The National Joint Board, with the subsequent approval of the negotiators of the Plan, created the additional standard of prevailing local practice. On individual issues the National Joint Board would have to decide whether the applicable standard was an applicable national decision, a widely recognized national trade practice, an applicable national agreement among contending trades, or a prevailing local practice. The board had to define the appropriate area and to evaluate the evidence presented by all parties to the case. The board was also authorized to consider the efficiency and economy of operations, or in the language of more recent agreements, "The board shall not ignore the interests of the consumer in settling jurisdictional disputes."

In making job decisions, the positions of the contending national unions and a detailed description of the disputed work, including drawings and specifications and views of the affected contractors, were required by the National Joint Board procedures. In the period May 1, 1948 to June 30, 1957, the National Joint Board held 375 meetings, making an average of approximately 10 job decisions a session.[14] In the years 1951–55 the statistics of the National Joint Board show that it handled 450 to 500 work stoppages a year by unions and another 40 to 50 cases a year in which contractors shut down work in a jurisdictional dispute. The issues in dispute that resulted in work stoppages and job decisions showed a considerable shift from year to year.[15] The contending unions and the sections of the country involved showed considerable variation. A special effort was made to settle by national agreement those issues that reflected continuing difficulty.

In the years 1948–57 six national decisions were made by the machinery provided for in the Plan,[16] and 33 new national agreements were negotiated between national unions,[17] with the involvement of affected national contractor associations in a number of cases. Most of these agreements involved my active mediation. As stated in a 1957 Summary Report to the negotiators of the Plan, "The record of the past ten years demonstrates that the national settlement of jurisdictional issues by agreement is the very best way to resolve these questions." In most of these cases joint committees of the contending unions developed the agreement, and the two unions were encouraged to designate a pair of jurisdictional administrators to settle disputes directly without resort to the National Joint Board and to keep the agreement current with new developments and problems.

Insofar as possible the machinery to make job decisions or national decisions in fact operated to work out practical solutions on a consensual and unanimous basis within the board and the hearings panels for national decisions. Indeed, in the course of handling thousands of job decisions and the few national decisions, I almost never cast a deciding vote as chairman. Contending unions and contractors are more likely, in my experience, to comply with "decisions" and settle future disputes of a similar nature if they have a consensual role in the process and in the result, even if the "decision" is adverse.

A cooperative working relationship was established throughout this period between the office of the General Counsel of the NLRB and the National Joint Board, providing notice of all charges filed within the scope of the private machinery. The objective was to settle all cases and secure the withdrawal of the charges. Periodic conferences were also held with the chairman of the NLRB. A body of public law appeared to be developing to assure stability for the private method of settling jurisdictional disputes in construction.[18]

The Machinery After 1957

The negotiators of the Plan decided to make the Chairman of the National Joint Board a full-time position after 1959. Rather than name an established arbitrator or mediator, the parties selected four successive contractor representatives with experience on the board to be chairman after 1957.[19]

The National Joint Board has continued to be influential in the restoration of work operations closed down in jurisdictional disputes by unions or contractors choosing to use the Plan (probably the vast majority of contractors under collective agreements). But the Plan has been less effective in resolving disputes on a mutually acceptable job basis by national agreements or decisions. Indeed, very few national agreements have been negotiated, and there have been no national decisions since the January 15, 1968 hearings panel decision on the installation of ceiling systems. The National Joint Board or the Impartial Jurisdictional Board seems not to have recognized adequately that consent and acceptability are indispensable or that "decisions" are not self-enforcing. The private machinery has been particularly unprepared in dealing with the NLRB after the 1960s.

It is in the relations between the private machinery and the NLRB and the courts that the most decisive damage has been done to the original conception of an industrywide jurisdictional machinery for labor and management engaged in collective bargaining in construction. The NLRB members and the succeeding General Counsels have shown relatively little interest in sustaining the private machinery. Thus, reporting immediately to the Washington office all charges on jurisdictional disputes or other charges such as secondary boycotts that may be designed to circumvent the private machinery is essential to the operation of private machinery as an effective instrument. This working relationship has ceased to be effective.

A number of conceptual difficulties have arisen in relating public law to the characteristics of the construction industry, particularly the operations of contractors and their national associations.[20] The view of the Board and the courts required that each contractor be stipulated to be bound by the machinery in order that the public procedures yield to the private machinery. (On the union side there was no such problem, since all national unions are bound by the constitution of the Building and Construction Trades Department and local unions are bound by their national union constitutions as to jurisdiction as a historical matter. Only if a national union left the Department could it escape the Plan.) With hundreds of thousands of contractors, with 15 or 20 per cent entry-and-exit rates per year, with ambiguities as to parties bound by thousands of local agreements, and with vast uncertainties and limitations on the constitutional powers of most national associations of contractors, it is most difficult to bind individual contractors to the National Joint Board when a union requests some action or when a contractor requests some relief that may affect another contractor on the site.

For practical purposes, after the mid-1960s, recalcitrant contractors were clearly able to have their choice on a project-by-project basis of the private machinery, with its advantages of speed and informality, or the NLRB and its injunctions and 10 (k) determinations. These determinations, in clear violation of the original intent of the legislation in my view, have supported virtually without exception any assignment of work made by a contractor unstipulated to be bound by the private machinery, regardless of the precedents in similar disputes under the private machinery. An invariant decision to support contractor assignments is not responsive to the mandate to "hear and determine the dispute" out of which the unfair labor practice arose. This state of affairs is completely at variance, moreover, with the support and design of the General Counsel and NLRB in 1947–48. Perhaps a more supportive position might have been maintained had the private machinery been better able to articulate, in opinions in cases involving litigation, the basis for its decisions.[21]

This is not the place to purpose remedies. The general labor law that developed around industrial plants, whatever its merits there, does not well fit construction. The NLRB and the courts have been loath to develop industry-specific applications, despite serious issues of application in a number of industries with highly specialized technological and market contexts such as those in construction and maritime. But the legal framework of collective bargaining in construction is so ambiguous and so remote from facilitating responsible negotiations at levels appropriate to the serious problems of the parties that a major reconstruction of collective bargaining is in order. There is no viable procedure to determine representation[22]; job-by-job elections are a travesty. Contractor associations have little capacity responsibly to represent or bind their members, since they can come and go almost at will. Labor-management relations on the typical project with many contractors remains a problem. Owners on large projects have come increasingly to be directly involved in industrial relations in construction.[23] The relative role of national and local parties needs a new assessment. It is only in the full review of the legal framework of labor-management relationships in construction that the jurisdictional machinery and its relations to public law should be remedied. To seek to consider the problems separately would be ineffective.

Endnotes

1. See my earlier writings on this subject: "Jurisdictional Disputes," *Proceedings of the New York University Second Annual Conference on Labor* (New York: Matthew Bender Inc., 1949), pp. 477–504; Note: "Jurisdictional Strike Statistics," *Review of Economics and Statistics*, (May 1950), pp. 162–63; "Jurisdic-

tional Disputes: 10 Types," *The Constructor* (July 1953), pp. 165 ff.; "Arbitration of Jurisdictional Disputes in the Building Industry," in *Arbitration Today*, Proceedings of the Eighth Annual Meeting of the National Academy of Arbitrators (Washington, D.C.: BNA Incorporated, 1955), pp. 161–66; *The Resolution of Jurisdictional Disputes in the Building Trades and Economic Prospects for the Industry*, Proceedings of a Conference, June 28, 1957, Institutes of Labor and Industrial Relations, Michigan.

2. John T. Dunlop and Arthur D. Hill, *The Wage Adjustment Board, Wartime Stabilization in the Building and Construction Industry* (Cambridge, Massachusetts: Harvard University Press, 1950). The Wage Adjustment Board operated as a tripartite agency in the period 1943–47.

3. See *Plan for Settling Jurisdictional Disputes Nationally and Locally*. The "Green Book" (starting in 1948) contains the text of this Agreement as amended over the years. The booklet is published by the Building and Construction Trades Department, AFL-CIO. The most recent edition is dated June 1, 1977.

   The General Counsel drafted Article VI of the original Agreement (Article XIII of the 1977 Agreement) which was designed to reflect the relationship mutually envisaged between the NLRB and the private machinery: "It is the sense of the parties hereto that the members and the Chairman of the Joint Board shall tender to the National Labor Relations Board their services as expert witnesses in any hearing held by the Board under the provisions of Section 10 (k) . . . and that no fees shall be charged for such service beyond the statutory witness fees and mileage allowance."

4. In 1926 the Lathers and Sheetmetal Workers entered into an agreement under which the Sheetmetal Workers secured particular types of metal cove base and metal window stool and frame. Two years later the Sheetmetal Workers transferred some of this same work to the Carpenters in an agreement. Agreements of Record, January 12, 1926 and March 21, 1928, Green Book.

5. Reinforcing rod work in concrete construction was agreed upon to be the Lathers, Local 46, in New York City rather than Iron Workers as elsewhere in the country; the work reverted to the Iron Workers in the merger agreement between the Carpenters and the Lathers, effective on September 10, 1979.

6. Outside of the Plan for Settling Jurisdictional Disputes nationally and locally, I served as mediator to resolve by agreement the long-standing major dispute between the International Association of Machinists and the United Brotherhood of Carpenters and Joiners of America. The agreement is dated September 18, 1954.

7. See the speech by Vice President Woll which clearly recognized this consequence of the Wagner Act. *Report of the Proceedings of the Fifty-Fifth Annual Convention of the American Federation of Labor*, 1935, pp. 528–34.

8. See Arthur J. Goldberg, *AFL-CIO Labor United* (New York: McGraw-Hill Book Company, Inc., 1956), pp. 141–45, 238.

9. Developments were also somewhat different in the railroad and airline industries, with the National Mediation Board and historically established class or craft certifications with continuing employment patterns.

10. Brown and Root, 51NLRB820. A pilot union shop election was held on May 10, 1948 in the heavy construction industry in Western Pennsylvania for a basic trades unit. No further area-wide elections were attempted. Relatively few project-basis representation elections have been held; the election process which is

otherwise standard procedure for determining questions of representation in American industry is not used in construction, as a practical matter.

11. See William Haber, *Industrial Relations in the Building Industry* (Cambridge, Mass.: Harvard University Press, 1930), pp. 180–190. The National Board for Jurisdictional Awards, 1919–27, is relevant.

12. See, for instance, Solomon Blum, *Jurisdictional Disputes Resulting from Structural Differences in American Trade Unions* (University of California Publications in Economics, September 27, 1913); Nathaniel Ruggles Whitney, *Jurisdiction in American Building Trades* (Baltimore: Johns Hopkins Press, 1914). William Haber and Harold M. Levinson, in *Labor Relations and Productivity in the Building Trades* (Ann Arbor, Michigan; Bureau of Industrial Relations, 1956), drawing on my 1949 New York University article cited above state only generally, "The business organizations of the construction industry must also accept some responsibility for the existence of interunion conflict," p. 231.

13. *Procedural Rules and Regulations of the National Joint Board for Settlement of Jurisdictional Disputes, Building and Construction Industry*, October 29, 1947 as subsequently amended. The latest rules are dated June 1, 1977.

14. The National Joint Board held 1104 meetings from 1948 to 1973, and the Impartial Jurisdictional Disputes Board has held 330 meetings since 1973.

15. See Annual Reports of the National Joint Board.

16. See Green Book.

17. Bureau of National Affairs, *Construction Labor Report, Construction Craft Jurisdiction Agreements*, 1957. Also see my Summary Report of July 25, 1957.

18. See "Statement of Interrelationship between the NLRB and National Joint Board for Settlement of Jurisdictional Disputes in the Building and Construction Industry," July 31, 1957, submitted by the National Joint Board, *Amicus curiae*, Case No. 8-CD-8, *In the matter of Wood, Wire and Metal Lathers, International Union and Local Union No. 2 and Acoustical Contractors Association of Cleveland.* The statement was submitted by Archibald Cox in behalf of the National Joint Board.

    A series of cases in the state courts and before the NLRB were supportive: *Judson-Pacific-Murphy, Guy F. Atkinson, Baltimore Plumbers,* and *A.W. Lee.*

19. R. J. Mitchell, 1957–62; William J. Cour, 1962–74; Fred J. Driscoll, 1975–79; and Dale R. Witcraft, 1979 to date.

20. For a discussion see Charles J. Morris, Editor-in-Chief, *The Developing Labor Law, The Board, The Courts, and the National Labor Relations Act* (Washington, D.C.: The Bureau of National Affairs, Inc., 1971), pp. 675–88 and subsequent supplements.

21. See the supportive decision of the NLRB in the *Don Cartage* case, Millwrights Local Union No. 1102 (Don Cartage Company), 160 NLRB 1061, 63 LRRM 1085 (1966). I personally mediated this very difficult and wide-ranging dispute between the Ironworkers and Carpenters nationally and issued, by the authorization of the General Presidents, an arbitration decision.

22. See Paul Weiler, *Reconcilable Differences, New Directions in Canadian Labour Law* (Toronto, Canada: The Carswell Company Limited, 1980), pp. 179–208.

23. See The Business Roundtable, *More Construction for the Money, Summary Report of the Construction Industry Cost Effectiveness Project* (New York, January 1983). Also see Report C-1, *Exclusive Jurisdiction in Construction* (July 1982).

Chapter 12

THE BASIC PROBLEMS IN
THE PUBLIC SECTOR

On establishing the Governor's Committee on Public Service Employee Relations on January 15, 1966, Governor Rockefeller requested it "to make legislative proposals for protecting the public against the disruption of vital public services by illegal strikes, while at the same time protecting the rights of public employees." This approach was in marked contrast to that taken in formulating the Condon-Wadlin Act. That legislation simply banned strikes by public employees and specified penalties to be invoked against employees for violation of the ban. There is now a widespread realization that protection of the public from strikes in the public services requires the designation of other ways and means for dealing with claims of public employees for equitable treatment.

Our assignment is thus broad in compass. Benchmarks for dealing with it are relatively few. However, because immediate changes in the Condon-Wadlin Act were so urgently necessary and so widely demanded as a consequence of the 1966 transit strike in New York City, the Committee had but limited time at its disposal. Nevertheless, with the assistance of a capable staff, it has been possible to make a thorough analysis of the problem.

We report a unanimous conclusion as respects the immediate legislative action that, we believe, should be taken. Legislation along the lines recommended should provide the basis upon which viable government-employee relationships in New York can be developed. Our report comes at a time of deep public concern about these matters.

From *Governor's Committee on Public Employee Relations, Final Report, March 31, 1966*, State of New York. The Committee was comprised of E. Wight Bakke, David L. Cole, John T. Dunlop, Frederick H. Harbison, and George W. Taylor, Chairman. The first draft of "The Basic Problems" was written by George Taylor.

The results of negotiations in New York City and elsewhere, conducted under strike threat pressures as well as actual resort to the strike, understandably gave rise to a widespread concern about employee-governmental relations and a determination that they should be conducted in a manner which would conserve vital public interests. In consequence, the following questions have been brought into sharp focus: How should collective negotiation in the public service be distinguished from collective bargaining in the private sector? What public policy problems are involved in according to public employees the right to representatives of their own choosing for collective negotiation purposes? Should such right be accorded?

Fundamental questions of employee-governmental relations are dealt with in this report. They include (1) the fragmented vs. the over-all unit for negotiations, (2) the complexities of varied government-employee relations, and (3) problems of effectuating the no-strike policy in public employment. They have come to a head when great increases are occurring both in the number of public employees[1] and in the variety of services provided by the State government and its numerous political subdivisions. This expansion coincides with a growing interest among public employees in participating more fully and more effectively than heretofore in the determination of their conditions of employment.

Fragmented Versus the Over-all Unit for Negotiations

The objectives of all employees in seeking collective negotiations are not identical. Changes are sought in the promulgation and administration of those civil service laws and other legislative enactments which apply uniformly to classified public employees in diverse occupational groups and performing varied functions. At the same time, public employees have been increasingly organizing themselves into unions to represent particular occupational interests—transit employees, school teachers and sanitation workers are but a few examples. The right to this kind of representation has been strongly asserted. It is the demand for collective bargaining, "as practiced in the private sector of the economy," about these occupational interests which presents the most difficult problems and the greater possibility of conflict with the ability of legislative bodies to perform their constitutional functions, especially as respects the budgeting processes and the levying of taxes.

Employee organization to advance the particular occupational interests through collective negotiation is fundamentally different from the civil service approach under which basic working terms and conditions are specified by state wide classification of public employees of the state and of its political subdivisions. Many of the most important terms of employment for public employees have long been established through legislative enactment, including laws governing the civil service. This will continue to be the case.

There are many who fear that the development of multi-unit collective bargaining in governmental service would enervate our institutions of representative government and undermine the usefulness of a long-established and effective civil service policy.[2] The term "collective bargaining" has thus come to connote a type of joint-determination by unions and private management which, for reasons to be detailed hereafter, cannot be transferred literally to the public employment sector. An objective evaluation of the questions before us will be assisted, we believe, by use of the term "collective negotiations" to signify the participation of public employees in the determination of at least some of their conditions of employment on an occupational or functional basis.

Collective negotiations as they have been carried on in New York State have resulted in quite diverse forms of agreement. There have been many informal memoranda of understanding, including agreements subject to validation by the appropriate legislative and administrative bodies. Only a few "full-fledged" collective bargaining agreements have been consummated.

Union representation and collective bargaining has been available to employees of New York City since 1958 under the terms of Executive Order No. 49,[3] issued by Mayor Wagner. Three formal arrangements have been consummated under authority of this Executive Order. As far as we have been able to ascertain, eight formal collective bargaining agreements have been made with public employees outside of the City of New York.

Impact of Fragmentation on Civil Service

Union objectives are quite at variance, especially at the state level, with the objectives of the Civil Service Employees Association. For many years, this organization has worked directly with legislatures and governmental officials in the formulation of changes in civil service statutes as well as in their administration. On behalf of a relatively large membership throughout the state (except in New York City) the officials of the Civil Service Employees Association espouse what they term the "industrywide" approach to representation of public service employees. They assert that the "fragmentation" of units of representation, implicit in the union approach, is quite contrary to the interests of public service employees as a whole and to the continuance of stable governmental-employee relations. They oppose legislation designed to make such fragmentation in collective negotiation possible but strongly favor legislation increasing the strength of their Association's voice in the formulation and the administration of civil service statutes, including the career and salary plan.

The conflict of employee views involves the role of the Civil Service Commission. It is responsible for applying, under legislative authority, a unitary rule system of job classification. Workers belonging to diverse occupational groups and performing quite diverse functions are found together in each job classification. If the employees are organized by occupation or by function, the results of negotiation on the multi-unit basis, autonomously for each group, are bound to be diverse. Employment terms will inevitably tend to be responsive to specific circumstances. Some observers have predicted that establishment of a pattern of multiple-unit negotiation in public employment will lead inevitably to a sacrifice of the unitary system established by civil service. They cite the dangers of so-called leap-frogging—that is, terms negotiated by an occupational group tend to be extended by "compulsive comparison." They are concerned that legislation will be ultimately fashioned by collective negotiation instead of the other way around.

Phrasing the problem in terms of collective negotiations, as previously defined, provides a constructive way, we believe, of getting at the heart of the matter,—that is, protecting the rights of public employees to representatives of their own choosing on an occupational basis without an unacceptable infringement upon the stability and viability of the Civil Service System.

In our considered judgment, occupational representation should not be denied and can be provided without undermining the Civil Service System. We believe that the right of public employees to representatives of their own choosing for collective negotiation should be recognized. At the same time, public employees have an obligation to recognize that collective negotiations must be conducted within the framework of our democratic political structure out of which the civil service idea has evolved. In fulfilling this obligation, careful attention must be given to defining the "appropriate unit" for representation, the subject matter of joint negotiations, and the nature of the negotiated agreement. It is not here suggested that ready answers to these perplexing questions are available. However, answers must be found because the right of employees to multi-unit negotiations cannot equitably be denied.

Complexities of Government-Employee Relations

The critical nature of the differences between the two approaches to public employee participation (on an "industrywide" basis or a "multiple-unit" basis) have to be thoroughly understood before legislation to supersede the Condon-Waldin Act can be effectively fashioned. Both forms of participation now exist in the State of New York, but in many variations.

Who are the public employees and how are their conditions of employment now determined? "State employees" constitute one category which, in the main, comprises employees of 20 state departments. The basic conditions of employment for classified employees in the executive departments (the large majority of employees of the state) are determined by provisions of the Civil Service Law as administered by elected and appointed State officials.[4] Other terms of their employment are specified by other legislation. There are also state employees in the legislative branch, a relatively small number, and in the judicial branch, comprising a larger number of employees. In the judicial branch, both wage and non-wage conditions are determined either by the State Judicial Conference or by a local government. Other "state employees" work for public authorities having more than local but less than state-wide jurisdiction. In many respects, the conditions of employment for these public authority employees differ from other employees in the executive branch although some participate in the New York State Employees' Retirement System and the New York State health insurance program. In still other ways they are treated like "state" employees.[5] Some public authorities provide essentially local services, such as a public housing authority within a city or the Transit Authority in New York City. They have generally been accorded by the legislature a wide latitude as respects the fixing of employment terms.

Most public service employees in New York are not employed by the state but by political subdivisions of the state. They include not only the employees of counties, towns, villages and cities[6] but also of school districts[7] and other political subdivisions, providing special services, such as water districts, sewer districts, and fire districts.[8]

In other words, there are many governmental employers with widely varying degrees of authority. They are also subject to diverse budgeting procedures. No one rigid procedure can be devised to effectuate a policy of according public employees the right to representatives of their own choosing for collective negotiation. Yet, these rights of association and negotiation must be accorded as a necessary counterpart to the prohibition of strikes by public employees.

Inapplicability of Strikes

Collective bargaining, including the right to strike, is recognized as an essential democratic right of employees in the private enterprise sector. Private employers have countervailing rights: they may lock out their employees or go out of business entirely. These are not simply private rights; the opposing economic pressures have a function to perform. They exert reciprocal pressures upon the parties to modify their positions to the extent necessary to bring about a private agreement. One objective is to insure a final conclusion without government intervention or dictation. Although both parties in private collective bargaining possess wide latitude of agreement in private negotiations, they are subject to constraints—the pressure of the market place where the consumer's power of choice is exercised. Jobs can be lost and production can be cut back if goods or services are priced out of the market. Whether or not market forces provide adequate restraints in the public interest has often been questioned. The so-called guideposts for wage and price determination, as enunciated by the Council of Economic Advisers, are central to the current debate. At any event, even in the private sector, doubts have been raised about the compatibility with the public interest of unrestrained use of private economic power in the establishment of wages as well as of prices.

Nor does the right of strike in the private sector prevail without limitation. Under the Taft-Hartley Act special procedures may be invoked in public emergency disputes. Nevertheless, the right to strike remains as an integral part of the collective bargaining process in the private enterprise sector and this will unquestionably continue to be the case. The according of this right to employees must be appraised, however, in the context of the private enterprise sector to which it applies.

In contrast to the private enterprise sector, the right of public employees to strike has never been recognized by the public, by the legislature, or by governmental authorities in the United States. There are solid reasons for the distinction. Nor can these reasons be epitomized by a simple assertion of the words "the rights of sovereignty." At any event, this is scarcely an apt term to apply to a system of representative democratic government, such as our own, which is responsive to the electorate. It is more realistic to inquire as to the manner in which public employees can participate in establishing their employment terms within the framework of our political democracy.

Instead of the constraints of the market place on collective bargaining (including the right to strike) which are in the private sector, negotiations in the public sector are subject to the constraints imposed by democratic political processes. A work stoppage in the private sector involves costs primarily to the direct participants. They also undertake considerable risk in fixing the terms of settlement; the volume of sales and opportunities for employment are at stake. On the other hand, a strike of government employees (there can scarcely be a countervailing lockout) introduces an alien force in the legislative processes. With a few exceptions, there are no constraints of the market place. The constraints in the provision of "free services" by government are to be found in the budget allocation and tax decisions which are made by legislators responsive to the public will. To be sure, a legislative body may delegate certain of its powers to subordinate officials and agencies to an extent consistent with the Constitution by which it is bound. As a matter of fact, considerable power has been delegated to public authorities, especially those which charge for services rendered to the public, as well as to executive agencies which are responsible for administering the prevailing wage laws for certain non-classified public works employees.

To a preponderant extent, however, the executive agencies are required to compensate their employees within the limits of the budgets for the state and for its political subdivisions. In New York, these budgets must balance—that is, taxes must be levied to cover estimated expenditures. It is the budget, rather than the market place, which constrains collective negotiation in public employment.[9]

It seems evident that orderly collective negotiations in public employment should be related to the budget-making processes of the appropriate legislative body—a legislature, a board of supervisors, a municipal council, or a fiscally-independent board of education.

Legislative Prohibition of Strikes by Public Employees

For reasons just outlined, "collective negotiation" in the public services is unlike collective bargaining in the private enterprise sector. The strike cannot be a part of the negotiating process. By constitutional interpretations in the courts and by application of the common law, strikes by governmental employees have been declared illegal and made enjoinable in jurisdictions from the federal to the local level. Virtually all representatives of public employees seem to be fully aware of the fact that strikes of public employees have always been enjoinable by the courts. Some insist, however, that there should be neither a legislative prohibition of strikes nor specified "punitive" penalties invocable upon violation. Some union officials believe that the ban on strikes of public employees constitutes the deprivation of a basic right. Many union representatives also express the conviction that a legislative ban on strikes and the prescription of "punitive" measures for violation has encouraged arbitrariness by the employing agencies which is a major source of friction in employee-governmental relations. These agencies, it is urged, will not seriously undertake the development of effective substitutes for strike action as long as they can presume that strikes will not occur. Union officials say, in effect, that the best way to protect the public against stoppages of public services is to eliminate the statutory ban on strikes. Only then, they assert, will there be meaningful negotiations.

Even though these union positions have self-serving characteristics, there is evidence that the cloak of "sovereignty" has been used to justify unilateral and sometimes inequitable decisions by governmental administrators. Moreover, legislative bodies and administrative agencies are traditionally inclined to retain as much of their rule-making jurisdiction as they can. Life seems to be easier that way. But decisions which are arbitrary or seem to employees to be arbitrary can give rise to employee reactions which impair the quality of service rendered and otherwise infringe upon the public interests. Despite the problems in this area and the frustrations they generate, ways and means other than the strike have to be found for resolving them.

The issue of the "retained rights" of the employer (related in public service to the proper performance of both the legislative and executive functions) is more difficult to deal with in the public sector than in the private sector. In the private sector, certain subjects are dealt with unilaterally by the employer on the assumption that this is essential to the proper performance of the managerial function. There are limitations to the scope of collective bargaining in the private sector which unions recognize. To a greater extent, moreover, the governmental employing agency lacks the power directly to negotiate with its employees or to have effective means for securing necessary consent to an agreement from higher levels of authority (from the executive officers of government and ultimately from the appropriate lawmaking body). As compared to the private sector, the authority to negotiate is less likely either to be granted in advance or to be promptly obtained when desired. Such restraints are a concomitant of operations in a democratic political context. Unlike the private business organization, government is more directly responsive to the demands of its constituency.

The need for validation of agreement in the administration of public agencies has a degree of comparability with the need for validation in the operation of democratic employee organizations.

Negotiating representatives of employees, in the private sector as well as in public employment, usually are limited in the authority they can exercise. Rules established by higher union organizational authority are sometimes an important limitation. The agreement they consummate, moreover, is almost universally subject to the democratic principle of ratification by the membership. This is not always pro forma. Indeed, retention by the employee membership of the ultimate authority to approve or reject a negotiated agreement can be a factor of considerable importance in fashioning the terms of settlement which are submitted for membership validation.

Governmental employing agencies secure their authority from legislative bodies representing the various public interests and they may have to secure a validation of agreed-upon terms from that body. In other words, the retained rights of government are defined, in the last analysis, by actions of the legislative body and executive officials who are subject to the restraints of the electorate. Employees may dis-elect their representatives and the public may dis-elect theirs. Collective negotiations in the public sector are obviously undertaken in an environment quite different, in important respects, from the private sector.

It follows from this analysis that, in order to spur the legislative bodies and the administrative agencies to accord more effective participation rights to public employees, doubts should not be raised about the firmness of the well-established principle that the strike, or the threat to strike, is not available to employees in public service. That might be the effect of legislation replacing the Condon-Wadlin Act if it were silent on this subject. The fact of the matter is that collective bargaining in the private enterprise context is markedly different in many respects from collective regulation in the governmental context. One difference is in the lack of appropriateness of the strike in the public sector.

We come to this conclusion after a full consideration of the views expressed to us not only by some union representatives but by others that public employees in non-essential governmental services, at least, should have the same right to strike as has been accorded to employees in private industry. We realize, moreover, that the work performed in both sectors is sometimes comparable or identical. Why, then, should an interruption of non-essential governmental services be prohibited?

To begin with, a differentiation between essential and nonessential governmental services would be the subject of such intense and never-ending controversy[10] as to be administratively impossible. There is, however, an even more telling reason. Careful thought about the matter shows conclusively, we believe, that while the right to strike normally performs a useful function in the private enterprise sector (where relative economic power is the final determinant in the making of private agreements), it is not compatible with the orderly functioning of our democratic form of representative government (in which relative political power is the final determinant).

An unequivocal recognition of this fundamental principle by the representatives of public employees, rather than the raising of doubts about it, would, we believe, elicit powerful public support for the stated fundamental objective of most public employee organizations, i.e., the development of substitutes for the strike which will insure adequate considerations of employee claims.

Summary

Despite many complexities, we believe it is both feasible and desirable to develop a system of effective collective negotiation in the public service. This can be achieved in a manner which is consonant with the orderly functioning of a democratic government. It cannot be achieved by transferring collective bargaining as practiced in the private enterprise sector into the governmental sector. New procedures have to be created. In subsequent sections of this report, recommendations are made as to some of the ways and means by which collective negotiation in the public service can be soundly developed.

Endnotes

1. From 1955 to 1965, New York State employees increased from 83,738 to 128,322, while local government employees increased from 325,524 to 472,028.
2. It will be recalled that the civil service approach was undertaken (initially about 75 years ago in New York) to provide job security to public employees and job status based upon merit and ability as a substitute for what was called "the spoils system."
3. This Executive Order superseded an earlier Executive Order issued in 1954 which established interim collective bargaining procedures.
4. An exception is made by Section 220 of the State Labor Law. This Section applies to "laborers, workmen, and mechanics" and specifies the payment of "prevailing wages and supplements" not only to employees of contractors engaged in a public works project but as well to *unclassified* public works employees of the State, its municipalities, and other instrumentalities of the State including public authorities.
5. Public authorities are engaged in the operation of bridges, highways, transit, water pollution control, parks, ports, and hydroelectric power as well as the construction of university facilities and low-cost housing. There is a "Statement

of Employee Relations Policy, New York State Thruway Authority, Nov. 21, 1960" (re-issued in Jan. 1, 1966) which has been signed by representatives of several employee organizations after collective negotiations. Even in the absence of specifically delegated authority, authorities may engage in collective negotiations when they are deemed by the authority to be necessary for the proper conduct of their business.

6. In New York there are 62 counties, 932 towns, 533 villages, and 62 cities.

7. There are 1,199 school districts in the state.

8. It is estimated that there are about 5,540 of these political subdivisions in the State.

9. The New York State Constitution (Article VII, Section 2) requires the Governor to submit annually to the Legislature a budget containing a complete plan of expenditures for the ensuing fiscal year beginning on April 1 and, at the same time, proposed legislation to provide revenue for meeting the proposed expenditures. The Constitution further requires that no money may be paid by the State except in pursuance of an appropriation made by law.

   The law governing counties requires a budget officer appointed by the County Board of Supervisors to estimate proposed expenses and anticipated revenue for each fiscal year which begins on January 1. Following a public hearing, a budget must be adopted no later than December 20 by the County Board of Supervisors. A similar budget-making procedure must be followed for village and town budgets. No single general law applies to the cities; each separate city charter determines the budget procedure.

   School district budgeting is subject to different procedures. In the larger cities (over 125,000 population), the tentative school budget proposed by the Board of Education, like other departmental requests, may be modified by the agency or official responsible for preparing the entire municipal budget, which is subject to enactment by the legislative body. Once the school budget is adopted, the Board of Education has sole control of expenditures without limitation as to the purpose initially appropriated. In the smaller cities, school districts are fiscally independent. Each school district outside the cities must seek authorization by ballot of the voters of the right to levy taxes sufficient to cover their proposed expenditures.

10. It has been suggested to us that an interruption of the services provided by public school teachers should be permissible because this would not create a public emergency. One can assume that this point of view is not widely shared.

Chapter 13

RESOLUTION OF DEADLOCKS IN COLLECTIVE NEGOTIATIONS[1]

The avoidance of the strike is substantially the perfection of procedures and policies to provide an effective alternative to conflict. The present chapter focuses upon the critical questions of the most appropriate alternatives to conflict in the event that collective negotiations appear to have reached an impasse. What then?

The design of dispute settlement procedures must constantly avoid at least two serious pitfalls. The first is that impasse procedures often tend to be overused; they may become too accessible, and as a consequence, the responsibility and problem-solving virtues of constructive negotiations are lost. Dispute settlement procedures can become habit-forming, and then negotiations become only a ritual. The second pitfall is that a standardized dispute settlement procedure is not ideally suited to all parties and to all disputes. Procedures work best which have been mutually designed, are mutually administered, and have been mutually shaped to the particular problem at hand.

Coordination of Collective Negotiations with Legislative/Budget Year

Collective negotiations in government employment need to be closely coordinated with the calendar of the legislative and budget year. Indeed, an impasse is typically identified by the failure to have achieved an understanding or agreement before the approach of

Governor's Committee on Public Employee Relations, Final Report, March 31, 1966, State of New York. The Committee was comprised of E. Wight Bakke, David L. Cole, John T. Dunlop, Frederick H. Harbison, and George W. Taylor, Chairman. The first draft of this chapter of the report was written by John T. Dunlop.

budgeting deadlines established by law. It is a fundamental principle in government employment that collective negotiations and the resort to procedures to resolve an impasse be appropriately related to the legislative and budget-making process. An impasse may be defined in terms of the failure to achieve agreement sixty days, or some longer period, prior to the budget submission date established by law for the agency or unit of government.

A wide variety of types of collective relations exist in public employment in the State of New York:

1. In some cases more than one employee organization is recognized in a single unit, while in others one employee organization has the right exclusively to represent all employees.
2. In some cases wages and conditions of employment are prescribed by the agency after discussions with employee organizations; in other cases they are set forth in memoranda or agreements signed by employee organizations after joint discussions but with final prescription by the government agency; in still other cases, agreements are formally negotiated by employee organizations and the agency and signed by both.
3. In some cases the range of subjects discussed with employee organizations is very narrow since many of the conditions of employment are mandated by legislation or administrative regulation, while in other cases the subjects discussed range as widely as in private industry.
4. In some cases wages and conditions of employment for non-classified employees are determined under legislative authority by reference or equivalence to the wages and conditions prevailing for other designated employees, while in other cases no such formula or principle has been authorized.
5. In some situations the budget available to the government agency is determined in advance and is fixed for the purposes of any collective discussions, while in other cases it is understood that the agency undertakes to seek the necessary funds; in still other situations discussions over wages and sources of funds proceed simultaneously.
6. In some cases the conditions of employment are determined for a single budgetary year, while in others these terms are fixed across two or more budget years.

This variety in the patterns of collective relations between government agencies and employee organizations in New York State, and the early stage of many of these relations, led this Committee to conclude that every opportunity and encouragement should be afforded each collective relationship to develop its own procedures and dispute-settling machinery. No single procedure or style of dispute settlement is likely to prove equally acceptable or effective. Moreover, parties may wish to experiment and to revise procedures in the light of experience. No procedure should be imposed by law without first affording the governmental agencies and employee organizations involved in collective relations the opportunity to develop directly their own procedures for resolving an impasse. It would be unwise to freeze so early in the development of collective relations in government employment a single pattern of dispute settlement and to deprive the future of a more varied and perceptive experience from which to choose.

The time to develop procedures to resolve an impasse is when there is no crisis. The processes of joint discussion and negotiations in each collective relation should be devoted to the development of procedures to resolve disputes and to avoid an impasse. Such procedures, designed to meet the needs of the particular parties and the public interest, should be regarded as a priority subject for collective negotiations. These agreed-upon procedures should be reviewed and perfected from time to time in collective negotiations in the light of experience.

Procedures to Invoke in an Impasse

The Governor's Committee proposes the principle and policy that every collective relationship between a governmental agency and an employee organization, which is reduced to writing, should incorporate a specific procedure which the parties agree to use to resolve disputes over conditions of employment in advance of budget submission or legislative deadlines. Where the collective relationship involves no written agreement or memorandum, the parties should nonetheless adopt such a procedure which they may elect to reduce to writing.

The Committee recommends that every existing collective relationship between a governmental agency and employee organization promptly undertake discussions seeking to establish a mutually agreeable procedure to be followed in a future dispute over employment conditions. This obligation to search for agreed-upon procedures should apply regardless of any specified term of current conditions or existing memoranda or agreement, but any agreed-upon procedure need become operative, if necessary, only with the expiration of the present term. Among the types of procedures the parties may wish to consider are the following. They may alter or combine these procedures in a variety of ways. Their resourcefulness and imagination may be expected to create still others more appropriate to their particular situation. The list which follows is identified without preferment or ranking. Any procedure must, of course, conform to provisions of law.

1. *The advance commitment to submit a dispute to arbitration.* Specific standards may or may not be designated.

2. *The determination to resolve a question according to a formula specifying that the wages, benefits, or other conditions of employment in the locality and type of work in question shall be governed by those prevailing in private or public employment in other designated localities and types of work.*

3. *The advance agreement to refer a dispute to fact-finding with recommendations, with or without the advance commitment by one or both parties to accept the recommendations.* The procedures may provide a number of variants. The negotiators may jointly agree in advance to accept the recommendations of the fact-finders and to urge their acceptance upon their principals. They may jointly agree in advance to take the recommendations to the appropriate legislative body to advocate jointly the requisite appropriation or change in regulations, recognizing the authority of such legislative body. The procedure to select the fact-finding and recommending body may also take a variety of forms.

4. *The advance agreement to establish one or more study committees to review together complex or difficult problems, such as wage relations among classifications, which may not be amenable to simple and immediate solution.* Such joint study committees should be expected to achieve mutually agreeable recommendations to their principals prior to the next budget submission or legislative deadline. Joint study committees have proved to be constructive in many private and public relationships. The study committees could well include several employee organizations depending on the scope of the issue.

5. *The advance commitment to utilize mediation procedures and to designate individuals or agencies, public or private, as the mediators.*

Procedures for Unresolved Impasses

Some of the parties to a current collective relationship may be unable to reach agreement on the procedures which they are to follow in the event of an impasse in collective negotiations. In such event, the Committee recommends that the following procedures be required to be utilized if an impasse exists not less than 60 days before the date required for the submission of the budget. These procedures may be invoked by the government agency, by the employee organization, or by the Public Employment Relations Board on its own motion.

1. The Public Employment Relations Board shall first ascertain whether an impasse exists, the issues in controversy, the status of the collective negotiations, and the steps which the parties have taken to resolve the dispute. The Board shall seek to resolve the dispute by further mediation, including the search for mutually agreeable procedures to resolve any remaining differences between the parties.

2. If an impasse continues, the Public Employment Relations Board shall appoint a fact-finding board, ordinarily of three members, each of whom is to be representative of the public, with power to make public recommendations. The fact-finding board shall be appointed from a list of recognized experts maintained by the Board and drawn up after consultation with representatives of employee organizations, state and local government administrators, and agencies with industrial relations and personnel functions. The Public Employment Relations Board may also appoint non-voting advisors to the fact-finding board from each of the parties, in appropriate cases.

3. The fact-finding board shall hear the contending parties to the dispute. It may request statistical data and reports on its own initiative in addition to the data regularly maintained by the Public Employment Relations Board. A majority of the members of the fact-finding board shall make a recommendation to resolve the issues in dispute no later than fifteen days prior to the submission of the budget or legislative deadline. The recommendations of the fact-finding board shall be used to facilitate agreement prior to the budgetary or legislative deadline; however, they shall not be binding on either the governmental agency or the employee organization, unless they so agree.

4. In the event that a fact-finding report with recommendations issued by a board established under procedure adopted by the parties, no further fact-finding board with power to make recommendations, as provided in paragraph (2) above, shall be appointed. However, the Public Employment Relations Board shall have the power to take whatever steps it deems appropriate to resolve the dispute, including the making of recommendations after giving due consideration to the recommendations and facts found by the first body.

This Committee has recommended the above impasse procedures and those incorporated below, because it has concluded that these are most appropriate and most generally applicable to public employment. Fact-finding requires the parties to gather objective information and to present arguments with references to these data. An unsubstantiated or extreme demand from either party tends to lose its force and status in this forum. The fact-finding report and recommendations provide a basis to inform and to crystallize thoughtful public opinion and news media comment. Such reports and recommendations have a special relevance when the public's business is involved. The public has a special right to be informed on the issues, contentions, and merits of disputes involving public employees.

The Committee has rejected the proposal for compulsory arbitration not merely because there may be serious questions as to its legality but because of the conviction that impasse disputes may arise less frequently and be settled more equitably by the procedures outlined in this report. In our judgment, the requirement for binding arbitration would likely reduce the prospects of settlement at earlier stages closer to the problems, the employees, and the agency; it would tend to frustrate the participation of employees in the determination of compensation and conditions of employment and tend to encourage arbitrary and extreme positions on both sides. Moreover, the procedures here proposed, we believe, are more effective in encouraging proposals which are likely to prove to be mutually acceptable and enforceable. They better preserve the autonomy and authority of the legislative process while achieving a balance between the rights of public employees and the public interest.

A collective relationship between a governmental agency and one or more employee organizations now applies to only a minority of government employees in New York. This Committee recommends that any collective relationship, which results in a written understanding or agreement in the future, incorporate in any such memorandum or agreement a procedure to be followed by the parties in the event of an impasse in negotiations. The parties should preferably design their own procedures, but they may elect to adopt the Public Employment Relations Board procedures outlined above.

This Committee recommends that the Public Employment Relations Board maintain and make available to employee organizations and government agencies, as well as to mediators and fact-finding boards, statistical data relating to wages, benefits and employment practices in public and private employment applicable to various localities and occupations. The Board should also provide data for joint study committees established by government agencies and employee organizations and assist them to resolve complex issues in their negotiations.

The Committee is of the view that the procedures outlined above, providing for the maximum participation by government agencies and employee organizations in the design and administration of the procedures to resolve an impasse, will make a major contribution to the orderly resolution of disputes. As either party is left the alternative to reject the recommendations of a fact-finding board, it is essen-

tial to state the views of this Committee as to appropriate procedures
in that event.

In public employment, responsibility for the final resolution of any
dispute, which has not been settled by the procedures outlined
above, lies with the local or state legislative body. The rejection by
the employee organization of the recommendations of the fact-finding
board does not make a strike legitimate or appropriate. The rejection
by a government agency of such recommendations does not constitute a final disposition of the dispute.

Economic coercion involving work stoppages is not to be applied in
our society against government. The proper course for the employee
organization to take any further complaint, after review and recommendations by a fact-finding board, is the legislative and political
arena representing all the people.

Similarly, if the government agency should reject the recommendations, as it too should have the right to do, the employee
organization and the administrators should take the remaining controversy to the legislative and political arena rather than to the
streets. In the ordinary course, the legislature reviews and evaluates
contending views in budgetmaking and in the specification of conditions of work for public employees.

The Show-Cause Hearing

This committee recommends that in the event of the rejection of a
fact-finding recommendation, the legislative body or committee hold
a form of "show cause hearing" at which the parties review their
positions with respect to the recommendations of the fact-finding
board. The appropriate budgetary allotment or other regulations are
then to be enacted by the legislative body.

It is ultimately the legislature and the political process which has to
balance the interests of public employees with the rest of the community, to relate the compensation of public employees to the tax rate,
and to appraise the extent and quality of public services and the
efficiency of their performance to the aspirations of public employees.
The methods of persuasion and political activity, rather than the
strike, comport with our institutions and traditions as means to resolve such conflicts of interest. It is these methods, moreover, that
have been utilized by the wide variety of employee organizations
which are indigenous to public employment.

In summary, four basic principles stand out in the design of machinery to resolve disputes which reach a deadlock in collective
negotiations. First, collective negotiations need to be closely coor-

dinated with the budget and legislative year; indeed, an impasse is to be defined by reference to failure to achieve an agreement not less than 60 days prior to the final date of the budgetary submission. Second, all written memoranda or agreements should include procedures which the parties develop themselves to invoke in the event of an impasse. Parties to such memoranda or agreements now in effect should be encouraged to incorporate such procedures. Third, in the event of an impasse which has not been resolved, the Public Employment Relations Board should appoint a public fact-finding board, ordinarily of three members, to make recommendations. And fourth, in the event of the rejection of a fact-finding recommendation by the employee organization or the governmental agency, the appropriate legislative body or committee should hold a form of "show cause hearing" at which the parties review their positions with respect to the recommendations of the fact-finding board prior to final legislative action on the budget or other enactment.

Endnote

1. The procedures considered in this part of the report do not apply to grievances of individual employees or groups of employees, nor to disputes over representation, but relate rather to disputes over the terms and conditions of employment generally which have not been settled in negotiations.

Part Four

JOINT CONSULTATION AND LABOR-MANAGEMENT COMMITTEES

Part One provided a generalized interpretation of what happens in negotiations and described the natural course of negotiations among continuing organizations, such as those that take place among labor and management organizations in the United States.

Part Two introduced the concept of an industrial relations system applicable to national, sectoral, or other configurations of labor organizations, managements, and governmental agencies. It then sought to explain the emergence and development of labor organization in this country and to identify the past and future tendencies in our industrial relations arrangements. The central unresolved problem of our industrial relations is that the legal framework for the establishment and operation of collective bargaining has been characterized by political power and conflict rather than consensus between labor and management, with public participation, and political approval.

Part Three focused upon the mechanisms designed by labor, management, and government to resolve a few types of disputes that arise between labor and management in particular industrial relations settings. In order to appreciate perceptively the design of the mechanisms, the larger setting of the particular industrial relations systems needs to be appreciated. Disputes do not arise in a vacuum. Mechanisms for the resolution of emergency disputes, jurisdictional disputes in construction, and disputes over terms of collective agreements in state and local government were examined in this framework.

Part Four is concerned with labor-management, as well as labor-management-government, interactions in problem-solving and dispute resolution. These activities are comprised of joint consultation and the operation of labor-management committees, with or without government participation. These committees on occasion may include procedures by which national leaders or statewide leaders facilitate the settlement of local collective agreements of their constituents. The specialized purposes, the diverse procedures, and the imaginative and productive approaches to issues through some joint committees are illustrated in the detailed accounts of three committees. In some political settings, the relations among labor, management, and government as well as various public policies may be established through a social contract. The future directions in the interactions of labor, management, and government constitutes a concluding chapter.

Chapter 14

LABOR-MANAGEMENT COMMITTEES: FUNCTIONS AND EXPERIENCE

Labor-management committees are not to be identified with collective bargaining, although most committees have arisen where employees are represented by labor organizations. Joint committees are to be distinguished from collective bargaining institutions in a number of respects. First, collective bargaining, as reflected in an agreement, encompasses a wide range of topics including wages, benefits and hours; rules respecting hiring, layoffs, and transfers; conditions of work including standards of discipline; and procedures to resolve grievances, as the text of any agreement reflects. Labor-management committees are typically concerned with a far narrower focus on a relatively few issues such as health and safety, quality of worklife, waste, absenteeism, production efficiency, training, or a general exchange of views.

Second, collective bargaining provides mechanisms to resolve disputes between the parties by a grievance procedure and arbitration, or resort to strike or lockout, while labor-management committees typically provide for study and exchanges of views, occasionally with assistance through mediation by a neutral chairman, but ordinarily without procedures to break a deadlock. Labor-management committees typically can lead to action only if labor and management are in agreement on the specific activity.

Third, there is a point of view which regards labor-management committees, and the cooperative relationship they reflect, as a means toward the full participation of employees as "partners" in the productive process and in the interests of the enterprise. Labor-management committees at the work place, in this perspective, are envisaged as quite different from collective bargaining that reflects confrontation and an adversarial relationship between particular labor and management organizations.[1]

Fourth, collective bargaining is in detail regulated by administrative law and the courts. The subjects of mandatory or voluntary bargaining, the data that are required from management to furnish to a union, the conduct of good faith bargaining, the prohibition of unilateral change in an established condition of work or procedure, and the definition and consequences of an impasse are all specified by government in collective bargaining. Such regulation, however, does not extend to labor-management committees.

And fifth, employee-management committees on a department or establishment level may exist without the formal union representation essential for collective bargaining. Such committees of employees and supervisors may consider and jointly propose changes in a variety of production, quality-oriented, and welfare operations or procedures. There may be some uncertainty as to the limits of the law where a labor-management committee, such as a quality circle, takes on some of the functions of a bargaining representative.

The British use the term "joint-consultation" to refer to the activities encompassed by labor-management committees, and their usage makes it clear that "joint consultation is to be sharply distinguished from collective bargaining. . . ."[2] The British unions have always insisted on playing a part in joint consultation; like U.S. unions they have perceived joint consultative bodies, and current Quality Circles, as potential rivals for the loyalty of workers and as a base for competing unions or management control. Thomas R. Donahue, Secretary-Treasurer of the AFL-CIO said, "Quality of worklife programs are no alternative to the collective bargaining process, and growing interest in the programs may be an attempt by employers to bypass or supplant unionization of the work force. . . . It is only the collective bargaining stature of the unions that establishes workers as 'real partners'."[3]

In the United States there is no obligation in law to bargain over the establishment of cooperative labor-management committees to operate separately from a collective agreement and grievance procedures. Beyond collective bargaining processes themselves, each relationship, each locality, and each industry may choose the forms of any joint committees and designate the subject matters of special concern as well as their methods. Or they may engage in no such joint consultation at all. Enforced consultation and cooperation would be a contradiction in terms.

Types and Features of Committees

The varieties of labor-management committees approach the diversity of the animal kingdom, although it may not be useful to use such classical categories as phylum, class, order, genera, and species or to develop Latin forms of nomenclature for various categories in the labor-management committee world.[4] But some classification of committees is essential to orderly discourse.[5]

Level of Committees

Committees range from those at the immediate work place or department, to those at the establishment level, to an industry in the locality, to a locality as a whole, to a sector regionally or nationally, to an economy-wide labor-management committee. The concerns and interests, membership and representation, methods of operation and relations to collective agreements are likely to be very different. Thus, departmental committees in a plant may well operate under procedures defined in a collective agreement, while a locality committee is not likely to be created in agreements between different unions and managements in the same locality. A few illustrations and references will better convey the different types of these committees.

Work Place or Plant Committees. These committees are the most numerous. Closest to the involvement of individual workers and supervisors, they are likely to be authorized and circumscribed by the provisions of an agreement when the work force is represented by labor organizations. These committees may exist in the absence of collective bargaining as with Quality Circles or other work place groups. Work place committees tend to concentrate on production problems, cost savings, quality of product, scrap, inventories, scheduling, suggestions and the like.

During World War II a large number of plant-level committees were established to help increase wartime production.[6] A number of plans since then have been introduced to encourage production and to share the gains with employees on a plant-wide basis, most notably the Scanlon Plan.[7] The Kaiser Steel Company and the Steelworkers established a Long-Range Sharing Committee with departmental committees in 1959.[8] The basic steel agreement provided for labor-management plant-level advisory committees, and often departmental committees as well, at each plant for a number of years.[9] The basic steel agreement of 1980 specifies the reasons for Labor-Management Participation Teams:[10]

The parties recognize that a cooperative approach between employees and supervision at the work site in a department or similar unit is essential to the solution of problems affecting them. Many problems at this level are not readily subject to resolution under existing contractual programs and practices, but affect the ongoing relationships between labor and management at that level. Joint participation in solving these problems at the departmental level is an essential ingredient in any effort to improve the effectiveness of the company's performance and to provide employees with a measure of involvement adding dignity and worth to their work life.

The TVA agreement with the Tennessee Valley Trades and Labor Council has provided for both a Central Joint Cooperative Committee and local joint committees from the early days of representation.[11]

These cooperative committees give consideration to such matters as the elimination of waste; the conservation of materials, supplies, and energy; the improvement of quality of workmanship and services; the promotion of education and training; the correction of conditions making for misunderstandings; the encouragement of courtesy in the relations of employees with the public; the safeguarding of health; the prevention of hazards to life and property; and the strengthening of the morale of the service. The committee shall, however, not consider and act upon subjects or disputes the adjustment of which is provided in Articles VI, VII and VIII of this agreement.

The 1980 National Memorandum of Understanding between A.T.&T. and the Communications Workers of America states:[12]

. . . recognizing the desirability of mutual efforts to improve the work life of employees and enhance the effectiveness of the organization, the Company and the Union express their mutual belief that activities and experiments initiated and sponsored jointly by Management and the Union can prove beneficial to all employees and the Company, and that by encouraging greater employee participation, work can be made more satisfying and organizational performance and service quality can be improved.
. . . The Company and the Union agree to encourage all levels of their respective organizations to cooperate in the design, development, and implementation of participative experiments, projects, and programs, in a spirit of mutuality and responsible leadership.

There have also been a number of scholarly studies of particular plant-level labor-management committees.[13]

Locality Committees. The principal focus of the locality type of labor-management committees has been their concern with the resolution of disputes over the terms of collective agreements expiring in the locality in order to reduce serious work stoppages, with labor-management cooperation to promote economic development and an influx of new enterprises and job opportunities to the locality. These locality committees often involve local political or governmental officials and their interest in a favorable climate for economic development. Locality committees have been active in such communities as Toledo, Louisville, and Jamestown, New York. The following account is typical of locality committees:

> *Labor-management relations in the Beaumont area once were so poor that there were 50 to 60 strikes yearly. After one nine-month strike, Maurice Meyers, the mayor then, put together a permanent union-management group that now has 23 labor and 23 business members who meet monthly. Jack Kennedy, the top labor representative, says the group "talks before the pickets go up." Last year, there were about 10 strikes; so far this year, only two.*
>
> *To attract new business to the area, the group has begun distributing literature about its program to corporate relocation firms. It also plans a public-relations campaign using radio and TV ads and billboards to sell the approach to more local businesses and workers. "We're erasing the negative image we had earned," says Meyers." (Wall Street Journal,* August 2, 1983, p. 1.)

The Labor Department listed 28 area-wide committees that had been established by January 1980.[14] Cooperative activity between the major banks and the municipal unions and their pension funds was a decisive factor in the leadership that avoided bankruptcy in New York City through cost restraints and pension fund loans in the late 1970s. The number of communities, however, with locality labor-management committees has never been extensive, and experience teaches they have in most cases operated for a limited period.

Industry Committees in a Locality. Labor management committees have been established to deal with rather specific problems in an industry or a sector of industry in a locality or in a region, at times governed by a common or identical collective agreement. The Cleveland Ladies' Garment industry during the period 1919–31 introduced standards of production and earnings through a board of referees. The New York hotel industry established a relationship after 1938 that reflected the special circumstances of that service industry.[15] The Chicago Construction Coordinating Committee, financed by the Federal Government in the 1970s, brought together labor and management and Federal Government procurement agencies in the Chicago area to deal with problems of seasonality and the cyclical unemployment created by variation in government construction. The program for a period was extended to Boston, Kansas City, Denver, and San Francisco.

Industry or Company Committees on a National Basis. The parties to collective bargaining agreements in a sector have on occasion set up committees on a national basis to consider common problems. Sometimes these joint committees have related to governmental agencies, on an *ad hoc* or continuing basis. For example, the private Construction Industry Joint Conference in the period 1959–68 brought together all national contractor organizations engaged in collective bargaining and the national construction unions to consider a wide variety of common problems, apart from the resolution of disputes over the terms of collective agreements.

The Armour Progress Sharing Agreement in the 1960s in the meat packing industry facilitated the shutdown of uneconomic plants. With the assistance of neutrals, it encouraged the adjustment process of the work force, including retraining, moving, job search, and counseling.[16]

The private Joint Labor-Management Committee of the Retail Food Industry was established in April 1974. It provides a mechanism to facilitate, with the aid of private neutrals, the settlement of disputes in any locality over the terms of collective agreements between retail food chain stores and the butchers, clerks, and teamsters. The Committee also engages in study and discourse over significant economic issues confronting the industry nationally, such as competition from unorganized stores in local markets, the issues growing out of part time workers, and changing patterns of store hours, related warehouse problems, health care costs, and certain OSHA regulations.

An Economy-wide Labor-Management Committee. These committees have been drawn from national labor and business leaders. Sometimes they have been assembled or appointed at the initiative of government stabilization agencies or by the President. On other occasions the initiatives for organizing or continuing a committee have come from the private organizations. The issues that have impelled business and labor leaders to meet are national and international economic policy questions including job creation, tax policy, inflation, energy policy, trade issues, housing, medical care, and physical infrastructure. Only on rare occasions have they been stimulated to meet on industrial relations questions. Presidents Johnson and Kennedy met with such committees in the 1960s[17] and President Ford established and met with a Committee regularly in 1974–75. A private labor-management group has continued with a partial interruption since 1976. A number of business leaders and union presidents affiliated with the Industrial Union Department met in the early 1980s on issues of trade and industrial policy.[18]

Involvement of Neutrals or Government

The above illustrations by level of committee make it clear that labor-management committees can also be classified into three groups according to whether they involve (a) no third party in their operations or decisions, (b) a private neutral as a third party, or (c) a government official as a third party. By virtue of these different arrangements, committees may be quite different in how they operate, whether their deliberations are open to the press and media, how they conduct serious discourse, the nature of staff work and access to data, and the use of the views and conclusions generated by the committee. Moreover, a third party may fulfill a wide range of roles as was developed earlier in Chapter 1, from merely a presiding officer to one of aggressive consensus building. But the role of any third party is certain to be partly shaped by the labor and management representatives; the third party is *not* ordinarily an entirely free agent.

Assignment and Scope of Duties

Labor-management committees may have a narrow assignment and an expected date for the completion of an assignment or they may have a broad and continuing reference, particularly when the committee is comprised of leaders rather than subordinates. Policy-making groups may extend their attention from one matter to others, and may thus tend to have a longer duration.

Labor-management committees may be staff groups designed to prepare an issue for negotiations or to carry out a particular provision of a recently negotiated agreement, often involving a problem that was postponed or not fully resolved in contract negotiations. Such committees are often comprised of subordinates of the top representatives of the parties. Pension data or health costs and benefit data may need to be gathered and factually agreed-upon to expedite negotiations and facilitate the agreement-making process. Or, the joint committee may be asked to propose for submission to the top leadership a revised job evaluation plan, a revised incentive plan, a training proposal, or a study of imports.

Labor-management committees may be comprised of policy-making leadership, whose action are likely to require some ratification before they can be implemented but who are prepared to discuss serious issues of organizational direction and alternative policies. The substantive content of the discussions, of course, varies with the level of the committee as noted above. It is useful to distinguish between staff groups and policy-making groups.

Generalizations from the History of Committees

Despite the wide variety in the types and features of labor-management committees, the record over many years supports the following generalizations. This general appraisal provides background to a discussion of labor-management committees in the current scene.

1. *Labor-management committees have functioned in only a relatively few collective bargaining relationships.* As Sumner H. Slichter concluded more than forty years ago, "In industry as a whole, the number of unions pursuing the policy of systematic cooperation is small . . . . The traditional view of unions is that getting out production and keeping down costs is the employer's responsibility. . . . Unions have been bitterly opposed by most employers and have had to fight for the right to exist. . . . Employers have not desired their help."[19]

2. *Labor-management committees appear to arise in response to threats to the economic viability and job opportunities provided by the enterprise, locality, or sector, or under the circumstances of special challenges and with the leadership of dedicated personalities who have the capacity to command unusual support in their respective organizations.* Dramatic technological and market changes, a long work stoppage, the growth of competitive imports, or other threats may impel a joint committee. ". . . the times when labor and management have cooperated over the years have been times when economic difficulties threatened the viability of both parties, or when international tensions necessitated cooperation in the interest of national security. In these periods of crisis, collective bargaining alone had proved to be an inadequate forum for addressing each and every pressing issue."[20] Slichter saw the main field of committees to be "in the high-cost establishments where equipment is semi-obsolete or the management is poor and where the union needs to do something to help its members hold their jobs."[21]

3. *Labor-management committees ordinarily have a limited life span, much shorter than collective bargaining relationships.* The central problem they were designed to consider may be resolved or pass; the special leadership may leave; the circumstances may change and a new set of urgent issues emerge; the vital neutral or the governmental official may disappear; or the willingness of both parties may not be sustained. Cooperation seldom has been a viable long-term or permanent policy with unchanged institutions outside the collective agreement.

4. *Labor-management committees, contrary to much popular writing, are not a recent phenomenon.* They go back to the early days of collective bargaining, and many cooperative or specialized activi-

ties performed by designated committees had been undertaken directly by the principal parties to the collective agreement. The interstate joint conference in bituminous coal mining,[22] the conciliation arrangements between the Bricklayers and the Mason Builders[23] in New York, Chicago, and Boston, and the impartial umpire institution in the clothing industries, going back as far as seventy to a hundred years, resemble joint committees in their attention to the basic problems of a sector and their discussions of cooperative means of meeting these issues, in addition to their function of negotiating collective agreements. Indeed, the two functions were often closely intertwined.

5. *Labor-management committees have existed in both private and public employment and in federal, state, and local government.*

6. *The federal government, particularly in wartime, has played a role in encouraging some labor-management committees.* The Federal Mediation and Conciliation Service, through its "preventive mediation" and other activities to encourage parties to avoid serious strife in the resolution of future agreements, has been instrumental in helping to establish some joint committees. The Labor-Management Cooperation Act of 1978 constitutes largely a public expression of the desirability of joint committees to improve communications, to study and explore innovative joint approaches, to assist parties in problem solving, and to enhance the involvement of workers in decision making. A small amount of funding was authorized to encourage joint committees. The overall impact of governments in the establishment and operations of labor-management committees, however, must be assessed to be relatively minor. Joint committees are largely the joint work of management and unions. Moreover, the financing of the work of the committees has come from the private parties, typically the joint costs shared equally.

7. *The third party, if present in the work of labor-management committees, can make a contribution in two respects.* A joint staff function with representatives of the parties serves to gather and interpret data relevant to the concerns of the parties, and agreed-upon courses of action on particular issues for the several organizations involved in the joint committee are mediated.

8. *Many of the most consequential results of labor-management committees are indirect.* They grow out of improved communications, better relations, mutual respect, and knowledge of the other organization, all of which can be applied to other issues than may have initiated the joint committee.

9. *Labor-management committees and their leadership on both sides are often bedeviled by conflicting issues of principle or perception.* Labor leaders can readily be undermined by policies, state-

ments, and appearances that are too collaborative or too responsive to management in the view of the work force (members). Such a stance may be suicide in the internal politics of the union electorate. Increasing productivity may be acclaimed in the press or the academic community, but workers (members) may identify productivity with speed-up, layoffs, or unshared gains of stockholders. Labor members of joint committees are likely to be sensitive to these perceptions on the part of their constituency.

Management members of joint committees likewise have concerns derived from long-held principles and attitudes. The sharing of data on the operations of units of management with employees does not come easily. There is no telling what informed employees may suggest, into what details they may probe, what established policies they may question, or how these ideas may affect subsequent collective bargaining negotiations. Cost data are highly sensitive and often regarded as proprietary. The style of management that directs and orders employees and finds security in its prerogatives is not readily changed to more cooperative and shared decision processes.

In sum, the moderation or abandonment of traditional attitudes and procedures is most difficult for representatives of both sides.

The Near-Term Future

In the last several years of the 1970s and in the early 1980s there has been vast public outpouring of material concerning labor-management committees, quality circles, work innovation, participative management, and a variety of other approaches to managing a work force, all designed to elicit greater output, quality, performance, loyalty, dedication, and responsiveness to the interests of the managers among the managed. There are a number of reasons for this surge. The economic difficulties of the period; the inroads of foreign competition in domestic and in foreign markets, particularly from the Japanese with what are thought to be cooperative labor-management relations in the work place; the intense public debate over re-industrialization programs with labor-management committees proposed as a major policy tool; the objective need for economic restraint in collective bargaining in major sectors threatened with serious questions of survival; the role of numerous consultants selling quality circles, work innovation, and forms of participatory management; the National Accord of September 28, 1979 between the Carter Administration and the AFL-CIO; and the re-industrialization proposals of 1980, with provision for tripartite committees. All these factors have heightened attention in the press and media and in business and professional journals as well. The emphasis on the need for new management methods is also derived from what are thought to be major new technologies, industries, and occupations combined with a work force that is better educated, comprised of more women and older workers, and including more individuals interested in part-time work.

These influences raise the question of whether the United States is in the process of developing "a new industrial relations" and "new methods of managing the work force" that are likely to constitute a watershed, or whether the period has created a series of largely passing fads. The question is whether the generalizations from the history of labor-management committees in the last section are in the main a useful guide to the future or whether we are entering a genuinely new age. An ebullient view of a new order is found in a special feature in *Business Week*:[24]

> *Quietly, almost without notice, a new industrial relations system with a fundamentally different way of managing people is taking shape in the U.S. Its goal is to end the adversarial relationship that has grown between management and labor and that now threatens the competitiveness of many industries.*
>
> *   *   *
>
> *Clearly, a changed social and economic environment in the U.S. demands that labor and management create a new relationship. The lessons provided by the pioneers of work innovations prove that changes in work processes and structures are not only possible, they can be highly successful. Most of all they show that the U.S. industrial relations system, so long arrested at primitive levels of development, can now evolve into a third stage—a participative stage.*

A little perspective, five or ten years, on the developments of the late 1970s and early 1980s is likely to yield a quite different appraisal. Many beginnings have faded away. Methods that suit a few relationships are not necessarily accepted by most managers and labor organizations. Economic recovery is likely to change labor and management attitudes and decisions, just as the threat of survival in deep recession created common bonds. In July 1983, on the return of profits, the UAW asked the Chrysler Corporation to reopen its collective agreement (scheduled to run to January 1984) and grant an immediate increase. These parties could not agree, and the union postponed its requests until it could use strike pressure. The company made an improved offer that was accepted, extending the agreement to October 1985. Peter J. Pestillo, Vice-President, Ford Motor Company, stated: ". . . the critical question is whether the spirit of cooperation that both sides claim was a part of the concession contracts of 1982 will survive an apparent return of prosperity."[25]

While the jury is out on the long-term consequences of contemporary developments, it is well to remember that American management, or some segments, have embraced a series of different approaches to the management of its human resources over the course of this century. Scientific management at the turn of the century emphasized work processes, time and motion study, individual incentives, and training. Welfare programs of the 1920s, until disrupted by the Great Depression, sought to relate the individual worker to the enterprise; and the human relations views of Elton Mayo, F. L. Roethlisberger, and other behavioral researchers provided the basis of subsequent emphasis on the small work group and performance. Each of these movements made vastly exaggerated claims as to effects on productivity, morale, and the relationship between workers and managers. Yet each of these movements has left a residue that had made a permanent contribution to the current philosophy and policies of managers generally toward their work force. It would, indeed, be surprising if the contemporary movement, stressing work innovation, participative management, and labor-management committees, would prove to be very different.

While the first sentence of the *Business Week* lead paragraph cited above is grossly inaccurate reporting, the second sentence is bad history: "Its goal (a fundamentally different way of managing people) is to end the adversarial relationship that has grown between management and labor. . . ." An adversarial relationship has not "grown between management and labor"; the relationship was already adversarial, and was probably more so in years past. The relationship has clearly become less violent; it may be no less adversarial but is constrained by legal procedures. The frontiers of new organizational campaigns and decertification cases yield some of the most bitter conflicts. Established relationships on balance have clearly tended over long periods of time to become less adversarial, although hostile environments may readily engender adversarial behavior.

As in the past, it would appear likely to expect that there will be a number, even some greater number, of labor-management relationships that are cooperative and participatory, although the number is likely to be relatively small. While there can be no quarrel with those who wish to spend time and energy expanding this small group, broad policy has to presume that the vast bulk of labor-management relationships contain and will continue to contain simultaneously significant mixtures of both adversarial and cooperative elements in varying proportions.

This view of labor-management relationships is embodied in the "Statement of Purpose" of the Labor-Management Group, comprised of top leaders of labor and large businesses, issued March 4, 1981. These excerpts are illustrative:[26]

> *The national interest requires a new spirit of mutual trust and coopera-*
> *tion, even though management and organized labor are, and will re-*
> *main, adversaries on many issues. . . . It is destructive to society and to*
> *business and to organized labor, if in our legitimate adversarial roles,*
> *we question the right of our institutions to exist and perform their*
> *legitimate functions. In performing these functions, we recognize that*
> *both parties must respect deeply held views even when they disagree.*

The perspective on labor-management relations embodied in this statement involves two observations about industrial conflict and adversarial relationships that are at variance with the simplistic objective of fully cooperative relations. The first observation is that industrial conflict often serves a useful social (and economic) purpose. Conflict may be the only way to change the minds of managements and workers on an issue. As Douglas H. Soutar, Senior Vice-President of ASARCO said, "For collective bargaining to work properly its adversarial nature must continue."[27] The withdrawal of services or job opportunities for a period constitutes a failure of organized buyers and sellers to agree in the labor market and is an essential element of a free society. The virtues of conflict, competition, and struggle are not to be underrated. The second observation is that labor and management relationships at all levels involve both adversarial and cooperative elements in our society. It is not one or the other. "Joint consultation may help to reduce antagonism and to solve difficulties before they become disputes; but antagonism and difficulties will remain. They are inherent in a free society."[28]

Labor-management committees live in an environment with elements of both conflict and cooperation.

Endnotes

1. Jerome M. Rosow and Robert Zager, *Productivity Through Work Innovations,* A Work in America Policy Study (New York: Pergamon Press, 1982). *Perspectives on Labor-Management Cooperation,* U.S. Department of Labor, Labor-Management Services Administration (Washington, D.C., 1982).
2. *The System of Industrial Relations in Great Britain, Its History, Law and Institutions,* Allan Flanders and H. A. Clegg, eds. (Oxford, Basil Blackwell, 1954), p. 320. (Chapter VI, "Joint Consultation" by H. A. Clegg and T. E. Chester, pp. 323–64).
3. Bureau of National Affairs, *Daily Labor Report* (January 25, 1982), p. A-15.
4. *Hearings Before Human Resources Committee, Human Resource Development*

Act of 1977, 95th Cong., 1st Sess., Subcommittee on Employment, Poverty and Migratory Labor (September 27, 1977), pp. 49–67, testimony of John T. Dunlop.

5. Some appreciation of the diversity is evident from National Center for Productivity and Quality of Working Life, *Directory of Labor-Management Committees* (October 1976), Washington, D.C.: U.S. Department of Labor, Labor-Management Services Administration, *Resource Guide to Labor-Management Cooperation*, Washington, D.C. (1982).

6. Dorothea DeSchweinitz, *Labor and Management in a Common Enterprise* (Cambridge, Mass.: Harvard University Press, 1949).

7. See Frederick G. Lesieur, ed., *The Scanlon Plan: A Frontier in Labor-Management Cooperation* (Cambridge, Mass.: M.I.T. Press; and New York: John Wiley and Sons, Inc., 1958); National Commission on Productivity and Work Quality, *A Plant-Wide Productivity Plan in Action: Three Years of Experience with the Scanlon Plan*, Washington, D.C. (1975).

8. James J. Healy, ed., *Creative Collective Bargaining* (Englewood Cliffs, N.J.: Prentice-Hall, Inc., 1965), pp. 244–81; Kaiser Steel Corporation and United Steelworkers of America, *The Long Range Sharing Plan*, Fontana, California (May 1965).

9. United Steelworkers of America, *The Joint Advisory Committee on Productivity* (November, 1971).

10. See *Agreement between Jones and Laughlin Steel Corporation and the United Steelworkers of America* (August 1, 1980), pp. 213–14.

11. *General Agreement between the Tennessee Valley Authority and the Tennessee Valley Trades and Labor Council, Covering Construction Employment*, Article X.

12. *Statement of Principles on Quality of Work Life*, from the CWA/AT&T National Committee on Joint Working Conditions and Service Quality Improvement (April 17, 1981).

13. The classic studies are Sumner H. Slichter, *Union Policies and Industrial Management* (Washington, D.C.: The Brookings Institution, 1941), pp. 393–571; Sumner H. Slichter, James J. Healy, E. Robert Livernash, *The Impact of Collective Bargaining on Management* (Washington, D.C.: The Brookings Institution, 1960), pp. 841–78. Also see, Jean Carol Trepp (McKelvey), *Trade Union Interest in Production*, Ph.D. dissertation submitted to Radcliffe College (1933). For a series of case studies, see, *Causes of Industrial Peace Under Collective Bargaining*, Clinton S. Golden and Virginia D. Parker, ed. (New York: Harper and Brothers, Publishers, 1953). For an evaluation of labor-management committees see William Gomberg, "Special Study Committees," in *Frontiers of Collective Bargaining*, John T. Dunlop and Neil W. Chamberlin, eds. (New York: Harper and Row, 1967, pp. 235–51).

14. U.S. Department of Labor, Labor-Management Services Administration, *The Operation of Area Labor-Management Committees* (Washington, D.C., 1981), p. 26.

15. Morris A. Horowitz, *The New York Hotel Industry, A Labor Relations Study* (Cambridge, Mass.: Harvard University Press, 1960).

16. Arnold R. Weber, "The Interplant Transfer of Displaced Employees" with Edwin Young, "The Armour Experience: A Case Study in Plant Shutdown," in Industrial Relations Research Association, *Adjusting to Technological Change*,

Gerald G. Somers, et al., eds. (New York: Harper and Row Publishers, 1963), pp. 95–143; 144-58. George P. Shultz and Arnold R. Weber, *Strategies for the Displaced Worker* (New York: Harper and Row, 1966).

17. See Jack Stieber, "The President's Committee on Labor-Management Policy," *Industrial Relations* (February 1966), pp. 1–19. Also see documents from Department of Labor Records Microfilm Reel #27 in the holdings of the Johnson Library.

18. See The Labor-Industry Coalition for International Trade, *International Trade, Industrial Policies and the Future of American Industry*, Washington, D.C. (1983).

19. See Sumner H. Slichter, *Union Policies and Industrial Management* (Washington, D.C.: The Brookings Institution, 1941), pp. 561–62.

20. U.S. Department of Labor, Labor-Management Services Administration, *The Operation of Area Labor-Management Committees*, Washington, D.C. (1981), p. 25. Also see, Joseph A. Loftus and Beatrice Walfish, *Breakthroughs in Union Management Cooperation*, Work in America Institute (1977); and Irving H. Siegel and Edgar Weinberg, *Labor-Management Cooperation*, W. E. Upjohn Institute for Employment Research (1982).

21. *Loc. Cit.*, p. 567.

22. Arthur E. Suffern, *Conciliation and Arbitration in the Coal Industry of America* (Boston: Houghton Mifflin Company, 1915).

23. Josephine Shaw Lowell, *Industrial Arbitration and Conciliation* (New York, G. P. Putnam's Sons, 1893).

24. "The New Industrial Relations," *Business Week* (May 11, 1981), p. 85.

25. *New York Times* (July 24, 1983), Section 3, p. F13.

26. Labor-Management Group, *Release* (March 4, 1982). Appendix B to Chapter 15.

27. "An Era of Challenge for Collective Bargaining" (May 5, 1983).

28. H. A. Clegg and T. E. Chester, *loc. cit.*, p. 364.

Chapter 15

THE WORK OF
LABOR-MANAGEMENT
COMMITTEES

The potentials, as well as the limitations, of labor-management committees can be better appreciated—beyond the general experience portrayed in the last chapter—by some more detailed review of the work of individual committees. A brief report and analysis follows on three currently operating committees[1] in which I have been involved: the first is on the state level in the public sector; the second is on the national level in a soft-goods sector; and the third is concerned with the economy generally. These more detailed reports permit a comparison of objectives, methods, and roles of participants and they show the wide variety of problems and activities addressed by committees. A final section of this chapter is concerned with consensus-building processes.

Massachusetts Joint Labor-Management Committee for Municipal Police and Fire[2]

Massachusetts law, effective July 1, 1974, provided that disputes over collective bargaining agreements between municipalities and police and firefighter labor organizations be resolved by mediation and fact finding with recommendations and, if still unresolved, by last-best-offer arbitration on a package basis involving all issues in dispute. The award was binding on both parties, including the municipal legislative body required to appropriate the funds.

This form of final and binding arbitration provides that the arbitrator is required to choose between the package of final proposals made by the union and that made by the city or town. Subsequently, legislation authorized the arbitrator to include in his options the package of recommendations made by a fact-finder, if there was one. The theory of the last-best-offer approach is that each party will be induced to move its position to be closer to the other, and perhaps even reach agreement, in order to avoid a win by the other side. This process is thought to stimulate direct agreement-making.[3]

By 1977 the municipal firefighter and police unions and the cities and towns were in deep conflict and acrimonious debate over the final and binding arbitration statute. The form of the arbitration made it easy to identify a winner and a loser, and the municipal managements scored heavy political gains against the process and the arbitrators by showing that the unions "won" twice as many cases as management. Never mind that the managements may not have put together realistic packages and that many were inexperienced in bargaining and third-party proceedings. The process was long and expensive for many cases. Cases that went through the last-best-offer arbitration process in the years 1975–79 required 15.2 months for resolution, and those settled upon issuance of the fact-finder's report required 8.8 months. The average for all cases was 6.7 months. There was extensive litigation in the courts over unfair labor practices and the arbitration process.

In June 1977 the Massachusetts legislature voted to extend the statute two years. Governor Dukakis vetoed the bill, and the legislature passed it over his veto. The cities and towns, unwilling to give up the political fight, decided to develop a referendum petition for signatures to place the issue on the ballot for the 1978 elections.

At this juncture after a significant number of signatures had been enrolled, representatives of the Massachusetts League of Cities and Towns and the Massachusetts Professional Fire Fighters approached me, through the City Manager of Cambridge, to serve as mediator to seek a resolution of the continuing dispute over the legislation and its administration. On August 30, 1977 I met with Kennedy Shaw and Demetrios Moschos, representing the League of Cities and Towns, and with T. Dustin Alward, Martin Pierce, and J. J. Jennings, representing the Professional Fire Fighters of Massachusetts and the major police union associations as well. I was without background in the Massachusetts experience.

By September 19, 1977 in the course of a few sessions, the parties reached full agreement on the text of a memorandum[4] that I had drafted outlining a new procedure for the resolution of disputes. They translated the agreement into statutory language, jointly presented it to the Governor and the leaders of the legislature, and they were instrumental in securing its passage and enactment into law on

November 15, 1977 without significant opposition. The law was truly the product of their agreement and joint efforts.

The agreement and the statute provided for a joint committee comprised of six municipal officials, drawn from the different components of municipal management—mayors, city managers, selectmen, finance committee members, and others—three representatives of municipal police, three representatives of firefighters, and a chairman (and later a vice chairman). These members were to be nominated by the respective organizations, and these members in turn were to agree upon the neutral chairman. The Governor was required to appoint the nominees of the organizations; the Committee members were not to be the usual political appointments in state government. The original Committee members asked me to chair the Committee and that appointment has continued since November 1977.

The Committee is assisted by a senior staff representative nominated by management and one nominated by the labor members and by (currently) four mediators. The committee members serve without compensation, but they are reimbursed for expenses. The neutrals are compensated on a per diem basis. The Committee expended $320,000 in fiscal 1983.

There are approximately 165 local labor organizations representing 11,700 firefighters and 252 local labor organizations representing 12,200 police officers in the 350 cities and towns in the Commonwealth.

The Committee members on both sides play a significant role in the dispute resolution process, in mediation, and in making the decisions as to any further steps that may be appropriate. The members of the Committee have proved to be very effective in promoting settlements with their constituents and in working as a team with an opposite number and a staff mediator or the chairman. A neutral can seldom approach a mayor, selectman, or finance committee member, for instance, with the perspective and the effectiveness of another mayor, selectman, or municipal official.

The Committee may refer a case to fact finding with recommendations by the neutrals on the Committee or by an outside neutral. But unlike the prior routine referral of cases to fact finding, the Committee engages in extensive mediation with staff mediators, senior staff, committee members, and the chairmen, and occasionally with outside mediators. The Committee designs a series of steps likely to encourage settlement in the particular case.

Prior to November 1980, the Committee referred to final and binding arbitration a relatively few cases that would not yield to fact finding and further mediation. In the period from January 1978 until September 1980 the Committee referred 45 cases to arbitration out of

221 cases, compared with the 105 cases that had gone to last-best-offer arbitration out of 648 cases in the period 1975–79. All of these 45 were settled by *de facto* agreement. The average time used in settlement under the Committee, 1978 to 1980, was 3.6 months, compared with 6.7 months under the prior arrangements. The average time for settlement under the Committee by fiscal year since then is as follows: 1980—4.6 months (85 cases); 1981—4.8 months (71 cases); 1982—4.5 months (83 cases); 1983—3.8 months (52 cases).

In November 1980 the Massachusetts voters approved by 59 per cent a referendum question that imposed a limit on state and local taxes on real estate and personal property equal to 2½ per cent of its full and fair cash value. The referendum question also included the repeal of the provision in state law for compulsory last-best-offer arbitration in municipal police and firefighter negotiations. The Committee was otherwise unaffected by the referendum petition; only its authority to order final and binding arbitration was affected. On February 10, 1981 the Attorney General of the Commonwealth issued an advisory opinion holding that the Committee continued to have authority to order final and binding arbitration on the executive officers of a city or town but not on a legislative body requiring it to appropriate the requisite funds. In these circumstances the Committee chose to avoid the uncertainties of any legal confrontation; it has simply continued to use only mediation and other non-compulsory methods. Some disputes have proved difficult, and a few have required inordinate time and effort to resolve.

Since the interest of this chapter is in the committee mechanism generally rather than in the details of the Joint Labor-Management Committee for Municipal Police and Fire, a series of general observations derived from this experience are in order. First, the Committee was created basically by agreement and consent of the parties. Although supported and made legitimate by statutes, the Committee was not imposed on the statewide organizations by the hostile fiat of state law. The Committee is manned by the parties, and the neutrals are selected by the members; it is operated by the parties with the aid of a staff responsible to the members and working with them in particular cases. Further, the parties have the *de facto* capacity to destroy the Committee by refusing to cooperate in furnishing members and in other ways. In every sense, it is *their* committee, and they have a sense of responsibility for it.

The concluding sentences of a volume examining the last-best-offer arbitration experience of Pennsylvania, Michigan, and Wisconsin stated: "It seems, therefore, that the ideal solution is the one designed by the parties themselves for their own use. It can be an amalgam of the various features of the system used elsewhere, but if self-designed, it will have a better chance for a longer life."[5] The Massachusetts procedures were designed by the parties.

The Committee reflects the internal differences within the management side of many communities. Finance committee members and selectmen may often disagree; mayors and city councils may be at odds. Disputes within management on fire and police issues may often reflect conflict over questions quite apart from personnel policy. Lawyers representing a community may often represent only the least common denominator, while a management member of the Committee may be more able to penetrate and help to resolve such internal conflicts within management. Contests for office and the endorsements by firefighter and police local unions may complicate issues, particularly in the shadow of elections. The internal complications of union organizations and the rivalries for provisions of agreements are better known; the committee structure is likewise designed to accommodate these real issues and obstacles to agreement making. Because the business of government includes politics, the dispute resolution machinery must be able to operate effectively in such an environment.

The representatives of the cities and towns and public safety unions both recognize that collective bargaining in the years ahead faces complex and difficult issues and that an attitude and relationship of greater constructive discourse and cooperation would be helpful to all parties and to the citizens of the state generally. The Committee was envisaged as a forum around which policy discussions could be held. Such long-term issues include the regionalization of fire and police services, the relations of civil service rules to collective bargaining, and the quality of appointments to labor relations posts in the state government. Some of these topics have been discussed in special days set aside for the topic, although the opportunities have not been fully utilized.

The Committee has appreciably reduced the cost of legal services involved in the settlement of agreements. Settlement times have been materially reduced and litigation has been sharply curtailed. It has developed a significant data base of collective agreements and data, which are stored in a computer for current use in the work of the Committee.

The Committee permits the coordination of dispute resolution between firefighters and police in the same community and among contiguous localities. This was not possible under the pre-1978 arrangements, where each case was largely a separate entity and comparative conditions were argued before separate factfinders and last-best-offer arbitrators. The whipsaw between firefighter and police negotiations can be substantially mitigated. The agreement and statute state, "The Committee shall have oversight responsibility for all collective bargaining negotiations involving municipal police and firefighters."

The Committee seeks to enhance the agreement-making process; it is relentless and dogged in its pursuit of new methods to agreement. Its approach to any formal proceedings, factfinding, or arbitration is to seek terms likely to be acceptable to the parties rather than something meritorious from a stack of exhibits. Its philosophy is, "Where would the bargaining of the parties come out if an agreement had been consummated instead of having been frustrated?" The approach is not to find what some formal criteria might abstractly yield in a proceeding. The Committee has performed its work without work interruption in the cities and towns of the Commonwealth. Moreover, as Chairman, I have virtually never cast a vote, but rather sought agreement within the Committee.

The Committee also resolves a number of cases that were previously handled before the Labor Relations Commission of the Commonwealth as unfair labor practice cases, particularly involving allegations of refusal to bargain or bargaining in bad faith. At the direction of the legislature these cases affecting firefighter and police issues are routinely referred to the Committee to be resolved in mediation with the substantive negotiations.

Over the course of its first six years the Committee has had to adjust its methods and approaches to a changing legal framework, to a changing economic climate, to different state government administrations, to a changing staff, to a changing Committee membership, and to shifting issues at collective bargaining tables. There is no assurance that the adaptation can continue indefinitely, particularly in the absence of closure authority, but the Committee has proved to be a flexible institution. It may also be observed that, as is often the case, the Committee provided the personal contacts and helped to create the attitudes that made possible the reform of the Massachusetts public pension and disability administration in 1983 (Chapter 630 of the Acts of 1982 and Chapter 661 of the Acts of 1983).

Tailored Clothing Technology Corporation (TC)^2

In October 1976, following negotiations in the shirt branch of the men's clothing industry, the Amalgamated Clothing and Textile Workers Union requested me to study the current extent of and the likely prospects for imports in the men's clothing industries. Limitation of imports had been a major issue in the shirt negotiations and seemed likely to be a significant issue in future negotiations with other branches of the industry, including the tailored clothing sector. The shirt contract negotiations had been resolved at the final hour with the agreement for a study.

With the understanding that the study would be made with the joint participation and cooperation of management, I agreed to organize the project. The study was undertaken by Professor Elisabeth Allison.[6] It pointed out that:

> In 1965 the wardrobe of the average American male was almost 100% American made. In 1976 it would be rare to find a wardrobe without foreign labels: 30% of the shirts, 30% of the sportcoats, 18% of the trousers and 12% of the suits sold were made offshore. Over the same period employment in the clothing industry declined by 25%, while economy-wide employment rose by 32%; the number of firms declined by 20%.

The report concluded that there would be continued rapid growth of imports, estimated to exceed 50% of all products by 1987. The report noted, however, that:

> One critical new factor for the next decade will be the massive increase in males in the 30-45 age group as the baby boom children enter their 30s. This growth will be sufficient to allow the domestic industry some absolute growth in volume for a limited period even with increased foreign penetration.

In the light of the results of the study and at the request of the parties in the tailored men's clothing industry, I suggested that they undertake three programs to address their long-term concerns. First, they should develop a joint training program in view of their high turnover in order to improve employee selection, to reduce training costs, and to improve average productivity. Substantial government funding would be available under CETA discretionary funds in the Department of Labor if the parties would support a change in the Congressional prohibition, by virtue of an exchange on the Senate floor in the 1960s, against the use of government training funds for sewing occupations. Second, they should seek support from the Commerce Department for funding of a program of modeling the production process, quality control, and piece-rate method of payment, as well as a program of supervisory training. And third, they should develop a genuine research and development program. Although the major interest of this section is with the research and development program, let us consider briefly the training program.

On March 2, 1978 the Amalgamated Clothing and Textile Workers and the Clothing Manufacturers Association signed a contract with the Labor Department establishing the first comprehensive training program for the tailored clothing industry. They established a Joint

Job Training and Research (JTR) non-profit corporation. The program came to encompass more than 60 companies in 14 major markets. While it was operating, the Labor Department invested more than $2 million a year in the program.

On June 28, 1977 the labor and management leaders of both the men's and women's clothing industries presented to President Carter their program "to initiate changes in these industries to make them more productive and competitive." The industry was well suited to achieve the objectives of public policy expressed in the CETA legislation. The tailored clothing industry is urban and employs a high proportion of women, minorities, and those with little formal education, and it is relatively high-wage among apparel sectors. The subsidy amounted to one-half the trainee's then starting rate (under the collective agreement) of $3.25 for 14 weeks.[7] The program was well organized and efficiently managed. After the election of 1980, the training program was phased out by the new Administration.

In the summer of 1979, in company with Professor Frederick H. Abernathy of the Division of Applied Sciences of Harvard University, I visited a number of tailored clothing plants and leaders of the industry to ascertain the potentials and interest in a five- or ten-year research and development program in the technology of men's suits. Professor Abernathy, a specialist in fluid mechanics, explored the technology potentials, recognizing that computer-based cutting of cloth had been introduced into the industry after 1970. I concentrated on the possible institutional arrangements to organize and support research and development work. At the end of the summer we held a workshop, August 28–29, 1979, with technical and production-oriented persons from the industry, including union people, from academic posts, and from the government to report our findings and to seek a consensus of views as to the more fruitful possibilities.[8]

These developments led to the establishment in October 1980 of a non-profit corporation, Tailored Clothing Technology Corporation, $(TC)^2$, with a board of directors drawn from clothing companies, textile companies manufacturing cloth, synthetic fiber companies, and others with an interest in the project. Each company and the union have contributed $50,000 a year and the Commerce Department has matched the private sector contributions from economic development funds appropriated for trade-afflicted industry. The non-profit corporation in turn developed a technical advisory committee from its constituent organizations. The board of directors provided funding beginning on April 24, 1981 to Charles Stark Draper Laboratory, Inc. (formerly a part of M.I.T. in Cambridge, Massachusetts) to design and develop a new system of sewing. The budget of the first year (1981–82) was $450,000 and has since been increased to $2.65 million a year in calendar year 1984 as additional companies have joined with matching government funds provided.[9]

By the end of the first year $(TC)^2$ and Draper had agreed upon a prototype machine to design and build, concentrating first on the sleeve.[10] Patents were applied for and, by the end of the second year, the machine had been successfully tested in the laboratory. By September 1983, two and one-half years into the project, the machine was in place on a production line in a clothing factory in Allentown, Pennsylvania, being tested under operating conditions.

There are a wide range of issues of technology, economic viability, manufacturing, and patents that confront the board of directors of $(TC)^2$ and its technical advisory committee. They can be studied in more specialized reports. The present interest is with the operations of the underlying labor-management committee and its institutional form in the board of directors.[11]

At the outset of the consideration of research and development activities, I discussed at length with President Murray Finley and Secretary-Treasurer Jack Sheinkman of the Amalgamated Clothing and Textile Workers the fundamental questions involved in promoting technological change that might improve international competitiveness by reducing direct labor costs but that might be expected to affect employment adversely. They responded that our study of imports suggested that there was little choice, beyond what was being done in trade policy to restrain imports, than to encourage technological innovation in cooperation with the clothing companies under collective agreement. The large general executive board of the Union has been kept informed of the research and development activity, and a vice-president serves on the technical advisory committees. If, and when, the time comes generally to introduce the new machinery, the Union will have contributed to its development and may be expected to have a significant say in the rate of introduction, retraining of workers (particularly maintenance personnel), and in sharing the benefits of gains and patent royalties.

Labor relations in the men's clothing industry have a long and well-known history of constructive and cooperative action, beginning with Sidney Hillman and Hart, Schaffner, and Marx.[12] But the inclusion in the management group of a number of companies without significant collective bargaining relationships and some with years of conflict with the Union is rather extraordinary. These companies producing clothing, cloth, synthetic yarn, or fabricated products all have a business interest in a more productive clothing industry in this country.

The clothing industry had no history of research and development—at least among companies under collective agreements. Companies building specialized sewing machines or pressing machines introduced innovations from time to time, but these changes suited the machine builders and their market configurations rather than the opportunities in the men's clothing industry. The technical advisory committee of (TC)^2 has impelled some clothing companies to appoint research and development officers for the first time as in Hartmarx Corporation. The first-hand association with DuPont and others with a long research tradition and capability has likewise stimulated research and development among the affiliated clothing companies.

The approach of (TC)^2 constitutes a significant precedent—or at least one possible model—for public policy concerned with issues of trade, research, and development in a sector of the economy. The idea of the project, its technical direction, and its leadership all arose in the private sector. The private parties have put up more than half the funding, including contributions in kind. Industry, labor, and a private laboratory are cooperating in the enterprise. The government support is encouraging technological development in a sector without previous activity, a sector vulnerable to more imports and politically capable of generating significant limitations on imports. The clothing and textile sector employs a very large work force largely comprised of women and with large numbers of minority workers; the industries are relatively low paying. Rapid dislocation would create serious hardship. The parties, it might be said, are seeking modestly to develop an element of their own industrial policy appropriate to the sector.

It might be observed that since the formation of (TC)^2 a number of countries have announced large-scale research and development programs in the textile and clothing industries. Japan, the European Community, and Sweden have announced multi-year and multi-million dollar programs supported by governments. The structure and experience with research and development of the clothing industry in the U.S. is inherently quite different from that in computers, chemicals, or even automobiles. The issue of appropriate response in U.S. public policy remains a political issue debated largely in ideological terms.

The work of (TC)^2 has taken some years to show any results, and the viability of the approach will not be evident for some time. Already (TC)^2 and Draper have identified a number of additional projects that seem worth while and that are anticipated to yield profitable returns to the cluster of industries. Research and development in the sector needs somehow to be institutionalized; no single firm in the past has regarded the activity as profitable. These issues lie ahead of (TC)^2.

The Labor-Management Group

A labor-management committee comprised of the leaders of the American labor movement (under the aegis of the AFL–CIO) and chief executive officers of large business enterprises such as those represented by the Business Round Table, has met, in varying incarnations, regularly since 1973 on a wide range of issues related to economic policy. For the period prior to early 1976 the Committee met with the President or top government officials, and since then the Committee has met as a private body without government involvement or status except when cabinet officials joined meetings for a period of six months in 1977. The ten years 1973–83 is a longer period of interaction between top labor and management representatives in a succession of forums, with some continuing personnel, than has previously occurred in this country. The President's Committee on Labor-Management Policy in the Kennedy-Johnson era, which had a quite different focus (largely on a number of labor-management issues except for inflation), met during the period 1961–67.

Labor-Management Advisory Committee

In January 1973 I was appointed Director of the Cost of Living Council to administer wage and price controls, replacing both the Price Commission and the tripartite Pay Board from which the AFL–CIO had withdrawn on March 22, 1972. In the belief that any continuation of wage and price controls, and more generally the shape of economic policy for the period ahead, required a significant direct contribution from the major business and labor communities, Secretary of the Treasury George P. Shultz and I organized a Labor-Management Advisory Committee.[13]

The Committee issued a major policy statement on February 26, 1973 (see Appendix A). It set forth a standard for "responsible wage behavior" considering the economy as a whole and stated that the members of the Committee were prepared "to use their good offices to create a climate favorable to the settlement of collective bargaining negotiations in major cases in 1973 and within the framework of stabilization policies in cooperation with appropriate government officials."

The Committee further stated, "Responsible wage behavior for individual parties in 1973 requires that more attention be directed than in the recent past to issues of long-term competitive conditions, productivity, and working conditions, wage relationships, and benefit costs as well as to the achievement of moderate settlements." The Committee stated it would advise the Cost of Living Council whether particular settlements were consistent with the goals of the statement or unreasonably inconsistent with the stabilization program.

The Committee was invaluable generally and specifically in the administration of controls during the period January 1973–June 1974, including its support for special tripartite committees in the retail food, health care, and construction industries. "The procedural fundamental of wage and salary stabilization in this country is the necessity for the sympathetic involvement of labor and management leaders."[14] "Non-cooperation and hostility from labor or management leaders can quickly put the stabilization authorities under siege with massive lawsuits, concerted legislative attack with endless amendments to the statutory authority and limitations on appropriations, and—most serious of all—labor disputes and work stoppages that are directed against the government and its stabilization program."[15] In the absence of cooperation, every collective bargaining strike in effect becomes a strike against the government—an intolerable position in a political democracy.

The Committee also became a forum, with top government officials, for a continuing frank discussion of the economic outlook and economic policy. Private sector current economic information on order books, prices, employment, and the like for major sectors is often not available to government officials and is reflected in published statistics only after several weeks.

The labor and management members of the Committee also served as members of a National Commission for Industrial Peace, with cabinet level government officials as ex-officio members and David L. Cole as chairman. This Commission made a number of recommendations to improve collective bargaining dispute resolution.[16]

On November 13, 1973 the Committee reiterated its view that "the stabilization act, which is scheduled to expire April 30, 1974, should not be renewed and that no legislative authority to administer wage and price controls should be enacted for the period thereafter."[17] The Committee ceased to function after June 30, 1974 with the expiration of the stabilization program.

President's Labor-Management Committee

In September 1974 President Gerald R. Ford asked me to recommend a labor-management committee. On September 30, 1974 he established the President's Labor-Management Committee.[18] The Committee was given a broad charter to advise and make recommendations to the President. The Committee met regularly with a prepared agenda. At these sessions, the Committee met alone or with cabinet officers and senior economic policy staff and then with the President. In the 15 months of activity, the Committee held 8 meetings and the President took part in 7 of them.

On January 10, 1975 the White House released the recommendations of the Committee on the distribution of a personal income tax cut, estimated to aggregate $15 billion a year, and an increase in the investment tax credit to 12 per cent, aggregating $5 billion a year. This was the first occasion on which organized labor had supported an investment tax credit. George Meany and Reginald D. Jones presented their views jointly to the chairman of the Ways and Means and Finance committees of the Congress. The Committee views were influential in shaping the tax-reduction measures of 1975. A statement of the Committee on National Energy Policy was also released on January 10, 1975.

The Committee had staff papers prepared and also adopted positions on housing and the financing of public utilities (released by the White House on June 13, 1975), on unemployment, and on the development of labor-management committees in private sectors. At each session with the President, the Committee also provided its view of the economic outlook.

Labor-Management Group

In January 1976, when I resigned from the Administration, the labor members of the President's Committee advised that they would not continue to participate. The management members explored with George Meany the idea that the labor-management committee continue as a private group with the same members and coordinator. The labor members readily agreed and the first meeting of the Group was held on March 15, 1976. The name "Labor-Management Group" was adopted to symbolize the change.

A sense of the interests of the Group is best conveyed by listing the topics identified as possible candidates for serious joint staff work on which consensus might be achieved: unemployment, jobs, and capital formation; housing; the regulatory process; energy; New York City's financial problems; health care; social security; international trade; national economic policy-making processes, illegal aliens, agricultural policy, welfare, the balance of clean air and water and economic considerations; wage and price controls and incomes policies; sectors with special problems; and the public understanding of collective bargaining. Among this group of policy issues the following were to become the issues of most detailed staff work, discussion, or public statements over the course of the next four years: job creation; inflation and incomes policy; health care; energy; illegal aliens, air quality, and economic considerations; and housing. The Group had reached a broad consensus on "Job-Creation: Labor-Management Recommendations" by the time of the elections of November 1976.

On April 15, 1977 in a major statement on Inflation, President Carter said:

> *If this battle against inflation is to succeed, I am, above all, convinced that it requires a close collaboration between business, labor, and the Government. This collaborative effort should consist of working together to advise government on its objectives for our economy, for job creation, and for inflation reduction, to help work out approaches to achieve these objectives and to monitor the results on a continuing basis. . . .*
>
> *Accordingly, I have asked the President of the AFL–CIO and the Chairman of the General Electric Company, to help to coordinate this new cooperation between labor, management, and the Government. Within the Government, I have asked the Chairman of the Economic Policy Group [Secretary of the Treasury Blumenthal] . . . to work with these gentlemen and other representatives of business and labor. . . .*

Accordingly, Secretary Blumenthal and Secretary Marshall came to part of the regularly scheduled meeting of the Group on April 18, 1977 to initiate a series of seven meetings over six months with the Labor-Management Group and a series of joint labor-management staff meetings with Government staff on inflation, government policies, and private restraints. The Government representatives to the full Group sessions involved five cabinet-level officials. These meetings were characterized by very detailed and intensive discourse; the labor-management group members focused attention on such sectors as health care, energy, food, industrial capacity, and construction, as well as on compensation and more general economic policies. The tripartite staff developed a major paper on the "Anatomy of Inflation."

In October, however, Secretary Blumenthal reported that the Attorney General had ruled that such meetings in private, not open to the press and media and the public generally, contravened the Federal Advisory Committee Act, and that they had to be discontinued or opened.[19] The discussions ceased. One of the enigmas of this episode and policy is that the Carter Administration found no difficulty in meeting for a sustained period two years later in 1979 with labor representatives alone on a wide range of major economic policy issues and entering into a "National Accord Administration–American Labor Leadership." (See Chapter 16.)

The Labor-Management Group issued a number of papers in 1977 on energy,[20] on illegal aliens,[21] and on health care costs.[22] It also adopted a statement against tax-based-incomes policies for subsequent use. General economic policy issues were focused subsequently in 1978 in papers on "Structural Unemployment: Economic Growth and Inflation Restraint" and "International Trade and Competition," treating particular sectors of the economy as well, and the subject of capacity restraints to economic growth with 10 industry studies. Joint support for the role of health maintenance organizations was evidenced by the attendance of Mr. Meany and Mr. Pilliod, representing the Business Round Table, at a national conference. The Group also encouraged the negotiations of the Nuclear Power Construction Stabilization Agreement effective March 1, 1978.

In the fall of 1978 the public acrimony on issues of labor-management relations and public policy rose many decibels, although the controversial matters had not been under discussion in the Group. In retrospect, this detachment may have been a mistake. The Carter Administration had not consulted business in a serious way or sought to reach a consensus between labor and management on the issues of labor-law reform. The Senate conservatives blocked the legislation, while organized business conducted a massive campaign against it. The leadership of the Business Round Table (Reginald D. Jones, Irving S. Shapiro, and Thomas Murphy), management members of the Group, were outvoted in their Policy Committee on their advice to take no organizational position on labor-law reform. Douglas Fraser publicly resigned from the Group and achieved a neutrality letter from General Motors. In these circumstances George Meany decided to postpone formal meetings, starting with the scheduled September 27, 1978 meeting.[23]

In the ensuing year there were a number of informal sessions with staff and several leaders of each side and the Coordinator. But the regular activities of the Group were in abeyance. President Carter entered into a National Accord on September 28, 1979 without business participation (see Chapter 16).[24]

The 18-member Pay Advisory Committee was created on September 28, 1979. It included Lane Kirkland on the labor side, Philip Hawley on the management side, and John T. Dunlop, as chairman.[25] The joint staff of the Labor-Management Group assisted the two sides of the Pay Advisory Committee. Every action of the Pay Advisory Committee in its 14 months was unanimous—a fact that served, in part, to restore a measure of the members' confidence in each other.[26] Numerous private sessions of these parties took place in this setting. By the early fall of 1980 more formal sessions were begun among the leadership to reconstitute the Group, with several of the key leaders intending to retire from their business posts.

A New Labor-Management Group

A reconstituted Group was formally announced on March 4, 1981, after several meetings in which a Statement of Purpose was developed (Appendix B). The membership was similar to that of the preceding Group, with some replacements for changes in the leadership of particular unions and businesses.[27] The Statement said, "The principal focus of the Group's discussion will be in the area of economic policy in which its collective experience is widely based." A paragraph reflected concern with the acrimonious public exchange of views on labor law reform:

> *The uniqueness of America lies in the vitality of its free institutions. Among these, a free labor movement and a free enterprise economy are essential to the achievements of social and political stability and economic prosperity for all. It is destructive to society and to business and organized labor if, in our legitimate adversarial roles, we question the right of our institutions to exist and perform their legitimate functions. In performing these functions, we recognize that both parties must respect deeply held views even when they disagree.*

The Group turned its primary attention to a number of themes centered on economic growth in the prospective setting of the 1980s: energy policy; competitiveness of American industry, concentrating on half a dozen specific sectors including automobiles and construction; the physical infrastructure of roads, bridges, potable water, and sewerage systems; unemployment and human resource development; and the continuing issue of illegal aliens. A new joint staff group proceeded to work on these issues.

The Group issued a major paper, "The Labor-Management Climate," which encompasses both the developments in the post-war period and the projections for the next decade related to demography, the labor force, employment, technology, competitiveness and the state of industrial relations. The paper is attractively presented and provides a setting for discussion of major economic policy issues confronting labor and management,[28] and government as well.

The Group then completed work on a study of the physical infrastructure problems of roads, bridges, potable water, and sewerage systems; the needs for further funding; and the methods to finance these costs.[29] It distributed the study widely. The Group also renewed its consensus on policy relating to illegal alien legislation and communicated its views to appropriate officials. The Group reached agreement on the extension of the Federal supplemental unemployment insurance program which was scheduled to expire September 30, 1983 and was influential in the enactment of this legislation. Work continues on the other topics, and new suggestions will no doubt be proposed.

The Group instituted a private forum in its staff to resolve disputes suggested for resolution by either side or to encourage opportunities for cooperation with the other side. Neither side would be obligated to resolve the case, only to consider a good-faith effort.

The experience with a national labor-management committee raises a number of larger issues that would require detailed treatment but can be briefly identified here. The question arises whether top labor-management discussions should regularly include the Government, in the light of the concerns reflected in the Federal Advisory Committee Act and of the fears that Big Labor and Big Business will only conspire against the public. While periodic public reporting is essential and practical, open meetings destroy any meaningful discourse and simply reiterate announced public positions. The fragmentation of business creates special problems in composing any forum, and union leaders need to be concerned with the charge of "class collaboration" from elements of the membership. There is also the observation that there are some considerable advantages to labor and management in meeting with government, as there are for government officials, while there are also some opportunity costs in being included in an official committee.

A few general observations on the experience since 1973 are relevant to the present purpose of understanding the operations of different types of committees. The joint staff functions are crucial to a labor-management committee of top officers. The relationships among the staff, as well as among the principals, are useful to direct communications on many matters beyond the work of the Group. Each side learns much about how the other works; it learns better to distinguish public rhetoric and organizational resolutions from negotiable positions; it learns some of the pressures on the opposing side's leadership. Personal relations among the principals may be transferred to other areas in the community or national organizations. There is deep genuine interest on both sides in the views of the other on the issues of the times, and there is a common concern with the international, strategic, diplomatic, financial, and trade position of this country. An agenda must leave some time for spontaneous discourse on these abiding interests as well as work on a prepared agenda. Good relations among top leaders of the business and labor communities would be vital in any serious emergency for the country.

As one leader of the management side privately characterized his experience, "Tedious, but mind sets do change on both sides; we must prevent a Britain where it got too late to get the proper dialogue." But, unlike many other Western democratic countries, the United States has no official forum for systematic discussions among business, labor, and government.

The Consensus Process

To achieve significant results beyond an exchange of views and dialogue, labor-management committees require a consensus on some issues. The consensus-building process may involve organizations in addition to labor and management, as in the group of six private organizations concerned with health care costs and access to health care, or the task force of private organizations, state legislators, and executives involved in seeking agreement on the reform of the Massachusetts public employee pension and disability system. While the diversity and the substantive problems no doubt make a difference in the approach and techniques of consensus building, some essential ingredients in the process are to be generally identified.[30]

Consensus building is problem solving and pragmatic. It relies heavily on the art of listening and on reading perceptively between the lines of formal positions. It is devoted to the quest for irreducible facts, for the actual and for the tendencies. It requires candor and mutual respect. It exhausts charity, patience, and persuasion. It does not presume rationality or order in the affairs of men and women. There is little place for grandiose plans or potential schemes except as a point of departure. It is comfortable with a mixed but acceptable system. It seeks agreement on a few matters and can live with respected differences on other questions.

Consensus building does not depend primarily upon political might or the exercise of governmental or market power. It does not thrive in strident tones or in programs or platforms. It is not congenial to doctrinaire adherence to the left or to the right. It does not rely on Keynes of Laffer. It is not simply the greatest good for the greatest number, insofar as it is sensitive to the interests of internal minorities. It has a special place for genuine representatives on the margin or at the boundaries of their organizations. Experience teaches that the consensus-building process is comprised of the following elements:

1. *A continuing forum.* An occasional symposium or assembly may launch an effort, or call attention to a problem, or provide a one-time platform for meritorious proposals or an opportunity for preachments. But a genuine meeting of minds or a compromise of vital formal positions on any important problems necessitates continuing and regular dialogue among the interests represented in the forum. There

must be a continuing discourse on neutral turf or under somewhat dispassionate auspices to reach common ground.

2. *Private or off-the-record discussions.* It is impossible for responsible leadership of various groups seriously to explore compromise of positions on economic policy or approaches to industrial policy in the glare of press or media or with destructive information leaks. Responsible leaders come to the forum with official positions enshrined in resolutions, traditions, and policies crafted to preserve internal balance or reflecting an ideological commitment. A hospitality to different views requires delicate discussions and explanations to major constituencies. An open meeting cannot generate a consensus, although it may record periodically the results of private discourse. There is a responsibility to report to a wider public on such private discussions.

3. *Professional staff work.* Continuing discourse is substantially facilitated by professional staff under policy direction which marshals the facts, breaks down the issues, and states dispassionately the areas of agreement and disagreement, including a statement of the reasons for contending positions. Staff that captures policy-making functions by default or ambition usually proves to be a disaster. Carefully prepared sessions for policy makers are likely to be vastly more productive in reaching consensus than a series of bull-sessions.

4. *Consensus on limited issues.* It is vital to recognize that consensus on some issues is likely to leave differences on many other questions. It takes experience and sophistication to recognize that groups may agree and cooperate on some issues and disagree and conduct limited warfare or take a neutral stance on other matters.

5. *Consensus and decisions.* Consensus development cannot be a substitute for the formal decision-making processes of the private or public sectors. It can only provide a sense of direction, smooth social conflict, and speed formal processes. Legislative and executive decision processes within the several organizations or the community need to take their normal public processes.

The consensus-building processes can often be extraordinarily constructive. Policies not envisaged initially by any participant may emerge in the course of it.

Endnotes

1. In addition to these three committees, the following current committees in which I am also involved might also have proved of interest in illustrating the range of fields, purposes, and policies of various committees:
   (1) Joint Labor-Management Administrative Committee under the Nuclear Power Construction Stabilization Agreement.

(2) Joint Labor-Management Committee of the Retail Food Industry.

(3) International Union of Bricklayers and Allied Craftsmen and the Mason Contractors Association of America (disputes over local agreements).

(4) Six national organizations concerned with health care.

(5) Working group on Massachusetts public employees pensions and disability.

2. See John T. Dunlop, "Commonwealth of Massachusetts Joint Labor-Management Committee for Municipal Police and Fire," *Massachusetts Business and Economic Report;* Vol. 8, No. 2 (Fall 1980); and Jonathan Brock, *Bargaining Beyond Impasse, Joint Resolution of Public Sector Labor Disputes* (Boston: Auburn House Publishing Company, 1982). Also see *Activity Reports* of the Joint Labor-Management Committee for Municipal Police and Fire for each six-month period.

3. James L. Stern, *et al.*, *Final Offer Arbitration, The Effects of Public Safety Bargaining* (Lexington, Mass.: Lexington Books, 1975).

4. Jonathan Brock, *loc. cit.*, pp. 257–60 for the text of the memorandum of agreement.

5. James L. Stern, *loc. cit.*, p. 197.

6. Elisabeth Allison, *The Impact of Imports on the Men's Clothing Industry* (April 1977), mimeographed.

7. JTR, *Subcontractor Manual* (May 4, 1978).

8. Frederick H. Abernathy and John T. Dunlop, *A Summer Study of Research and Development Needs of the Tailored Clothing Industry*, Division of Applied Sciences, Harvard University (January 1980), National Science Foundation, Grant No. 1SP-79-20288.

9. The Companies in the program are Celanese Fibers Marketing Company, E.I. duPont de Nemours, Inc., Hartmarx Corporation, Milliken and Company, Burlington Menswear, Surgikos, Genesco, Inc. and J.P. Stevens and Co., Inc. The Amalgamated Clothing and Textile Workers of America has been involved from the outset. In January 1984 there were 12 companies and the union participating.

10. *Final Report on the First-Year R&D Program for the Men's Tailored Clothing Industry*, 5 volumes (May 23, 1982). Prepared for the Tailored Clothing Technology Corporation by The Charles Stark Draper Laboratory, Inc.

11. Professor Frederick Abernathy and I continue to be involved as associate (non-voting) members of the board.

12. See David L. Cole, *The Quest for Industrial Peace* (New York: McGraw-Hill Book Company, Inc., 1963).

13. The labor members of the Committee were George Meany (with Lane Kirkland in attendance), I. W. Abel, Frank Fitzsimmons, Paul Hall, and Leonard Woodcock. The management members were Stephen Bechtel, Jr., Edward Carter, R. Heath Larry, James Roche, and Walter Wriston.

14. John T. Dunlop, "Wage and Price Controls As Seen by a Controller," Industrial Relations Research Association, *Proceedings of the 1975 Annual Spring Meeting, May 8–10, 1975, Hartford, Connecticut*, p. 463. Also see, *The Lessons of Wage and Price Controls—The Food Sector,* John T. Dunlop and Kenneth J. Fedor, Eds., Harvard University Press (1977), pp. 233–60.

15. *Ibid.*, pp. 458–59.

16. *The National Commission for Industrial Peace, Report and Recommendations,*

May 1974, Washington, D.C., Executive Office of the President. The Commission was established by Executive Order 11710 on April 4, 1973.

17. *Hearings Before the Committee on Banking and Currency, House of Representatives, 93 Cong., 2d. Sess. on H.R. 13206, March 6–8, 1974*, p. 70.

18. Executive Order 11809. The labor members of the Committee were George Meany, I. W. Abel, Murray H. Finley, Frank E. Fitzsimmons, Paul Hall, Lane Kirkland, Arnold Miller, and Leonard Woodcock. The management members were Stephen D. Bechtel, Jr., Richard C. Gerstenberg, John D. Harper, Reginald D. Jones, R. Heath Larry, Rawleigh Warner, Jr., Arthur M. Wood, and Walter Wriston. John T. Dunlop was appointed coordinator. See *The Conference on Inflation*, held at the request of President Gerald R. Ford and the Congress of the United States, September 27–28, 1974 in Washington D.C., pp. 291–92.

19. For a discussion, see Henry H. Perritt, Jr. and James A. Wilkinson, *The Georgetown Law Journal* (February 1975), pp. 725–50.

20. Statement of the Labor-Management Group on "Assuring an Adequate Domestic Energy Supply" (May 23, 1977). The statement was sent to President Carter and to concerned Cabinet officials.

21. November 4, 1977 press statement on illegal aliens.

22. *Labor-Management Group Position Papers on Health Care Costs* published as a 37-page booklet in 1978 and widely distributed to labor and management organizations.

23. Bureau of National Affairs, *Daily Labor Report* (August 30, 1978), No. 169, pp. C1–C4.

24. Bureau of National Affairs, *Daily Labor Report* (January 21, 1980), No. 14, pp. C1–C3.

25. For a full list of the 18 members, see note 26, *Final Report*, p. 9.

26. Joint Economic Committee, *Final Report on the Anti-Inflation Guidelines by the Pay Advisory Committee, 1979–80*, 97th Cong., 2d Sess. (December 31, 1982); also see, Council of Wage and Price Stability, *Evaluation of the Pay and Price Standards Program*, Washington, D.C. (January 16, 1981).

27. The labor members of the Group were Lane Kirkland, Thomas R. Donahue, John H. Lyons, Lloyd McBride, Martin J. Ward, William H. Wynn, Glenn E. Watts, and Douglas A. Fraser. The management members were Clifton C. Garvin, James H. Evans, Philip M. Hawley, Ruben F. Mettler, Irving S. Shapiro, George P. Shultz, Roger B. Smith, John E. Welch, and Walter B. Wriston. John T. Dunlop continued as coordinator. Key staff to the Labor-Management Group have been as follows: For labor, Frank Pollara, Rudy Oswald and Kenneth Young; for management, Gordon Binns, Mark D'Arcangelo, Jim Graham, and Henry Lartigue.

28. "Labor-Management Climate, November 1981," reproduced in AFL–CIO, *American Federationist* (January and March 1982).

29. The Labor-Management Group, *A Consensus on Rebuilding America's Vital Public Facilities, Highways, Bridges, Urban Water Supply, Wastewater Treatment*, October 1983.

30. This section is adapted from John T. Dunlop, "The Consensus: Process and Substance," *Toward a New U.S. Industrial Policy?*, Michael L. Wachter and Susan M. Wachter, eds. (Philadelphia: University of Pennsylvania Press, 1981),

pp. 497–500. Also see Martha R. Cooper, *The Search for Consensus, The Role of Institutional Dialogue between Government, Labour and Employers, The Experience of Five Countries,* OECD (1982).

Appendix A: Statement of the Labor-Management Advisory Committee

1. The economic environment created by government decisions for the ensuing year is decisive to the operation and to the results of any economic stabilization program. The application of appropriate monetary and fiscal policy in a time of rising output and employment is essential to price and wage moderation. Price and wage controls that have been used in the past 18 months at some cost in efficiency and freedom to private decision making and to collective bargaining cannot substitute for responsible government policy on budgets and money supply in the economic climate of the year ahead.

2. The rapid and continuing rise in food prices at the wholesale level of agricultural products and at retail is a major problem to economic stabilization and to responsible collective bargaining in the year ahead. The prices of agricultural products are susceptible to various governmental decisions. Strong and effective measures to increase agricultural supplies and to contain and cut back prices are essential to responsible wage decisions in 1973.

3. Considering the economy as a whole, responsible wage behavior requires continuing stabilization in the average rate of wage and benefit increase (total compensation per manhour) in 1973 compared to 1972 so as to be consistent with the goal set by the President of getting the rate of inflation down to 2.5 percent or less by the end of the year.

4. The members of this Labor-Management Advisory Committee are prepared to use their good offices to create a climate favorable to the settlement of collective bargaining negotiations in major cases in 1973 within the framework of stabilization policies in cooperation with appropriate governmental officials. The settlement of negotiations over major agreements in 1973 without extended work stoppages or inventory dislocations can make a contribution to orderly economic expansion and stability this year.

5. The parties to collective bargaining agreements should address themselves both to short-term and longer run structural problems which they confront in their industries, localities and particular economic environments. Collective bargaining is pre-eminently a method of problem solving through negotiations. No single standard

or wage settlement can be equally applicable at one time to all parties in an economy so large, decentralized and dynamic.

6. Economic and industrial relations stability is encouraged in 1973 by collective bargaining agreements of more than a year's duration, and in most situations the large first year catch-up that developed from rapid inflation in recent years may not be appropriate in 1973 negotiations.

7. Responsible wage behavior for individual parties in 1973 requires that more attention be directed than in the recent past to issues of long term competitive conditions, productivity and working conditions, wage relationships, benefit costs, as well as to the achievement of moderate settlements.

This Labor-Management Advisory Committee is to advise the Cost of Living Council as to whether particular settlements are consistent with the goal (par. 3 above) for the rate of increase in wages and benefits for the economy as a whole or are unreasonably inconsistent with the goals of the Economic Stabilization Program. In this way parties will be better able to judge responsible wage and benefit behavior in addition to the general regulations.

8. If 1973 is to be a transitional year to a period without formal wage and price controls, with expanding employment and output, the moderate wage behavior described above, and correlate price behavior, is essential in the months ahead.

9. This is an initial statement of the Labor-Management Advisory Committee. The statement is advisory to the Cost of Living Council.

February 26, 1973

Members:

Labor	Management
I. W. Abel	Stephen Bechtel, Jr.
Frank Fitzsimmons	Edward Carter
Paul Hall	R. Heath Larry
George Meany	James Roche
Leonard Woodcock	Walter Wriston

Appendix B: Labor-Management Group Statement of Purpose

The U.S. faces a period in its history when non-inflationary economic growth and full employment are essential to the maintenance of a free and healthy society.

American labor and business see these as necessary mutual goals to provide our society with new and expanded job opportunities, increased living standards, international competitiveness in an interdependent world and the capacity to meet social commitments.

With these objectives in mind, the Labor-Management Group will meet on a voluntary basis to search for solutions to a wide range of issues.

The principal focus of the Group's discussions will be in the area of economic policy in which its collective experience is widely based. In framing its discussions, the Group is mindful that it is but one of many groups whose opinions may be sought in shaping the nation's policies. The Group's recommendations must consider its obligations to the aspirations of all Americans, including the just demands for equity by minorities, women and those for whom social justice is still a dream.

The national interest requires a new spirit of mutual trust and cooperation, even though management and organized labor are, and will remain, adversaries on many issues.

The uniqueness of America lies in the vitality of its free institutions. Among these, a free labor movement and a free enterprise economy are essential to the achievement of social and political stability and economic prosperity for all. It is destructive to society and to business and organized labor, if in our legitimate adversarial roles, we question the right of our institutions to exist and perform their legitimate functions. In performing these functions, we recognize that both parties must respect deeply held views even when they disagree.

One recognition of the legitimacy of our respective institutions is demonstrated in the process of free collective bargaining. We believe that both the democratic right of employees to determine the issue of representation and the process of collective bargaining must not be threatened by occasions of excessive behavior by employers or unions.

The Group will use the wider relationships its individual members have in the business and labor communities to broaden its knowledge of issues, to improve the overall labor-management climate and to communicate the results of its deliberations to its respective associates.

The complexity of issues suggests the Group may not find complete consensus on all the issues it explores. When it does, it will communicate its views publicly. Otherwise, the participants reserve to themselves the privilege to address issues in their individual capacities.

The Group intends to look closely at the issues it knows best and how they are affected by public policy. These are the issues that grow out of our experiences in industries and localities. Further we intend to explore a wide range of issues with particular emphasis on revitalizing the nation's economic base, rebuilding the private and public infrastructure on which our productive capacity as a nation depends, and stimulating safe and efficient means for meeting the nation's energy needs.

February 3, 1981,
Released March 4, 1981.

Chapter 16

THE SOCIAL CONTRACT

The General Council (of the British Trade Union Congress) believe that much progress has been made in implementing the social contract, which was first envisaged in the TUC-Labor Party joint statement of February 1973.[1] *... The General Council are confident that the further development of the social contract set out in this report will commend itself to unions and to Congress, and so enable the Government to proceed with progressive policies in the industrial, economic and social fields.*[2]

As with many other concepts and institutions involving the relations of labor, management and government, including collective bargaining itself, the origin of "social contract" is British. The experience, however, is older than the 1970s and has counterparts in Scandinavia, Austria, the Netherlands, and elsewhere, depending upon the precise definition. Is a social contract, however, limited in its application to countries with a parliamentary form of government so that a compact with government can readily be enacted? Are there features of the social contract that can be applied to the problems of the interaction of business, labor, and governments in the setting of the United States?

A social contract is more than an incomes policy that places restraints on the rate of increase of compensation, prices, or other sources of income, although an incomes policy may be an element of a social contract with a variety of other provisions, such as tax policy and particular social services to budgetary expenditures. An incomes policy alone may be imposed by legislation over the opposition of one or more of the "social partners," to use a European formulation to refer to labor movements, business interests and agricultural organizations.

Drafted October 9, 1979 as a commentary on the National Accord of September 28, 1979.

A social contract is accordingly an accord or a broad understanding reached after discussion and negotiations between representatives of a government and one or more social partners respecting a range of questions of social and economic policy that may include an incomes policy and respecting some measures to be taken by government and some by private parties. The discussions involve not only consultations but also a measure of agreement upon a set of policies with an understanding to cooperate and facilitate their administration.

Basic Problems of a Social Contract in the U.S.

In a parliamentary government a social contract, with even one social partner, may assure the legislative enactment of those terms of the accord that require new laws. In the United States, however, an accord with all the major groups might facilitate legislation, but a social contract with one group alone might well face severe legislative hostility and even make enactment the more difficult. The legislative implementation of a social contract with or by a government that has a parliamentary majority is likely to be much simpler than in a presidential system.

In the United States setting it is essential to identify another major impediment to the development of a social contract that has grown in severity in the past decade: the advisory committee act[3] and its oversight by the government operations committees of the Congress. This policy appears to preclude continuing private meetings between government representatives and those from business, labor, agriculture, and other social groups. The mandate that such meetings ". . . shall be open to the public"—that is, to the press and the media—seriously impedes or negates effective consultation and negotiations. In the view of labor and management representatives, it virtually forecloses any interest on their parts in systematic participation with government in a continuing labor-management top policy committee. While some exceptions to open meetings under the statute are possible under some circumstances,[4] in discussions of some subjects, or with the use of some data, there is little applicability of these exceptions to general economic policy or labor-management relations. Further, there has been little disposition in recent years by government administrations to seek to close meetings. No group, after all, is interested in appearing to circumvent the statute or to favor changing it, since no one wishes to be put in the unpopular position in these post-Watergate political times of opposing "open government," regardless of how counterproductive the statute may be.

It is understandable that top leaders of labor, business, or agriculture are not likely to change publicly enunciated positions on sensitive questions in the course of public discussion. Such leaders may be willing to recede from a position in exchange for a new position from other groups or as a consequence of some assurances from government, but these moves need to be explored privately and leaders will want to explain in their own words and with their own arguments changes in positions to their own constituencies. Communications and explanations to constituent bodies and members through the press and media simply will not do.

In a very important sense the United States has handcuffed itself in dealing with its most serious economic and social policies by precluding continuing, frank, and direct exchanges between top government representatives and leaders of the social partners, as well as direct discussion among representatives of these groups and with government. Every other advanced industrial country of the world encourages and welcomes such exchanges. In the language of an OECD report, ". . . We believe that trade unions, employers' organizations, and similar bodies have, in an appropriate legal framework, a socially useful and stabilizing role to play in a pluralistic society."[5]

Moreover, under political conditions in this country in which it is necessary for any administration to mobilize political support for the policies it seeks to enact and to administer, this limitation is the more debilitating. The statute encourages formalistic consultation, which amounts to no more than enunciating what government is going to do rather than genuine involvement in a decision with the consequent responsibility for initiating and supporting efforts to achieve agreed-upon results. Negotiations over a social contract encompass a wide variety of issues related to economic policy. This broad scope permits trade-offs and accommodations that would not be likely on a single item.

Contrast the approach to tax-based incomes policies (TIP) in 1978–80 with the procedures for handling amendments to Social Security in 1982–83. TIP was proposed with a nonnegotiated wage standard and a proposal for a legislated tax refund schedule. For some persons this approach was described as a form of social contract. "Tax reductions aimed at working-class incomes can be offered as an inducement for wage moderation in a social compact with labor."[6] Such a formulation bears little resemblance to discussions or negotiations over a social compact. President Carter publicly announced to Congress a proposal for a program of "real wage insurance" shortly after some of the leaders of labor had been advised of the presidential decision. The proposal had no support and could not be expected to secure support among any of the social partners.[7] Nothing ever came of the proposal. In contrast, the Social Security amendments of 1983 grew out of the National Commission on Social Security Reform appointed by the President, the Majority Leader of the Senate, and the Speaker of the House of Representatives and included representatives of business and labor and members of both parties in both Houses of the Congress under the chairmanship of Alan Greenspan.[8] The Commission carefully crafted a "consensus" package which permitted dissents on a few sensitive issues but which provided a broad agreement for the enactment of legislation.

Precedents in the United States

Although the term was never used, the World War II relations among labor organizations, management, and government could well be described as government by a form of social compact. President Roosevelt convened a conference of 12 labor and 12 management leaders, with William H. Davis and Senator Elbert Thomas as moderator and associate moderator, that met from December 17–23, 1941. These leaders agreed that there should be no strikes or lockouts during the war and that disputes should be resolved by a tripartite War Labor Board. But the compact was not complete because the parties disagreed strongly over the prospective resolution of the union security (closed shop-union shop) issue, and President Roosevelt merely accepted the "general points of agreement" and left, by implication, the union security question to be resolved by the board on a case-by-case basis.[9]

As Chairman Davis said at the end of World War II, "The significant, and the deeply encouraging, fact stands out that this tripartite Board did, throughout the critical national wartime emergency, effect by voluntary procedures a very substantial stabilization of industrial production and of the national wage structure."[10] Despite legal authority subsequently derived from statute, the *de facto* role of the War Labor Board and its effectiveness in dispute resolution and in compensation stabilization derived largely from the social compact of December 1941.[11] The viability of the economic stabilization program was particularly dependent upon the political compromises executed by Justice Byrnes in the spring of 1943 with the veto of the Bankhead Bill (that would have raised agricultural prices), the food subsidy program, and the tightening of price and wage stabilization standards.[12]

In peacetime, the only social accord in our experience was that announced by President Carter and Lane Kirkland, representing the AFL-CIO, on September 28, 1979.[13] It may be instructive to sketch briefly the background and the negotiations over the accord. In the early months of 1979 the relationship between George Meany and President Carter had deteriorated to the point that there was little communication on policy questions of common interest and there was considerable public acrimony. It was agreed, and reduced to writing, that a mechanism of contact would be a monthly meeting between Vice President Mondale, Secretary of Labor Marshall, the Director of the Domestic Council Eisenstat, and Landon Butler of the White House staff, on the side of the government, and Lane Kirkland and Thomas Donahue, and such associates as they might bring, representing the AFL-CIO. The first several meetings were held in the late spring and early summer 1979 (including May 18, 1979). The government's representatives were interested in having the labor unions call off their attack on the economic policies of the government, particularly their deep hostility to the wage guidelines. The union spokesmen indicated the guidelines were far down on their list of priorities, and they sought other changes in government economic policy.

In the summer the union spokesmen, speaking from penciled notes on folded ruled paper, indicated that they were willing to discuss participation in the stabilization program as a part of a general accord on other issues of economic policy. The list of their concerns included the following:

- Support for Humphrey-Hawkins full employment legislation already enacted.
- No tax cuts with recession; rather, increased expenditures on CETA, housing, public works, etc. (by $25 billion).
- Energy.
- Foreign trade policy.
- Trade negotiation administration arrangements.
- Extended federal benefits under unemployment compensation as unemployment increases.
- National health insurance.
- Federal status for workers' compensation.
- Restraint on illegal aliens.
- No reduction in social security benefits.
- Greater restraint on price increases and more monitoring of prices under the stabilization program.

In addition, the labor representatives identified four areas of special concern in particular sectors that would require attention:

- Federal pay, which had been limited by the President to 5.5 per cent despite the comparability statute.
- Maritime policy and the application of the Jones Act to the Virgin Islands.

- The application of OSHA to federal government agencies.
- Increased trade adjustment assistance ($240 million increase).

The Administration also met with a group of Democratic members of the Senate and House, on June 29th. From time to time Secretary of the Treasury Blumenthal met separately with business leaders about general economic policy. The notion of a social accord was not discussed with either business or legislative leaders.

When the AFL-CIO Executive Council met in Chicago on August 6–8, 1979, Lane Kirkland reported to the Council on the general discussions. He secured authorization to proceed with the discussions and to report back to the Council before any agreement was concluded. He said that he wished to involve a series of committees of Council members in the discussions with the Administration. Eventually committees of the Council were designated on macro-economic policy, wage standards, price standards, trade policy, federal government employees' pay, and maritime policy.

The discussions between the Administration and the labor spokesmen became intense with the arrival of Secretary Miller at the Treasury. He became the principal representative of the Administration and the draftsman of the National Accord with Lane Kirkland; the wage-price procedural understandings were worked out with a wider group of Administration representatives, and I joined these discussions in August, 1979 at the request of Secretary Miller.

The President was required by statute to make a decision on the pay increase for federal government employees by August 31st, and the Administration had announced that it would issue by September 15th revised wage and price guidelines or standards to become effective October 1st. The labor representatives made it clear to the Administration that continuing with 5.5 per cent for federal government employees in 1979–80, a decision that had been announced in 1978, or issuing as a final the draft wage standards on October 1st would break off all discussions with labor. Intense negotiations developed between the Administration and the labor committees, with a series of tight deadlines. There were, however, only minimal discussions between the Administration and representatives of the Business Roundtable over price or wage matters, and there was no consultation other than through the written comments on the draft wage and price standards from other business groups. Nonetheless, a "National Accord Administration-American Labor Leadership" was announced jointly on September 28, 1979:

All Americans share a common commitment to achieve our Nation's economic goals of full employment, price stability, and balanced growth as set forth in the Full Employment and Balanced Growth Act of 1978" (Humphrey-Hawkins). . . .

> *Inflation is a clear and present danger. It threatens our ability to achieve full employment; it reduces real incomes and values; it dries up job-creating investments; it impedes productivity; it breeds recession; and it falls most heavily on those least able to bear the burden.*
>
> *The war against inflation must be the top priority of government and of private individuals and institutions. There is no quick or simple solution. The war must be waged through a comprehensive strategy on all fronts on a continuing basis. But it should not mean acceptance of higher than otherwise levels of unemployment.*
>
> *The current recessionary conditions developed following the large increase in world oil prices in the second quarter. Policies should be directed toward moderating and reversing the resulting downturn.*

If the recession deepened, the Accord called for being ready to shelter the poor from inflation and recession with programs including public works, expanded job programs, access to capital for housing, and appropriate tax relief to offset inflation (without specifying any aggregate amounts), on one hand while contributing to anti inflation on the other hand through job creation, productivity improvement, and cost reduction.

The National Accord also had paragraphs treating international trade and maritime policies, support for major elements of the President's energy program, improvement of the human environment, and provision for continuing consultations.

Factors Influencing the 1979 National Accord

The Carter Administration was clearly deeply concerned with its low showing in the polls, 14 months before the next national elections and 4 months before the intensive season of state primaries. Repeated public criticism from leaders of the AFL-CIO was a source of very considerable embarrassment to the Administration, quite aside from any estimate of the impact of labor leadership views on rank-and-file votes in primary or national elections. The increasing likelihood that Senator Kennedy, with widespread support in labor leadership and among the rank-and-file, would challenge the President made the situation the more desperate. Something dramatic was imperative in political terms. From the perspective of the stabilization program, the limitations of a "voluntary program" without the overt participation of labor and business were becoming increasingly evident even to the economic advisers. The legal basis of the program had been challenged unsuccessfully in the courts. But further declines in respect for the program were in prospect, and the internal contradictions of a 7 per cent wage standard as the cost-of-living index continued to rise at an annual rate of 13 percent could not be escaped.

The program required second-year standards, and they were supposed to be announced by September 15 and to be in place by the start of the second year on October 1, 1979. A new Secretary of the Treasury provided a new face and the opportunity for a new beginning in the stabilization area.

Labor movement interest in the accord arose form a variety of considerations that were somewhat less transparent. The hostility to the President tended to divide the federation as the 1980 campaign dates approached. Unions aligned themselves with various candidates, or chose to remain neutral. The federation would not endorse a candidate until after the party conventions in the summer of 1980. The accord was seen as a device to hold the unions together and to reduce internal union conflict, while the political year developed without an endorsement for president. Indeed, the National Accord provided an explicit standard to criticize or even to part company with the President, should the Administration be judged to have abandoned the high aspirations of the National Accord. The federation and its President, George Meany, would no longer be vulnerable to the charge (of importance internally), that they could not get along with the President.

The National Accord was an interesting experiment for labor. It provided a showplace for the considerable skills of Lane Kirkland, who would be the new president of the AFL-CIO should George Meany not run for another term, as indeed he announced that he would not do on September 28th, the day the National Accord was approved by the AFL-CIO Council and made public. The National Accord was seen as further limiting and discrediting the charge that labor was responsible for inflation, since it was prepared to participate now in the government's anti-inflation program even as business appeared to be reticent to join the machinery. The National Accord provided a measure of recouped prestige from the defeat of labor law reform and served notice that, as the election drew near, a Democratic President would have to deal more sympathetically with labor. In the previous year, business—which had not helped to elect the President—was on the inside at the White House, and labor—which had helped to elect him—was on the outside. The National Accord would in part redress this situation.

The business community was largely ignored in the discussions over the National Accord. Indeed, it was not directly informed of the negotiations by the government and no effort was made to make the accord a three-way undertaking. In the aftermath of the Labor Law Reform fight, labor would have been unwilling to participate in a joint labor-management effort. The leaders of the Business Roundtable were consulted informally by the Secretary of the Treasury about wage-price policies, and they registered their strong protest over the original form of the price committee. They had no discussions with the government over the provisions of economic policy in the National Accord. These business leaders were, however, kept fully informed regarding wage-price policy developments from early August, when I had been selected to head the Pay Advisory Committee. The leaders of the NAM or Chamber of Commerce were not contacted directly. Accordingly, the hostility, the suspicions of politics, and the public opposition of large parts of the business community to the National Accord is understandable in light of the absence of any genuine involvement.

Toward an Understanding of the Social Contract

It is important to understand the theory of a social contract, how it is said to work, and the cases that can be made for it and against it, recognizing that social contracts may differ substantially in their provisions, in the parties to the agreements, and in the political and economic setting in which they arise. This discussion does not imply favor or opposition in principle to the social contract.

A social contract always involves direct negotiations between government and one or more social groups over a range of problems that might otherwise be considered the exclusive domain of the legislature or the executive branch of government. A social contract introduces private party representatives directly into the political process; it is a supplement or a substitute for other political processes and other private market processes. The process requires political sophistication among the social partners and the government. The absence of cohesion in the business community and the unwillingness to treat issues of general economic policy in an organized and coherent political manner limits the possibilities of political negotiations for business representatives.

During the 1970s the political parties and the political process in the United States apparently have become less able to deal with the problems of the times. As those processes have become more divided and immobilized, the search has begun for other ways of reconciling conflicting interests in the society. Many of the consensual ideas and values that underlay previous political solutions have given way to conflict and impotency, creating a need to seek a larger measure of consensus for national policies through direct negotiations rather than through the ordinary political processes.

In assessing the potentials of a social contract, it is well to remember that the AFL-CIO as a federation does little, if any, collective bargaining, and that negotiations are in the hands of the constituent national unions and their locals. In any social contract the federation may exercise influence and persuasion, but it has no direct control over constituents. But such influence, if genuinely exercised, is not to be deprecated or undervalued. It is ordinarily exercised privately, not publicly, but it can be quite effective in many situations because the federation can bring to bear a variety of pressures and services beyond the influence and moral authority of the century-old labor center. The public and the press do not understand these processes, alternating between the views that the federation is all-powerful and that it is impotent.

On the labor side, a social contract tends to involve a trade of some economic or collective bargaining power for other desired objectives, such as public policy on economic or social policy issues, budget expenditures, unemployment insurance, health policy, and other measures for the relatively poor or disadvantaged. The inherent trade-off is to exercise restraint in the high-wage strategic highly organized sectors in collective bargaining in exchange for social and legislative measures secured by legislation or executive action. In the August–September 1979 negotiations over the National Accord, the labor representatives perceived this very clearly without explicit reference.

A social contract carries the potential of increasing the social and economic pie. The view that negotiations over a social contract are only concerned with dividing the pie is in serious error. An economy beset with declining rates of productivity and considerable potential to improve training, introduce new technology, control labor costs, and so forth has an interest in providing at a national level a setting in which industry, company, and plant-level initiatives in these areas are given high priority and encouragement.

On the American scene a social contract involving business and organized labor, with government, is likely to be more successful in achieving results in the areas of economic policy and stabilization, in contrast to a social contract negotiated with only one partner. An economic package negotiated with one side is likely to create opposition on the other side, almost regardless of the provisions.

A social contract, particularly if negotiated with one partner, carries the potential of perverting the democratic political process by favoring one major social group compared with others. The same concerns, of course, exist in the absence of a social contract through the regular political processes, but a social contract—particularly if negotiated with only one partner—contains further potentials for this result.

One of the features of a social contract is that a general framework can be set in which to stimulate joint activities on a sectoral or industry basis, where appropriate policies to constrain wages and prices (apart from monetary and fiscal policies) or to increase productivity potentials vary from sector to sector. Public measures achieved by political and legislative processes tend to be far too uniform and standardized, but private parties can shape their efforts in very particular ways. Moreover, frequently the most effective measures toward stabilization or productivity gains require new institutions, new approaches, and new ways of relating to other groups which cannot be ordered by governmental fiat.

A fundamental feature of the social contract is recognition of the limitations on compulsion in a Western society. A social contract seeks to secure the voluntary involvement of leaders and members of economic groups in public policies and purposes to overcome the limitations of governmental compulsion. In the language of Victor Feather, former General Secretary of the TUC, ". . . we will not cooperate in carrying out a policy that is imposed on us."[14] In a complex democratic society even desirable economic policy cannot be imposed for long. Therein lies the art of economic governance and leadership.

In many areas of public policy, including inflation restraints and energy conservation, it is apparently not possible to marshal support for policies directly through the political mechanisms and process. Direct involvement of the various interest groups, including where possible agreement on a social contract, is necessary to achieve public objectives. It is increasingly clear how little government and the political process can accomplish by itself in the arena of economic policy and economic or social regulation. American interest groups and citizens simply will not comply with many policies simply imposed on them without their active support and the involvement of major organizations and groups.

Whether or not an overt social contract is negotiated, in many areas of economic and social policy, the active support and involvement of economic interest groups is essential to public objectives. The concerns over more rapid economic growth and greater competitiveness at home and abroad in the decade of the 1980s constitutes a potential focus of common discourse.

Endnotes

1. ". . . It will be the first task of (the next) Labor Government on taking office, and having due regard to the circumstances of that time, to conclude with the TUC, on the basis of the understandings being reached on the Liaison Committee, a wide-ranging agreement on the policies to be pursued in all these aspects of our

economic life and to discuss with them the order of priorities of their fulfilment." "Economic Policy and the Cost of Living," in *Report of the 105th Annual Trades Union Congress, held in the Opera House, Blackpool, September 3rd to 7th 1973,* p. 315.

2. Trade Union Congress, *Collective Bargaining and the Social Contract* (June 26, 1974), para. 40, p. 11.

3. Federal Advisory Committee Act, as amended. Pub. L. 94–409, 5(c), Sept. 18, 1976, 90 Stat. 1247.

4. *Administrative Procedures,* Chapter 5, para. 552b, pp. 214–15.

5. OECD, *Toward Full Employment and Price Stability,* a report to the OECD by a group of independent experts. Paul McCracken, Chairman (June 1977), p. 216, para. 381.

6. George L. Perry, "Stabilization Policy and Inflation," in *Setting National Priorities, the Next Ten Years,* Henry Owen and Charles L. Schultze, eds. (Washington, D.C., The Brookings Institution, 1976), p. 320.

7. See *Economic Report of the President,* January 1979, pp. 9, 82–84; for some of the reasons for opposition to TIP, see Albert Rees, "New Policies to Fight Inflation: Sources of Skepticism," *Brookings Papers on Economic Activity,* 2:1978, pp. 453–77.

8. "Report of the National Commission on Social Security Reform," *Social Security Bulletin* (February 1983), pp. 3–38; "Social Security Amendments of 1983: Legislative History," *Social Security Bulletin* (July 1983), pp. 3–48.

9. Bureau of the Budget, *The United States at War,* Historical Reports on War Administration, 1946, p. 192. Also, see United States Department of Labor, *The Termination Report, National War Labor Board, Industrial Disputes and Wage Stabilization in Wartime, January 12, 1942-December 31, 1945* (1946).

10. *The Termination Report, loc. cit.,* p. xv.

11. See W. Ellison Chalmers, "Voluntarism and Compulsion in Dispute Settlement," In *Problems and Policies of Dispute Settlement and Wage Stabilization During World War II,* Bureau of Labor Statistics Bulletin 1009, pp. 26–71.

12. John T. Dunlop, "The Decontrol of Wages and Prices," in *Labor in Postwar America,* Colston E. Warne, ed. (Brooklyn, New York: Remsen Press, 1949), pp. 3–4.

13. For a critical view, see, *Business Week* (October 15, 1979), pp. 32–34, 1978.

14. *Collective Bargaining and the Social Contract, loc. cit.,* p. 57.

Chapter 17

LABOR, MANAGEMENT, AND GOVERNMENT IN THE 1980S

The Changing Environment of the 1980s

It is imperative to begin with an appreciation of the major qualitative changes that have taken place in the past several decades and those that can reasonably be expected in the next decade in terms of human resources, technologies, and competitiveness in the markets that confront the American economy and our industrial relations system. The purpose is to provide in brief compass, by a series of "bullet" items, some sensitivity to the rapidly changing environment and the structural changes certain to shape the behavior of our major institutions and their interrelations.[1]

Human Resources

- The rate of growth in population during the 1980s will be two-thirds as fast as the 1960s and one-half as fast as the rate in the 1950s. Our population was 76 million in 1900 and is expected to reach 260 million, as a moderate estimate, by the year 2000.[2]
- The decline in the birth rate in the 1970s to a fertility rate of 1.7 (births per woman of child-bearing age) from a baby-boom peak in the post-World War II era of 3.8 has been offset in part in its effects on population by the large increase in legal and illegal immigration.
- Life expectancy has increased from an average of the middle 50s in 1920 to 77 for women and 69 for men today.
- As a nation we are growing older. In 1970 the median age was 28;

Part of an earlier draft was presented at Lehigh University on February 1, 1983 under the title, "Forging New Relationships Among Business, Labor, and Government" in 1980 the figure was around 30; and at the end of the century the median age is projected to be 35.5 years.

- In the 1980s the 18–24 age group is expected to decline; the fastest growing age group will be those between 35 and 44. The over-65 age group will grow by 5 million in the next decade. This group will be growing nearly three times as fast as the general population.
- The civilian labor force is expected to grow over the next two decades at a much slower rate than in the 1960s and 1970s, at a rate of 1.4 per cent a year in the 1980s and 0.5 per cent in the 1990s, in contrast to 2.5 per cent in the 1970s.
- Women accounted for 60 per cent of the growth in the labor force in the period 1960–75, and they are expected to account for two-thirds of the growth in the 1980s.
- Women and minorities are projected to account for 74 per cent of the growth of the labor force in the 1980s.
- Population increases are expected to be much more rapid in the South and West as compared with the Northeast and Midwest. The population center of the United States moved west across the Mississippi River in the 1970s. Population increases of 16.4 and 14.9 per cent in the South and West, compared with 4.6 and 5.3 per cent in the Northeast and Midwest, are projected in the period 1978 to 1990.
- Unemployment rates were much higher in the 1970s than in the two previous decades. Unemployment in the 1980s started at the highest levels since the Great Depression. There are significant differences in unemployment rates by race, sex, age, and occupation.
- In 1960 over 50 per cent of the labor force had less than four years of high school. By 1990 the figure is projected to be 19.8 per cent. The BLS estimates that there will be a surplus of 2 to 3 million college graduates entering the labor force in the 1980s.
- There is a steady increase in the proportion of the labor force who are college graduates: 9.2 per cent in 1960 to an estimated 21.7 per cent in 1990. By 1983, 24 per cent of the labor force in the age bracket 25 to 64 had completed four years of college.
- Employment in goods-producing industries (agriculture, mining, construction, and manufacturing) was 28.9 million in 1969 and is expected to be 33.7 million in 1990, while employment in the service sector was 57.4 in 1969 and is projected at 88.3 million in 1990—a much more rapid rate of growth.
- The fastest-growing industries in the 1980s in terms of employment expansion are in the service sector, with health services and a variety of business and professional services leading the way.

- Sales and clerical occupations in the 1980s will grow fastest among white collar occupations; craft jobs will grow faster than other blue collar occupations; service worker occupation growth rates will exceed both.

Technology and Productivity

- The economy is enmeshed in significant changes in technology, particularly those related to information manipulation and control, electronics, manufacturing processes, communications, biomedical processes, and space and military applications. These technologies will demand new skills and training.
- Technological developments emerge and spread world-wide, and their applications are diffused quickly across national economies.
- Rates of increase in productivity vary a great deal among sectors, with the greatest increases in the past two decades in synthetic fibers, telephone communications, air transportation, pharmaceuticals, and utilities, while coal mining showed actual declines.
- The rate of productivity growth in the United States has steadily declined since the mid-1960s. Real gross domestic product per employed person for the total economy increased 2.4 per cent during 1950–65, 1.7 per cent during 1965–73, and 0.3 per cent during 1973–80. A variety of factors account for this retardation since 1973 for example, a period of low economic growth, adaptation to high energy prices, low capital investments in new plant and equipment, low research and development expenditures, and regulations requiring environmental outlays that are not reflected in output. The rate of productivity growth in the early stages of the 1983 recovery has reflected a typical cyclical pattern of substantial improvement.
- But the rate of increase in productivity has also declined in our major industrial competitors since 1973. In Japan the rate of increase in real gross domestic product per employed person was 7.2 per cent during 1950–65; 8.2 per cent during 1965–73, and 3.0 per cent during 1973–80; in Germany the corresponding figures are 5.6, 4.3, and 2.9 per cent.
- Productivity in our major industrial competitors has increased at a more rapid rate in the post-World War II era than in the United States, but the level of productivity in the United States is still on the average above that of our industrial competitors. There are, however, marked differences among sectors, with Japanese productivity markedly higher in some sectors such as steel.[3] In 1950, after the destruction of World War II, Japan's real gross domestic product per employed person was only 15.5 per cent of that of

the United States; by 1980 it was 67 per cent. In 1950 Germany was 37.3 per cent of the United States; by 1980 it was 88 per cent.

Competitiveness

- Despite a doubling of average hourly earnings in the private, non-agricultural sector in the United States, money hourly earnings did not keep pace with the rise in the cost-of-living index in the years 1973–82, as a consequence, real hourly earnings did not rise in the 1970s—a marked contrast to earlier decades since World War II.
- The United States had a trade surplus in only three years of the 1970s. Total exports grew from $42 billion in 1970 to $182.0 billion in 1979; agricultural and capital goods exports grew five- and four-fold respectively. Meanwhile, imports grew from $40 billion to $211.5 billion, with petroleum imports rising twenty-fold from $2.9 billion to $60 billion.
- The competitive position of the United States economy in many sectors was seriously affected adversely in the decade of the 1970s. These sectors entered the 1980s with impairments that have been exacerbated by the severe recession of 1981–83 and adverse exchange rates. Automobiles, steel, and agricultural implements are only the most prominent. These and other sectors confront major secular readjustments.

Implications for Labor, Management and Government

The changing environment of recent decades will have a wide variety of potential consequences on the economy of the 1980s and on each of the major actors. A few illustrations will indicate some pervasive consequences.

- It was noted that 74 per cent of the growth of the labor force in the 1980s will be comprised of women and minorities. If the labor force grows 14.6 million in the 1980s as projected, 8.2 million are expected to be white females, 1.7 million minority females, 1.4 million minority males, and 3.3 million white males. Managements obviously need to be much better prepared to hire, train, and promote women and minorities. Labor organizations are finding a different clientele and market to which to appeal. Both need to consider more responsively the difficult and complex issues of comparable worth.[4] The government's own employment policies and issues of the work place may be expected to be greatly affected by this shift in the constitution of the labor force.

- The rapid growth in the population over 65 has already begun to influence economic policy and the politics of our times. The legal age for mandatory retirement was suddenly raised from 65 to 70 in 1977, and one should not be surprised very soon to see the elimination of any mandatory age for retirement. The country has seen in the headlines of the past several years the extreme political sensitivity of issues of the financing of the social security system. These changes in the age structure of the population are bound to bring a host of major issues before labor, management, and government in its several branches and levels, including retirement policy, funding of pensions, financing of social security, age discrimination, health care costs, medicare and medicaid, nursing homes, and continuing education.

- Formal education and training arrangements in the United States are decisively impacted by the range of structural changes outlined earlier. The number of teachers and schools have declined as the younger-age cohorts have declined with the "baby bust" of the 1970s. Despite the growth of technical and professional occupations, higher education programs and the employment of faculty may be expected to decline through the mid-1990s.[5] Many private school systems can expect extreme market and financial pressures. At the same time, rapid technical, regional, and industrial changes will require widespread transformation in vocational educational arrangements—already too often obsolete.

   These problems are compounded for our educational and training arrangements by other constraints and challenges. Twenty per cent of American adults today are functionally illiterate; they are unable to read a job notice, fill out a job application, or make change in money.[6] In many communities there has been—and will continue to be—a very rapid growth in the use of the Spanish language, complicating the task of education and communication and management at the workplace. Interest in post-retirement learning is on the rise, reflecting higher levels of education and the fact that in 1970 the average male had 10 years of retirement life, in contrast to 3.1 years in 1900, and these years can be expected to grow in number in the decade ahead.[7]

- The enormous disparities among regions, localities, and companies in the incidence of plant shutdowns, serious dislocation of employment, unemployment, and erosion of social services as a result of economic and technological changes—arising within the country or reflecting changing patterns of international trade—

have created many strains on retraining institutions and our capacity to shift resources without extreme personal and social costs.[8] These strains and burdens became unbearable in too many situations during the prolonged recession of 1981–83. The vast changes in industrial, occupational, and regional structure ahead in our country, combined with rapid changes in the work force, require a widespread retooling of the American work force.

- The federal-state unemployment insurance system, which expended $25 billion in 1982, is designed to sustain a measure of income for employees with work experience, but it is not intended to make any contribution to retraining, relocation, or major reshaping of the work force for the structural changes described earlier. Indeed, payments under the system are restricted to the partial make-up of lost wage income; they cannot be made for training services or relocation even if it is immediately apparent that no future jobs are available in the locality, specialized occupation or the sector. The major transformations ahead in our work force could be facilitated by a more supportive and adaptive unemployment insurance system.

- The secular decline in competitiveness in certain American industries, growing out of differential increases in productivity and newer technology, differential increases in energy costs, governmental trade and subsidy policies, monetary and exchange rate policies, among other things, also has significant implications for business managements and for collective bargaining relationships in these sectors. As has been the case historically, changing competitive conditions materially influence in due course the long-term relative compensation and other policies of parties to collective bargaining. In the present setting, it is not always possible to distinguish readily the influence of long-term structural changes that may require permanent adaptations, including those in the structure of bargaining. The same is true of the effects of a serious recession, such as in 1980–83, which creates reductions in output and employment and reversible short-term policies relating to compensation and labor costs.

In sum, the consequences of the ongoing and the projected structural changes cited above require that business, labor, and government develop—if possible, together—institutional arrangements in the form of education programs, retraining while in employment, economic and trade policies, collective bargaining policies, an unemployment insurance system, and the like to facilitate and encourage the vast transformation in industries, occupations, and locations that lie ahead for the American work force. The adaptations should be aimed towards what is likely to be, not toward that which has been.

There is a widespread view that, with so much unused plant capacity and so much labor unemployed now in the economy, the path of increasing output can be sustained for a long time without inflationary bottlenecks in labor and skill supply. There is a good deal of evidence, however, to show that in the 1970s there was a growing mismatch in the demand and supply for labor skills as a consequence particularly of a shift to new locations, new occupations, and industries.[9] Without major new policies among labor, management, and government— given the widespread transformation required in the work place and the changing character of the work force—an even more severe mismatch is a potential for the 1980s, with adverse effects in the form of inflation, low output, and unemployment.

Public and Private Policies for the 1980s

There appears to be widespread concurrence in the view that the long-term national objectives of the 1980s should be sustained economic growth, with high employment and reasonable price stability. Political programs of all shades embody such goals, without specification of quantities or rates. The path to follow from a deep recession in the changing environment of the 1980s outlined above to a plateau of desirable and sustainable growth is likewise uncharted in specifics. Nonetheless, the conflict is not fundamentally over objectives.

Debate and conflict develop rapidly, however, as related goals are expanded and made more specific—for example, goals for particular regions or categories of the labor force—and as the choices among policy instruments or tools are weighed. The centerpiece of the debates, often technical as well as political, concerns the extent and forms of public policy intervention or governmental activities, to use a more neutral term.

There is wide agreement that attention to economic growth should be accorded first to four related areas of public policy often encompassed under the heading of macro-economic policies: (1) public expenditures and tax policies, called fiscal policy; (2) monetary and interest rate policies; (3) exchange rate policies; and (4) international trade policies respecting tariffs, subsidies, and other measures. Every national economy carries on activities in these areas, and the coherence and effectiveness of these activities for the stated objectives is an appropriate field of public discourse and academic analysis. Moreover, the discipline of economics and the debates on public policy among economists are largely cast in terms of these aggregative policies. The discipline has helped to prejudice and to shape the policy approaches. Economists are trained from their first lessons in these aggregates and the related agencies. Few of them have much familiarity with more specific and sectoral institutions.

It is most difficult to secure concurrence on technical grounds alone as to the appropriate mix of the four areas of macro-policies for optimum long-term growth or for a course to move the economy from deep recession to such a long-term path in the changing environment of the 1980s. Nonetheless, in my view it is essential both in analysis and public policy decisions to identify explicitly the most appropriate macro-policy, because there is a considerable tendency and temptation to substitute specific regulatory and sectoral measures for the most appropriate macro-policies. Thus, as I have often said, one of the major problems with wage and price controls, is that political leaders will regard controls as an effective bulwark against inflation and fail to adopt a sufficiently tight fiscal and monetary policy. In the language of George P. Shultz, "The great vice of wage and price controls is not so much that they work poorly or that they are an inappropriate response to inflation . . . but rather that they induce government to relax monetary and fiscal policy.[10] In the same way, the 1982–83 mix of fiscal and monetary policy that yielded high interest rates and low economic growth in many sectors should not be corrected by an industrial policy without first providing attention to a more appropriate mix of macro policies, including a smaller budgetary deficit and less stringent monetary policy.

One does not have to believe that macro-economic policies alone will resolve all ills and set an adequate environment for the private sector to insist that in both analysis and policy making every practical alternative be explored to consider ruthlessly the most appropriate and effective mix of macro-policies for the objective of sustained economic growth. The political temptations are often to let up on, rather than to bear down on, these policy tools and to choose a mixture that is less offensive to significant political constituencies. The first requisite must be optimal macro-policies in an appropriate mixture.

For several reasons, that does not end the process of policy making. First, it is rare, indeed, that the optimal macro-policies are politically preferred and are likely to be put in place in the political processes of the executive and legislature. This process sets the stage for continuing proposals, second- or third-best solutions, and a variety of more specific measures, particularly in a rapidly changing environment such as the one described earlier in the 1980s. Government policy making comes to be a continuous and changing process of measures rather than the setting of a stable framework or a clear course.

Second, macro-policies have quite differential effects on particular sectors of the economy. The simplest case, for instance, is the consequence of interest-rate changes on different industries, with housing so interest-rate sensitive. Economists need to study more generally the differential consequences of macro-measures.

Third, it is not often appreciated how extensively penetrating are the decisions of governments in the sectors we choose to call private and how often these decisions are changed by actions of legislative bodies, administrative agencies, and the courts. Business leaders appear much more comfortable anticipating or adjusting to changes in technology or markets that are regarded as impersonal forces than they do dealing with changes that appear to originate with politics and governments. If they were more familiar with political processes, they might be more likely to include them in their forecasts.

I have often compared the modern economy to a good steak with extensive striations of fat. Government is very widely diffused through the whole economy, not simply a large separate sector. Follow the production process through any major industry and you will see the frequent and extended ways in which government regulations, activities, and purchases today impact the sector and its surrounding factor and product markets. Specific governmental activities thus are seldom something new.

In view of the changing environment of the 1980s and beyond the issues of the appropriate macro-economic policies for sustained economic growth, a mixture of institutional building measures involving both public and private sectors in varying proportions is required for the intermediate period ahead. These measures do not constitute in themselves an industrial policy, although they should facilitate industrial growth and rehabilitation, whether envisaged as a consequence of purely market forces or overt governmental activities. In my view these general institutional measures ideally should be begun apart from specifics of macro and industrial policies and their contending programs. Moreover, these institutional measures have wide support in the business and labor communities and are essential for sustained economic growth in the environment of the 1980s. The priorities are as follows:

1. A substantially higher rate of expenditures in the private and public sector is required in the intermediate term for basic research, research and development, and technological innovation than in the past. The potentials of expanding sciences and the urgency of international competition dictate this course, which will require public measures affecting expenditures, tax policy, and some anti-trust actions relevant to cooperative research. We will also need new institutions that meld public and private activities.

2. The physical infrastructure of the country has been deteriorating. Long-term modernization of such facilities as roads, bridges, potable water supplies, and sewerage plants is essential for renewed and sustained economic growth. Responsibility for the facilities is long recognized as lying in the public arena, with mixed roles for local, state, and federal governments. The political temptation to place a higher priority on new structures than on maintenance in governments, as well as the absence of capital budgeting, must be resisted in order to avoid further deterioration or short-term emergency programs without continuity.

3. An energy policy that enjoys substantial consensual support is essential to long-term economic growth. Resolution of deep policy disputes and procedures to resolve promptly particular cases in controversy over the use of coal, nuclear energy, natural gas, and imported oil are requisite to economic growth—particularly in times of international crisis. The easing of upward pressures on oil prices, caused by the deep world recession and an expansion in output, should not create a false sense of security or divert attention from the continuing necessity for a long-term energy policy.

4. The skills, training, and education of the present labor force is not well suited to the necessities of the future and the projected directions of growth. Part of the complex problems can be met through improvements in basic education, part can be achieved through training in industry, and part can be addressed by institutions which bring together private and public parties for these purposes in particular settings. The Job Partnership Act of 1982 (which replaced CETA) and the private industry councils were envisaged to encourage such cooperation at the local level. Institutional building in the educational-work interface for various categories of student-workers is an enormously difficult undertaking, and we are not likely to succeed with a new political beginning every 8 or 10 years. It is possible to be encouraged, however, by the fact that the Job Partnership Act of 1982 was a bi-partisan creation.

Under collective bargaining agreements, training programs should become as frequent and central as health and welfare, pension, or apprenticeship programs in craft unions. Examples of what can be done are provided by Ford Motor Company and the UAW, and AT&T and the Communications Workers.

5. The public unemployment insurance system which has, in general, served the country well since 1935 needs adaptation to encourage requisite adjustments in the employed labor force. Except in California and Delaware, the U.I. benefit system can be used only to pay benefits for a partial makeup of wages lost through unemployment. The Federal Government should encourage other states to follow the experience of California and Delaware in permitting ex-

penditures in training allowances, counseling, and other measures to facilitate the readjustment of employed workers.

6. In negotiation of collective bargaining agreements, reference to the standard of competitiveness should become more frequent and insistent. This concern should not be confined to international competitiveness, for economic health and economic growth are related to all competitive forces, including those arising entirely within the domestic economy and from deregulation as in the trucking and airline industries. Moreover, international competition should be viewed from the perspective of long-term rather than short-term exchange rates and the appropriateness of trade policies of trading partners. Detailed study and understanding of the competitive setting of each major agreement is a responsibility of the two sides jointly and is an appropriate subject for a labor-management committee to operate between the periodic negotiations.

7. The revival and growth of the central core of major metropolitan areas is a vital ingredient of potential national economic growth. In traveling from one metropolitan area to another, one is struck by the wide diversity in economic health among core cities. Some have steadily gone downhill, while others have shown remarkable capacity for resurgence and modernization. Economic opportunities, private development, and political leadership have no doubt played roles. These should be largely local initiatives.

It may be argued that the market alone and unaided can accomplish all the objectives proposed for the institutional building measures just outlined. I do not know any definitive way to prove or disprove the assertion that neither macro-public policy nor the market alone in the 1980s is likely to perform well and to create the proposed results, or that public policy measures and cooperative private-public activities within ordinary standards of performance and competence are requisite to achieve the objectives proposed for the group of seven institutional building measures. But labor, managements, and governments need to address these issues together.

These modest institutional building proposals of general application leave for further consideration and debate the more political and large-scale issues of industrial policy. The country seems determined to battle over industrial policy ideologically and politically before it chooses under that label to address any substantive issue. In the meantime we continue to have various activities of governments that are in fact uncoordinated industrial policies.

Endnotes

1. See Labor-Management Group, *Labor-Management Climate* (November 1981). Reproduced in AFL-CIO, *American Federationist* (January and March, 1982).

2. *Employment and Training, Report of the President* (1981), Table E-1, p. 247.
3. American Productivity Center, *Comparative Productivity Dynamics, Japan and the United States* (November 1982).
4. See E. Robert Livernash, *Comparable Worth, Issues and Alternatives* (Washington, D.C.: Equal Employment Advisory Council, 1980).
5. See *Princeton University, Report of the President, Graduate Education in Arts and Sciences: Prospects for the Future* (April 1981), pp. 11–28; "The Long-Run Academic Labor Market Outlook," in *Academe* (July-August 1982), pp. 6–8.
6. Pat Choate, *Retooling the American Work Force, Toward a National Training Strategy* (Washington, D.C.: Northeast-Midwest Institute, July 1982), p. 1.
7. Fred Best and Barry Stern, "Education, Work and Leisure: Must They Come in That Order?", *Monthly Labor Review* (July 1977), p. 4.
8. Richard F. Schubert, "Postwar Changes in the American Labor Market," in *The American Economy in Transition*, Martin Feldstein, ed. (University of Chicago Press, 1980), pp. 402–07.
9. James L. Medoff and Katharine G. Abraham, "Unemployment, Unsatisfied Demand for Labor, and Compensation Growth, 1956–80," in *Workers, Jobs and Inflation*, Martin Neil Baily, ed. (1982), pp. 49–88. James L. Medoff, "U.S. Labor Markets: Imbalance, Wage Growth, and Productivity in the 1970s," *Brookings Papers on Economic Activity*, I (1983), pp. 87–128.
10. George P. Shultz and Kenneth W. Dam, *Economic Policy Beyond the Headlines* (Stanford: Stanford Alumni Association, 1977), p. 21.

INDEX